T0271188

EUROPE AFTER ENLARGEMENT

Where is Europe going? Prominent European economists here offer essays on five big challenges to the development of the European Union (EU), namely, the new European Constitution, European finances and the euro, the need to boost economic growth, competition in both new member states and countries further to the east, and the goal of forming a cooperative and productive relationship with countries on the European periphery. Charles Wyplosz argues that enlargement and deepening are not substitutes but complements. Georges de Ménil worries that the Constitution could lock in Europe with excessive social entitlements. Vito Tanzi questions the Keynesian foundation of the Growth and Stability Pact. Fabrizio Coricelli suggests that the standards of this pact are neither relevant nor sufficient for the new member states. Daniel Gros criticizes the minimal achievements within the Lisbon Agenda. Patrick Lenain records small but positive reforms of European labor markets. Yegor T. Gaidar warns that recovery growth in the East may be temporary. Anders Åslund claims that Russian and Ukrainian oligarchs differ little from U.S. "robber barons." Susanne Milcher, Ben Slay, and Mark Collins discuss the EU's European Neighbourhood Policy, and Johannes F. Linn and David Tiomkin ponder long-term economic integration in Eurasia.

Anders Åslund is a Senior Fellow and specialist on post-communist economic transformation, especially the Russian and Ukrainian economies, at the Peterson Institute for International Economics in Washington, D.C. From 1994 to 2005, he worked at the Carnegie Endowment for International Peace, first as a senior associate and later as Director of the Russian and Eurasian Program. Dr. Åslund is an adjunct professor at Georgetown University and has also served as an economic adviser to the Russian government from 1991 to 1994, to the Ukrainian government from 1994 to 1997, and to President Askar Akaev of the Kyrgyz Republic from 1998 to 2004. He is the author of six books, including *Building Capitalism: The Transformation of the Former Soviet Bloc* (Cambridge University Press, 2002), *How Russia Became a Market Economy* (1995), *Gorbachev's Struggle for Economic Reform* (1989), and *Private Enterprise in Eastern Europe: The Non-Agricultural Private Sector in Poland and the GDR, 1945–83* (1985). In addition, he has edited eleven books, most recently, *Revolution in Orange.*

Marek Dąbrowski is a founder and Chairman of the Council of the Center for Social and Economic Research (CASE) in Warsaw, Poland. He also chairs the Supervisory Board of CASE Ukraine in Kiev and is a member of the Board of Trustees of the Institute for the Economy in Transition. Dr. Dąbrowski has actively participated in discussions on economic reforms in Poland since 1978. From September 1989 to September 1990 he was the First Deputy Finance Minister of Poland, and he later served as a Member of Parliament (1991–1993), as Chairman of the Governmental Council of Ownership Changes (1991–1996), and as a member of the Monetary Policy Council of the National Bank of Poland (1998–2004). Dr. Dąbrowski has been involved in policy advice, policy research, and training for the World Bank and UNDP and for sixteen European and Asian nations. He is an author or coauthor of numerous publications on the European Union and European Monetary Union.

Europe After Enlargement

Edited by

ANDERS ÅSLUND

Peterson Institute for International Economics
Washington, D.C.

MAREK DĄBROWSKI

Center for Social and Economic Research
Warsaw, Poland

Shaftesbury Road, Cambridge CB2 8EA, United Kingdom

One Liberty Plaza, 20th Floor, New York, NY 10006, USA

477 Williamstown Road, Port Melbourne, VIC 3207, Australia

314–321, 3rd Floor, Plot 3, Splendor Forum, Jasola District Centre, New Delhi – 110025, India

103 Penang Road, #05–06/07, Visioncrest Commercial, Singapore 238467

Cambridge University Press is part of Cambridge University Press & Assessment, a department of the University of Cambridge.

We share the University's mission to contribute to society through the pursuit of education, learning and research at the highest international levels of excellence.

www.cambridge.org
Information on this title: www.cambridge.org/9780521872867

First published 2007
First paperback edition 2012

A catalogue record for this publication is available from the British Library

Library of Congress Cataloging-in-Publication data
Europe after enlargement / edited by Anders Åslund and Marek Dąbrowski.
p. cm.
Includes bibliographical references and index.
ISBN 978-0-521-87286-7 (hardback)
1. European Union countries – Economic policy. 2. European Union countries – Social policy. 3. Monetary policy – European Union countries. 4. Constitutional history – European Union countries. 5. European Union countries – Foreign relations. 6. Europe – Economic integration. I. Åslund, Anders, 1952– II. Dąbrowski, Marek, 1951– III. Title.
HC240.E8117 2007
337.1′42 – dc22 2006023233

ISBN 978-0-521-87286-7 Hardback
ISBN 978-1-107-41051-0 Paperback

Contents

List of Charts, Tables, and Boxes

Charts

Tables

Boxes

Contributors

Anders Åslund is a Senior Fellow at the Peterson Institute for International Economics and the chairman of the CASE Advisory Council. He is also adjunct professor at Georgetown University and former director of the Russian and Eurasian Program at the Carnegie Endowment for International Peace, Washington, D.C.

Mark Collins is an economist at the United Nations Development Program's Regional Center in Bratislava.

Fabrizio Coricelli is professor of economics at the University of Siena, Research Fellow at the Center for Economic Policy Research, London, and William Davidson Institute, University of Michigan. He was also an economic adviser to the European Commission from 2001 to 2002.

Marek Dąbrowski is the Chairman of the CASE Foundation Council and one of its founders. He is also Chairman of the Supervisory Board of CASE Ukraine in Kiev. He has worked as a consultant for the World Bank, UNDP, and other international organizations actively engaged in economic reforms in many post-communist countries.

Yegor T. Gaidar was deputy and acting Prime Minister in charge of economic policy in Russia from 1991 to 1994. At present, he is the director of the Institute for the Economy in Transition in Moscow.

Daniel Gros is the director of the Center for European Policy Studies in Brussels and an adviser to the European Union.

Patrick Lenain is Head of Division at the Organization for Economic Cooperation and Development. Prior to joining the OECD, he spent ten years with the International Monetary Fund. His last IMF post was senior resident representative in Ukraine.

Johannes F. Linn had a long career at the World Bank, ending as vice president for Europe and Central Asia. Currently, he is the executive director of the Wolfensohn Initiative at the Brookings Institution.

Georges de Ménil is professor of economics at the École de Hautes Etudes en Sciences Sociales, Paris, and a member of the governing board of Paris-Jourdan Sciences Économiques, a research center that he helped to found. He is also a visiting professor at New York University.

Susanne Milcher is a policy specialist for poverty reduction and economic development at the United Nations Development Program's Regional Center in Bratislava.

Ben Slay is the director of the United Nations Development Program's Regional Center in Bratislava. Formerly, he was an assistant professor in the Department of Economics at Middlebury College, Vermont.

Vito Tanzi is a senior consultant at the Inter-American Development Bank, Washington, D.C. He had a long and distinguished career at the International Monetary Fund, serving as the director of the fiscal affairs department for two decades. He has also served as under-secretary for economy and finance in the Italian government.

David Tiomkin is an MBA and Masters in Public Administration/International Development candidate at Harvard University.

Charles Wyplosz is a professor of international economics at the Graduate Institute of International Studies in Geneva, where he is director of the International Centre for Money and Banking Studies. He is also director of the International Macroeconomics Program at the Centre for Economic Policy Reform, London.

Acknowledgments

This volume presents the most interesting papers from the International CASE Conference on "Europe After the Enlargement" held in Warsaw on April 8–9, 2005. CASE, the Center for Social and Economic Research, is a Warsaw-based international think tank dealing with the problems of European integration, the global economy, and post-transition development. It has an extensive network of daughter and associated organizations in Central and Eastern Europe and the former Soviet Union, as well as close partnerships with many U.S. and Western European research organizations.[1]

Three previous international CASE conferences concentrated on the problems of economic and political transition in the former Soviet bloc, plus some broader development issues, such as sources of economic growth, monetary and exchange rate regimes, tax reform, social and pension reforms, privatization, corporate governance, and migration.[2] In 2005, European integration and Europe's economic and social future were the main conference topics. Seven thematic sessions and four keynote addresses involved 250 of the best economists and political scientists from more than thirty countries. Key international organizations were represented as well. The debate concentrated on long-term pan-European challenges rather than short-term problems of individual countries. This volume contains ten major contributions selected out of almost forty delivered during the conference.

We want to thank the conference sponsors for their generous support. The main sponsors of the conference were the World Bank, the United Nations

[1] Marek Dąbrowski is Chairman of the CASE Foundation Council. Anders Åslund is Chairman of the CASE Advisory Council.

[2] The first international CASE conference, "Economic Scenarios for Poland," was held on January 18, 1997; the second conference, "Years After: Transition and Growth in Post-Communist Countries," took place October 15–16, 1999; and the third, "Beyond Transition: Development Perspectives and Dilemmas," was held April 12–13, 2002.

Development Program, and the Polish savings bank PKO BP SA. Support was also provided by the Konrad Adenauer Foundation, the Dutch Ministry of Foreign Affairs, the insurance company PZU SA, the National Depository of Securities of Poland, the pension fund "Skarbiec," and the energy company STOEN RWE Group. We are also grateful to the organization team, including Agnieszka Paczynska, Wojciech Paczynski, Joanna Binienda, Anna Maciazek, and several other CASE people, who worked hard for almost one year to prepare this important event.

Both the authors and editors of this volume express their gratitude to conference participants who gave numerous valuable comments and remarks, which we have tried to incorporate. The editors also want to thank Matthew Gibson, Roman Ginzburg, and Julija Remeikaite for their excellent and diligent assistance in preparing the manuscript for this volume.

Anders Åslund would also like to express his gratitude to Adolf and Eva Lundin as well as Hans and Märit Rausing for their great and generous support of his work. He also wants to thank the Peterson Institute for International Economics for providing congenial conditions for completing this work.

April 2006 Anders Åslund and Marek Dąbrowski

Introduction

Anders Åslund and Marek Dąbrowski

Over the last fifty years Europe has gone through a unique historical process of economic and political integration, sharply contrasting with the tragic first half of the twentieth century. The last fifteen years, in particular, have brought remarkable progress. The Single European Market and the common currency (euro) have significantly deepened the prior integration, which was limited to little more than trade. Meanwhile, the European Union (EU) has gone through subsequent enlargements. The latest and biggest enlargement of the EU in May 2004 expanded the number of member states from fifteen to twenty-five.[1] As a consequence, the EU's economic and geopolitical importance has increased. Most of Europe's nations and population are now contained in the Union.

Several other countries are in various stages of EU accession (Bulgaria, Romania, Turkey, and Croatia) or would like to start this process in the not too distant future (western Balkans, Ukraine, and Moldova).[2] The Rome Treaty established that all European countries have the right to apply for EU membership, signaling that future EU borders will move farther to the east and southeast.

Despite the obvious achievements of integration, the European economy and European institutions face serious challenges. This volume concentrates on five big ones. The first task for the EU is to find a new legal shape and adopt a European Constitution. The EU decision-making process is ineffective and

[1] EU-15 refers to Belgium, France, Germany, Italy, Luxemburg, the Netherlands, Denmark, Ireland, the United Kingdom, Greece, Portugal, Spain, Austria, Finland, and Sweden, which formed or joined the EU in five waves. The ten additional members were, from north to south: Estonia, Latvia, Lithuania, Poland, the Czech Republic, Slovakia, Hungary, Slovenia, Cyprus, and Malta. Of the ten new member states (NMS), eight, all but Cyprus and Malta, are former socialist countries.

[2] Sometimes the expression EU-28 is used. It refers to the current twenty-five members of the EU plus Bulgaria, Romania, and Croatia, whose entry is mostly seen as a given.

lacks sufficient democratic legitimacy on the European level. The summer 2005 referenda in France and the Netherlands, which rejected the proposed European Constitution, re-opened this question.

At present twelve countries use the euro, and Euroland is supposed to expand to the new member states in due time.[3] But the management of the European finances and the euro is a second major challenge. The 2005 reform of the Stability and Growth Pact will seriously undermine European fiscal discipline. Moreover, the crisis of the overextended welfare state is going to deepen in the future as the European population ages.

The need to boost economic growth is a third formidable European test. Three of the four big European economies are close to stagnation, and Europe as a whole is losing out in competition with the United States, Asia, and the Pacific region. The Lisbon Agenda, an ambitious EU program that aims to revitalize the European economy, has been little but a dead letter.

A fourth challenge is to face up to competition from new member states and countries farther east. Many old member states are hesitant to continue deepening the Single European Market, especially in the service sector, and want to impose stifling regulations and taxes on new member states as well as neighbors. The risk of protectionism looms, as always.

Finally, the EU must form a cooperative and productive relationship with countries on the European periphery. The Union has neither a clear vision of further enlargements nor a plan to help less developed countries on Europe's periphery to close the development gap and modernize their economic and political systems. Many Western European societies are increasingly critical of further EU enlargements, trade liberalization, and immigration, which they fear will undermine their very high standard of living.

The rejection of the European Constitution in the French and Dutch referenda should serve as a warning signal that at least a part of Europe is not ready to meet the challenges facing our continent. This makes both further enlargement and deepening of the EU more difficult, because the Constitutional Treaty would have consolidated the prior accomplishments of integration and made the EU decision-making process more efficient.

The first two chapters in this volume discuss aspects of the draft European Constitution. In the first chapter – "Has Europe Lost Its Heart?" – Charles Wyplosz argues that enlargement and deepening are not substitutes but complements. Enlargement does not necessarily dilute the EU, but it requires adjustment of the decision-making process. Contrary to many assertions,

[3] Austria, Belgium, Finland, France, Germany, Greece, Ireland, Italy, Luxemburg, the Netherlands, Portugal, and Spain.

the EU is growing closer through enlargement, because the new members tend to be the greatest champions of common European values. A new acceleration of European integration is now required, but it needs to be carefully prepared.

In chapter 2, "Economic Implications of the Social Provisions of the Stalled EU Constitution," Georges de Ménil analyzes the Charter of Fundamental Rights of the Union (a part of the Constitutional Treaty) and, particularly, its Title IV ("Solidarity") containing social entitlements. He shows that if an activist European Court of Justice interprets these constitutional commitments generously, they could harm European productivity and competitiveness. Such a court interpretation could force national governments to increase the level of social and labor protection and put Europe in a social welfare trap.

The next thematic bloc analyzes the fiscal policy rules of the enlarged EU. Vito Tanzi 's chapter 3, "Fiscal Policy and Fiscal Rules in the European Union," provides devastating criticism of fiscal activism in the Keynesian tradition. He illuminates numerous conceptual, methodological, and political traps associated with a countercyclical fiscal policy and fiscal discretion. Tanzi concludes that countercyclical fiscal policy is justified in depressions, but doubts whether countries already suffering from precarious fiscal conditions, as are numerous EU countries, should try it. Therefore, the EU Stability and Growth Pact should be not softened but rather reinforced.

Fabrizio Coricelli takes this discussion further to the new member states in chapter 4, "Design and Implementation of the Stability and Growth Pact: The Perspective of New Member States." He suggests that the standards of the Stability and Growth Pact are neither relevant nor sufficient for the new member states. They cannot allow themselves such large debts in relation to GDP, because their domestic financial markets are shallower and the volatility of their output growth and public finances is likely to be greater. But fiscal discipline is key to high growth and their swift economic convergence with the old member states. He warns that the recent loosening of the Stability and Growth Pact and the growing arbitrariness in its implementation reduce the incentives for fiscal adjustment in the new member states, which is particularly harmful for these countries.

This book also scrutinizes Europe's low economic growth and slow structural reforms. In chapter 5, "Perspectives on the Lisbon Strategy: How to Increase European Competitiveness," Daniel Gros deals with the complex issue of the Lisbon Agenda's failure, as reflected in the rather poor recent performance of the European economy. He focuses on three questions – demographic deterioration, the productivity slowdown, and the crumbling of both fiscal and structural policies – and underlines how profound Europe's economic problems are. Alas, the reform of the Stability and Growth Pact indicates that policy makers are moving in the wrong direction, looking for excuses not to undertake necessary reforms.

Chapter 6 by Patrick Lenain, "Is Europe Reforming? Evidence from Cross-Country Structural Indicators," concurs with this somber tone. However, according to Lenain, the real picture is more mixed. He undertakes a careful analysis of labor market developments in the whole of the EU, finding that some EU members have at least partially deregulated their labor and product markets, and most countries are moving in the direction of less regulation. Although developments are tardy, these observations arouse the hope that the second half of the Lisbon Strategy decade may be less disappointing than the first.

The rest of the book moves to the east of the EU. One group of chapters discusses the development challenges facing the EU's eastern neighbors. In chapter 7, "Recovery Growth as a Stage of Post-Socialist Transition," Yegor Gaidar analyzes recovery growth in transition economies after a prolonged output decline in the final stage of communism and the first years after its collapse. He warns that such growth tends to arrive unexpectedly after some disarray, and it is usually strong, but that growth potential can be exhausted if it is not reinforced by structural reforms that stimulate investment.

Chapter 8 by Anders Åslund, "Comparative Oligarchy: Russia, Ukraine, and the United States," addresses the controversial topic of "oligarchs" and their property rights in some post-communist countries. The author claims that Russian and Ukrainian oligarchs differ little from the "robber barons" in the United States in the second half of the nineteenth century. Åslund argues that the emergence of the super-rich is nearly inevitable under the conditions of large economies of scale and ineffective legal systems. He analyzes the policy options for dealing with this phenomenon in a way consistent with the market-oriented reforms.

The final thematic group contains two studies on the external relations of the enlarged EU. Chapter 9, by Susanne Milcher, Ben Slay, and Mark Collins, "The Economic Rationale of the 'European Neighbourhood Policy,'" concentrates on future EU relations with the post-Soviet countries. Their main concern is whether the EU's European Neighbourhood Policy will be sufficiently attractive to induce the Commonwealth of Independent States (CIS) governments to adopt the economic and governance reforms that were implemented in the EU new member states during their accession. Consequently, the authors reckon that the uncertain perspective of eventual EU accession is the main weakness of the European Neighbourhood Policy.

The tenth and final chapter, by Johannes Linn and David Tiomkin, "Economic Integration of Eurasia: Opportunities and Challenges of Global Significance," takes a broad perspective. It explores the opportunities for increasing economic cooperation across the entire Eurasian supercontinent, a possibility opened by the collapse of the communist system in the former USSR. The authors analyze energy and non-energy trade and transport, illicit drug trade, investment and capital flows, migration, and communication and knowledge sharing. They find ample opportunities for development, but the obstacles remain significant.

When looking at present-day Europe, observers are struck by two contrary impressions. On the one hand, much has been done to bring Europe closer together. The expression "Europe whole and free" has acquired a real meaning. On the other hand, the frustration with the remaining problems is growing to a crescendo. The EU decision-making system works poorly; the revision of the Stability and Growth Pact may endanger fiscal stability; the old EU countries are failing to undertake the necessary structural reforms of tax systems, social benefit systems, and labor market regulations to stimulate economic growth; low nativity combined with resistance to immigration reduces growth potential; and the EU appears to see predominantly danger rather than opportunity to its east.

Yet, as this book demonstrates, this critique has reached a new acuteness. A new restlessness is spreading through Europe. Criticism of fundamental European problems is no longer swept under the carpet. An understanding has matured that these problems will not go away and can no longer be passively accepted. In many cases, the cures are known, and their application cannot be indefinitely delayed. Importantly, the new member states are challenging one another as well as the old EU members with tax competition and the successful deregulation of labor markets. While the EU delivers a stage for competition through its single market, national governments both inside and outside the EU use this large stage to prove the competitiveness of their economic policies. Sooner or later, the *acquis communautaire* may adjust.

This resolute criticism of European economic policies gives hope that Europe is becoming ready for truly radical reforms.

ONE

Has Europe Lost Its Heart?

Charles Wyplosz

Introduction

Once upon a time Europe was a small group of like-minded countries, determined to integrate politically and economically in order to eliminate war. After centuries of recurrent devastation, this was an ambitious project. It was built on Jean Monnet's prudent step-by-step strategy, now called neo-functionalism.[1] Integration always progressed in fits and starts, but achieved amazing results. Not only is war all but ruled out, but also economic and political integration has deepened to a degree undreamt-of even by most Euro-enthusiasts. More amazing still, the project has spread. Nearly the entire continent is now part of the Union, and Turkey might join by the end of the decade. Two hundred million people share the same currency and enjoy borderless travel.

But success has its price. Twenty-five countries do not cooperate as six used to. Each enlargement gives the impression that the undertaking is being diluted, resulting in more weight given to national interests and less willingness to take the next integrative step. This perception is misguided. The EU-25 group is considerably more integrated than the original EU-6 ever was. Enlargement does not cause dilution, but it brings to the fore institutional failures that were present all along.

Now Europe needs to clean up its institutions and practices. Fifty years of negotiations have led to agreements both good and bad. Some of

[1] Classic references on neo-functionalism are Haas (1958) and Mitrany (1975).

This chapter draws in part on joint work with Erik Berglöf, Barry Eichengreen, Gérard Roland, and Guido Tabellini, but I alone am responsible for the views presented here. I am grateful for useful comments provided by CASE conference participants, especially my discussants Erik Berglöf, Josef Zieleniec, and Anders Åslund.

the old *acquis communautaire* is outdated. The European Constitutional Convention offered a unique opportunity to sort out this legacy, but this opportunity has been squandered. The Convention refused to open the Pandora's box of past agreements and fix them. Its wholesale adoption of all the *acquis communautaire*, good and bad, left many of the important issues untouched. Then the ratification process was managed badly in France and in the Netherlands. These two countries' rejection of the Constitution has opened a new window of opportunity, however. Will the European leaders now concentrate their efforts on a more modest but deeper project? A changing of the guard is under way and it remains to be seen what the next generation will deliver.

This chapter reviews a number of political-economic issues. The second section sets the scene by offering a broad review of task allocation principles. The third section examines the links between widening and deepening, concluding that the two are not substitutes, but rather possible complements. The fourth section presents some solutions that go beyond current debates.

Task Allocation in the EU

Principles from Fiscal Federalism

As summarized in Berglöf et al. (2003), the theory of fiscal federalism provides the starting point for allocating tasks (the provision of public goods) to the EU level –"centralizing" them. The theory develops two criteria to recommend centralization, and two to discourage it. Centralization is appropriate for (1) public goods subject to increasing returns to scale or scope and (2) public goods subject to externalities. The first criterion against centralization can be broadly defined as "heterogeneity." If national preferences differ, some countries will dislike any "one size for all" policy. The second is information asymmetries. The center typically knows less about local needs than national or subnational levels of government. Centralized decisions and implementation procedures may rest on a faulty appraisal of end-user needs.

Real-Life Governments

The previous reasoning assumes national governments are benevolent, striving only to maximize their citizens' welfare. Difficulties start when we allow for citizens to hold differing opinions. The simple fix is to assume that democracy provides an elegant solution: elections determine how collective preferences emerge from individual disagreements. Unfortunately, the recent literature shows this assumption is too simple.[2]

To start with, elections are not one-dimensional. European issues fly below radar in domestic political debates, particularly in larger countries. As a result, governments are not really accountable for decisions made and positions taken in "Brussels."[3] Moreover, according to one view, governments are not benevolent but captured by special interest groups.

What do such political failures imply? Does centralization mitigate or enhance these political distortions? There is no general answer. Under decentralized policy making, only (or mainly) domestic lobbies distort national policy. Under centralization, foreign lobbies also wield influence. As argued by Bordignon et al. (2003), the economies of scale created by centralization can actually encourage political lobbying. If the foreign and domestic lobbies have the same interests, then policy is doubly distorted. If instead the two lobbies have opposite interests, then they offset each other and the distortion is mitigated.

As soon as political failures are recognized, a new consideration emerges. The public choice literature has emphasized that one of the best responses to political capture is political competition.[4] Checks and balances among different levels and branches of government can increase political competition. Economic competition can raise the costs of political capture.

Europe's Way

The decision to allocate a particular task to the EU level is rarely black and white. The four benevolent-government criteria – economies of scale, externalities, heterogeneity, and information asymmetries – often send different signals, and political distortions must be factored in as well. In the end, any decision will necessarily involve hard-to-evaluate trade-offs. Different people are likely to reach different conclusions not because they fundamentally disagree, but because they may weigh the relevant considerations differently.

Whether by design or by luck, European integration has proceeded in steps. It has first centralized those tasks for which the fiscal federalism criteria were the least ambiguous, where capture by interest groups was more limited

[2] For a general survey, see Persson and Tabellini (2000).

[3] Direct democracy, in particular single-purpose referenda, deals with this problem. Unsurprisingly, perhaps, Switzerland, the country that has the most extensive direct democracy system, has not joined the EU. Similarly, Sweden, which has an open-government practice, is not too pleased with collective decision making in Europe.

[4] The classic reference is Buchanan and Tullock (1962). The other response from the public choice school is to keep government small. Openness is yet another recommendation.

or likely to be reduced by economic competition. The common market is the relevant example. Economies of scale and scope characterize modern industry, so developing a large internal market was a natural step. In this area, preference heterogeneities are minimal and there are few information asymmetries, at least in the long run.[5] Political capture is a serious issue, but the presumption is that economic competition is the right antidote. As the recent debates on state subsidies and industrial policies show, these aspects linger, but the burden of proof has now been reversed. Now special interests have to make a case for exemptions from single market principles. Since such interests are rarely aligned across EU member countries, their power has declined precipitously.

The creation of a monetary union also illustrates these principles and further shows that integration has a dynamic of its own. Increasing trade integration made EU member countries more similar, including in the timing of their business cycles. It reduced the ability of countries to use the exchange rate as a policy tool. By reducing national heterogeneities and alleviating information asymmetries, trade integration made it desirable to exploit the economies of scale and scope that a single monetary policy provides. At the same time, the emergence of independent central banks – partly inspired by the superior performance of the Bundesbank – underscored the desirability of reducing special interest influences on monetary policy. The adoption of a single currency became natural.

Europe's pragmatic approach has not led to centralization of the other tasks for which the balance of arguments is less clear cut. Having dealt with the most straightforward cases – the single market, a common trade policy, the single currency – Europe finds itself considering more contentious areas. New initiatives emerge in part because previous integrative steps changed the balance of arguments for and against centralization in areas such as taxation, labor mobility, common security policy, and common foreign policy. They also emerge because partisans of an "ever closer union," including the structurally pro-integration European Commission, seek to further their goals. It should not come as a surprise that the debates are becoming more contentious. Europe has lost its heart, but it has already done the obvious things. Further integration will be more difficult because it is less obviously justified. In addition, with a few important exceptions, economic integration is nearly complete. The next steps either tackle the hard economic core

[5] Transitions are different, though, since they involve deep restructuring. While transition costs are likely to be small in relation to long-term gains, the existence of losers and winners implies redistributive politics that play out very differently at the local level.

(agriculture, services, labor mobility, environment, taxation) or concern other areas (education, diplomacy, internal security, defense, culture) where heterogeneities loom large. In addition, enlargement challenges a number of established practices. This is the issue that is considered in the rest of this chapter.

Widening Versus Deepening

One often hears that Europe's current difficulties spring from the enlargement process.[6] Decision making has become more difficult, it is argued, because of the larger number of voices and increased heterogeneity (Baldwin and Widgrén, 2003). In this view, Europe can overcome this problem by allowing "clubs of pioneers" that may decide to deepen integration among themselves, leaving the door open to currently reluctant countries. This would mimic the previous evolution, when a core of "pioneer countries" created the European Community and nearly the entire continent gradually joined later (Moravcsik and Vachudova, 2003; Grabbe, 2005).

Another view derives from the observation that economic integration is now nearly complete (Berglöf et al., 2003). Does this mean that the EU should focus on eliminating the last barriers to the four freedoms (mobility of goods, services, capital, and people) and then consider its aims achieved? This view, which clashes with the "common house" views of the founding fathers, used to be popular before the "re-launch of Europe" in the 1980s. It aimed at the establishment of a perfect common market unencumbered with wider political objectives. Today we have passed this stage. Having fulfilled most of the economic integration objectives, Europe is asking itself how to move on to non-economic integration. Even though the issues at stake include areas such as internal security, foreign affairs, research, and education, the principles developed in the previous section remain relevant.

Costs of Enlargement

Decision making does not have to become more difficult as the number of countries grows. The EU voting rules have always been arcane, relying on qualified majority voting (QMV) rules, where member countries receive weights that are the result of deft bargaining and where the threshold required to adopt a decision does not seem to respond to any other logic than the need to conclude a negotiation. These rules reflect a standard feature of federal systems: they magnify the weights of the smaller entities,

[6] See, e.g., Gilbert (2004).

which fear the loss of decision power. The advantage of complex rules – in contrast to one country, one vote rule, for instance – is that they can be adapted to meet changing conditions.

The general principle, though, is that a decision-making rule is effective when there are few blocking minorities. Under majority voting with one country, one vote, 50 percent plus one government is needed to block a decision. With QMV and a higher threshold for adoption, many more opposing coalitions, each with fewer countries, can block decisions. Baldwin and Widgrén (2003) compute the number of blocking minorities according to decision-making rules. They show how the number of blocking minorities has increased following previous enlargements. They also show how EU voting rules can be adapted to enlargement.

The current stalemate is not the automatic consequence of enlargement. It reflects a number of concerns, most of which are not explicitly recognized. One is prestige, which led to the disastrous decision in the Nice Treaty and which has also played a role in undoing Nice in the framework of the draft Constitution.[7] Many countries fear losing their veto right, even indirectly as members of blocking coalitions. Their natural inclination, then, is to increase the number of blocking coalitions. Such indirect attempts to maintain sovereignty make decision making unwieldy. It is perfectly natural that some countries are reluctant to really transfer sovereignty, even in areas that have been identified as shared competences, but there are better solutions than distortion of the decision-making process. It is better to carefully identify the areas that become shared competences, allow for smooth decision making in these areas, and retain veto rights on the other issues, a topic to which I return below.

The view that heterogeneity increases with the number of member countries, preventing centralization, is another red herring. As far as the more contentious non-economic issues are concerned, there is no evidence in favor of this view, as Charts 1.1 and 1.2 and Table 1.1 demonstrate. Chart 1.1 shows that the new EU members have not increased the dispersion of views on a common defense policy. Table 1.1 shows that the same applies to a common foreign policy. Chart 1.2 shows the percentage of respondents who feel "national" as opposed to feeling European. Nationalism has not dispersed more with enlargement.

[7] The Nice culprit was France, which insisted on the same number of votes as more populous and economically larger Germany. Poland, which along with Spain has resisted any reduction in the number of its own votes, made a positive contribution in the end. France and the Netherlands buried the Constitution for unrelated reasons.

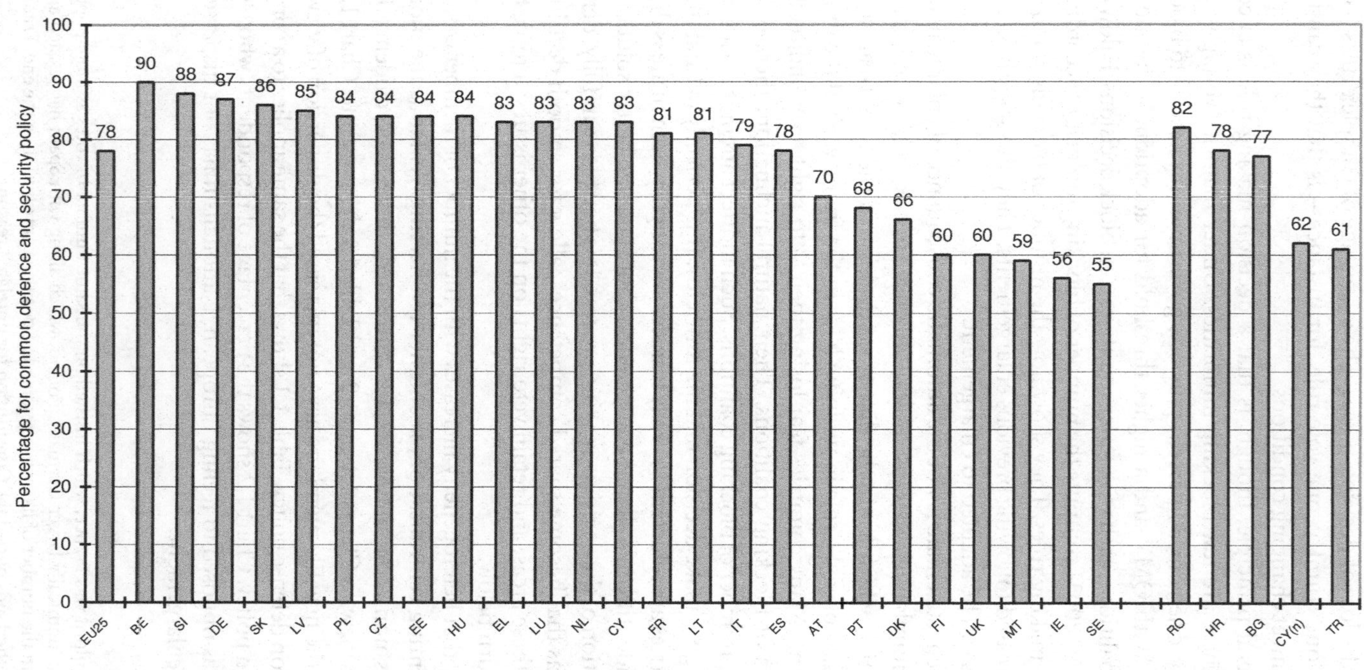

Chart 1.1. Support for a common defense and security policy among the member states of the European Union, 2004. *Source:* Eurobarometer.

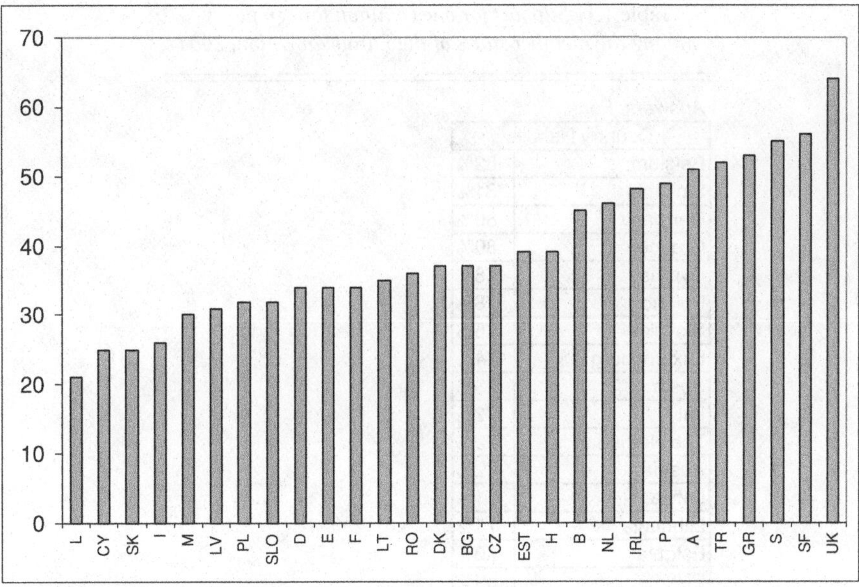

Chart 1.2. Percentage of citizens "feeling national," 2003. *Source*: Eurobarometer EB59.

So where does the perception of increased heterogeneity come from? Some argue that governments are keen to retain their powers in domains that have traditionally been considered as constitutive of sovereignty, even though their own citizens realize the importance of increasing returns from centralization. This hypothesis also encompasses capture by local interests (diplomacy and defense establishments). As special interest incentives are unlikely to be aligned, centralization would seem to be, *ceteris paribus*, the proper response to the hypothesized political failure.[8]

Enlargement should heighten all the usual economic benefits from trade integration, particularly for countries that are initially more diverse. This is a statement about the long run, though, which ignores adjustment costs and the winners and losers from trade integration. However, if trade integration is Pareto improving, the way to deal with transition costs is to organize Pareto transfers, not to oppose enlargement. Much of the grass-roots opposition to enlargement comes from groups that realize they will be among the losers and do not trust their own governments to deliver transfers. Here again, we face a political failure. One solution would be to centralize the Pareto transfers. Information asymmetries, however, warn us that centralization might be inefficient. Past experience with regional and structural funds, which were

[8] Initially, most central bankers were lukewarm, at best, toward the monetary union.

Table 1.1. *Support for one common foreign policy among the member states of the European Union, 2004*

Answers: For

Country Results	
Belgium	82%
Slovenia	81%
Germany	80%
Greece	80%
Cyprus	78%
Poland	78%
Slovakia	75%
Luxembourg	74%
Spain	73%
Italy	72%
The Netherlands	72%
Austria	72%
Latvia	71%
Lithuania	71%
Estonia	70%
EU25	69%
France	69%
Hungary	69%
Ireland	62%
Finland	61%
Denmark	60%
Czech Republic	59%
Portugal	58%
Sweden	52%
Malta	50%
United Kingdom	47%

** Cyprus North (55%)*

Source: Eurobarometer.

partly captured by special interest groups and even countries, confirms this fear. If Pareto transfers are unlikely to be offered, should we still advocate enlargement (past and future)? On economic terms, yes, since permanent gains always outweigh transitory costs. On political terms, one would have to weigh the risks of increasing opposition to and disenfranchising citizens from European integration.

Europe as a Common Market

The view that economic integration is nearly complete and that we should stop there is superficially convincing. To start with, it ignores the primary goal of establishing peace on the continent; the undertaking has always been wider than trade. The strategy of making each citizen a stakeholder in peace through economic interests has worked beautifully. Whether economic interests suffice is an open question.

More important, perhaps, is that integration generates its own dynamics. We cannot operate a common market without common institutions. The well-publicized democratic deficit of European institutions reminds us that common decisions cannot be left to bureaucracies. Europe is attempting to address this problem via the intergovernmental method, but the existence of political failures at this level – discussed above – indicates that this approach is not sufficient.

Economic integration is not limited to the movements of goods and services. Labor mobility is a crucial element, as is made clear by the optimum currency area literature (Mundell, 1961).[9] This means Europe de facto has a common border, which is a source of an important externality as terrorism and large-scale immigration amply illustrate. Labor mobility naturally begets a common internal security policy.

In addition, economic integration spills over into different policy domains, such as education and research. There is increasing recognition that Europe's failure to catch up with the United States economically is related to its inferior education and research institutions. This is a complicated issue that goes beyond the present chapter, but two observations illustrate the issues at stake. First, research is subject to increasing returns to scale. Second, higher education cannot reach top-level quality without robust competition. In both cases, the question is what the proper scale for the relevant policies is. In principle, competition can take place at the level of each country. Competition is the norm in some countries, but elsewhere state control – including key areas such as student admission and hiring of professors – all but eliminates competition. The solution, therefore, lies at the country level, but Europe has a role to play for two reasons. First, many countries are too small to achieve the required scale and reap the benefits from increasing returns. After all, there cannot be twenty-five world-class universities in Europe. Second, in those countries where competition is sorely lacking, reforms are unlikely because of capture by established state universities. Following Bordignon et al. (2003), European initiatives can overcome such a political failure, as long as competition is the guiding principle.[10]

[9] Trade theory, in its basic version, establishes that trade and labor mobility are substitutes. This assumes away market failures, for example, the existence of involuntary unemployment.

[10] These remarks concern higher education. Primary and secondary education involves considerable preference heterogeneities and is better organized at the national – or subnational – level.

Finally, many other policy domains have important economic aspects. For instance, defense absorbs a sizable share of public spending. Defense is subject to increasing returns, and spillovers are very large in a geographically compact area. A European army would certainly be more efficient than the medley we now have. Efficiency-conscious governments need to balance this consideration with other non-economic issues, and the rational answer might well be a common defense policy. This has been a perennial issue, going as far back as 1952, to the stillborn European Defense Community. Much the same can be said about foreign policy. To be sure, true preference heterogeneities exist, but one might reasonably suspect the critical opposition originates with powerful vested interests. As shown in Charts 1.1 and 1.2, 67 percent of citizens favor a common foreign policy, while 78 percent favor a common defense and security policy.

Dilution?

Is enlargement diluting the Union? The most visible difficulty relates to decision making. As noted above, it is entirely possible to adapt voting procedures to avoid an inefficiently large number of blocking coalitions. The evidence in Chart 1.3, which shows passage probabilities under existing voting rules, confirms that past reforms have not prevented a sharp decline in decision-making effectiveness.[11] The cost of fixing the problem is that individual member countries, especially but not only the smaller ones, may end up unable to form or join blocking coalitions.

The second source of concern is growing heterogeneity. This is not a necessary consequence of enlargement, only a possibility. It can be explored empirically but this has not been done systematically. The evidence presented here is therefore sketchy. It exploits the biennial survey carried out by the Commission and published in Eurobarometer since 1973. Unfortunately, the coverage and questions have changed over the years, thus a long-term series is not available. Chart 1.4 shows the evolution of perceived benefits from EU membership, a series that can be traced back to polls conducted between April and May 1983, that is, after the first and second enlargements, and October 2004, shortly after the fifth enlargement. The answers can be interpreted as a measure of satisfaction with EU membership. Available data cover three enlargements, listed under the chart and indicated by vertical lines. The thicker curve shows the unweighted EU average. The thinner curve displays the standard deviation across countries and can be interpreted as

[11] Passage probabilities are computed using the normalized Banzhaf index, which measures the probability that a proposal will be accepted on the basis of random voting by member countries. For details, see Baldwin and Widgrén (2003).

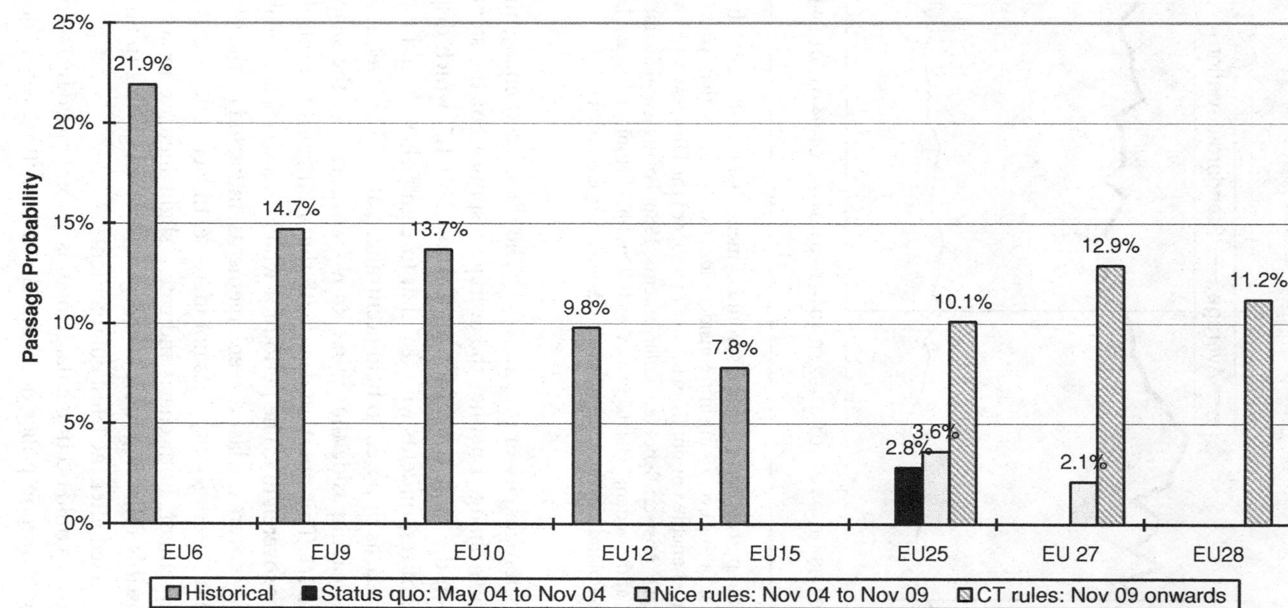

Chart 1.3. Passage probabilities in the EU. *Note*: The figures show the "passage probability," which measures the likelihood that a randomly selected issue would pass in the Council of Ministers. *Source*: Baldwin and Widgrén (2003).

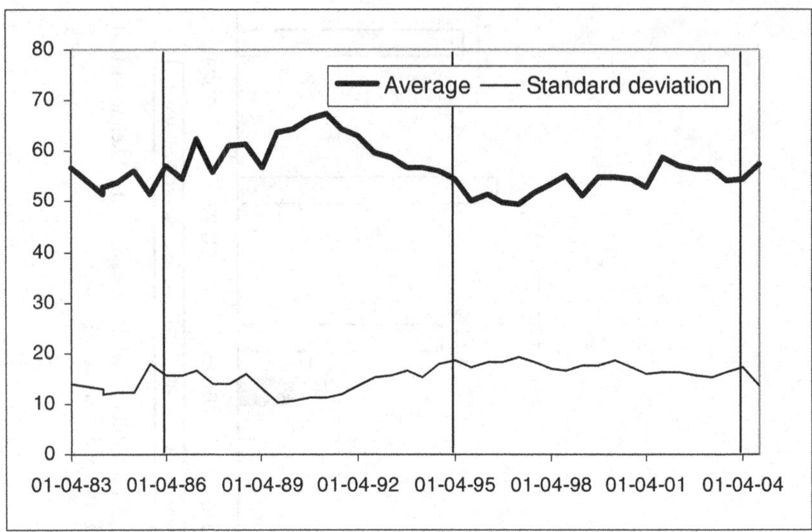

Chart 1.4. National perceptions of benefits from EU membership, 1983–2004, by percentage. Question: Taking everything into consideration, would you say that (your country) has on balance benefited or not from being a member of the European Community (Common Market)? Answer: Benefited. Enlargements: 1986: Portugal and Spain; 1995: Austria, Finland, and Sweden; 2004: Cyprus, Czech Republic, Estonia, Hungary, Latvia, Lithuania, Malta, Poland, Slovakia, and Slovenia. *Source*: Eurobarometer.

a measure of heterogeneity of preferences.[12] The three latest enlargements have significantly changed neither the average response nor the standard deviation. Much the same conclusion applies to Chart 1.5, which displays the percentage of respondents who feel that foreign policy should remain in national hands, as opposed to being centralized at the EU level. It is the complement – leaving aside the "don't know" answers – to the snapshot shown in Table 1.1. This question deals with the willingness to centralize a key attribute of sovereignty. The period for which this series is available is shorter and only covers the last two enlargements, indicated by the vertical lines. Here again, heterogeneity does not increase. In fact, it decreased after the latest enlargement. Both charts indicate a slight increase in standard deviations, possibly reflecting more heterogeneity (though this trend may have briefly reversed after the latest enlargement).

Finally, dilution could occur if enlargement is accompanied by less cohesion in existing common policy domains. By construction, this is not the

[12] Using the unweighted average is desirable for examining national preferences. Obviously, the number of countries included in the polls increases following each enlargement.

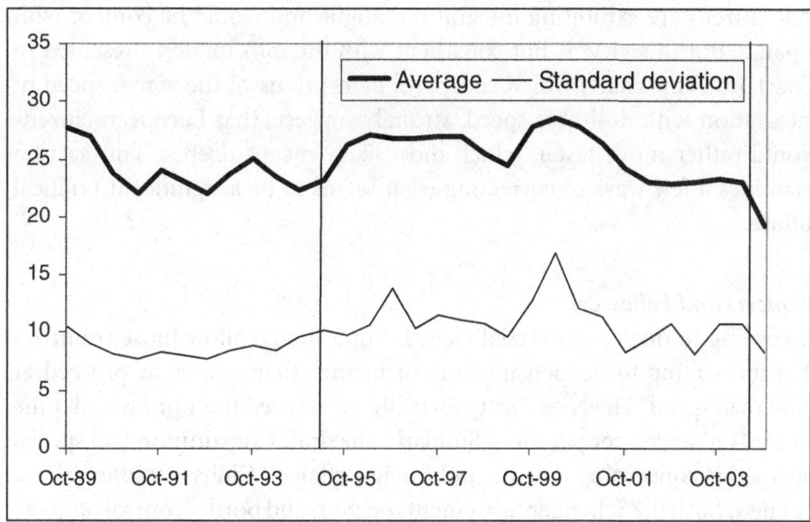

Chart 1.5. Preference for National Foreign Policy, 1989–2003, by percentage. Question: Foreign policy toward countries outside the European Union should be decided by the (national) government/mainly at national level. Answer: Yes. Enlargements: See Chart 1.4. *Source*: Eurobarometer.

case. New member countries must take on board the whole of *acquis communautaire*, which have become considerably more extensive over the years. In this respect, the EU-25 is considerably more homogeneous than the original EU-6 as far as actual policies are concerned.

On the basis of this limited information, dilution appears not to be an automatic implication of enlargement, but rather the result of a political failure. Governments seem less willing to reduce their individual influence in order to preserve the effectiveness of collective decision making. This is not surprising, as governments are often keen to preserve their powers. On the other hand, governments respond to incentives. The next section examines what could encourage them to trade off some autonomy in the pursuit of more efficient collective decision making.

Making a Large Union Work

A recurrent theme so far is that enlargement need not occur at the expense of deepening. This chapter has also argued that limiting the integration process to economic issues – that is, to completing the Single Market – is both unrealistic and unlikely to match citizens' preferences. One often hears that citizens are exhibiting integration fatigue and would be content with a pause, but this view is not consistent with the information presented in Chart 1.6. This chart, which compares perceptions of the actual speed of integration with desirable speed, strongly suggests that European citizens would rather move faster, which most likely means deeper. This section examines a few ways of correcting what seems to be a significant political failure.

Pioneers and Followers

According to one controversial view, Europe should allow those countries that are willing to deepen integration further than others to proceed at their own speed. The Nice Treaty formally introduced this option under the label of enhanced cooperation. Similarly, the draft Constitution had special provisions concerning defense and foreign affairs. "Clubs of pioneers" are not new. Both the Schengen agreements on visas and border controls and the monetary unions are instances where a subgroup of countries has proceeded on its own.

This could be an antidote to rising heterogeneities. As previously observed, there is little evidence that heterogeneity has increased as the result of enlargement (Charts 1.4 and 1.5), but Chart 1.6 shows that, on average, citizens want faster integration. Heterogeneity arguments predict that averages conceal important national differences, which Chart 1.7 confirms. This chart plots national averages of perceived and desired integrative speeds.[13] Along the line actual and desired speeds are equal. In the few countries below the diagonal – chiefly the Nordic countries and Austria – citizens would rather see integration slow down. Most of the new EU members are far above the diagonal.

The logic of establishing pioneers' clubs is related to the previous discussion. In the presence of significant heterogeneity regarding the desirability of deeper integration, we need to have an effective decision-making process. The deterioration of effectiveness, documented in Chart 1.3, makes clubs appear to be an attractive alternative to decision-making reform.

The idea of pioneers' clubs provokes serious opposition, especially in countries that are not willing to proceed faster. Opponents often argue against an EU with two classes of member countries, but what does this really mean? One possible interpretation is that pioneers may enjoy welfare gains at the expense of those that stay out.

[13] Note that those who want to see acceleration also tend to perceive actual speed as low; i.e., there is a negative correlation between perceived and desired speeds.

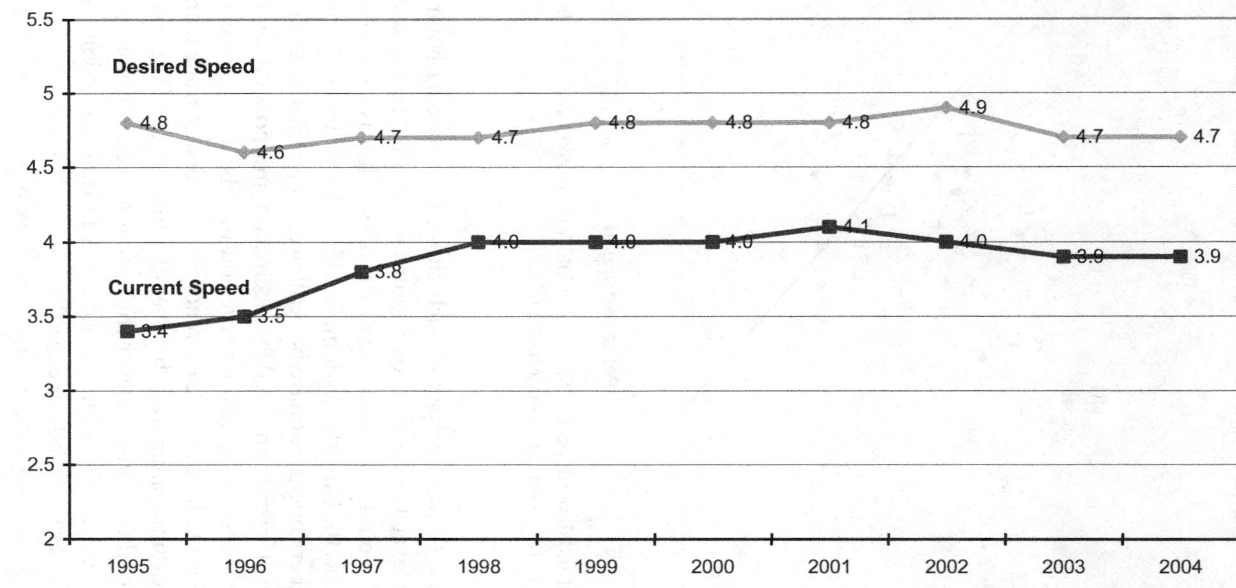

Chart 1.6. Actual and desired speeds of European integration, 1995–2004. Scale is from 1 (standing still) to 7 (running as fast as possible). The average is present here. *Source*: Eurobarometer 62.

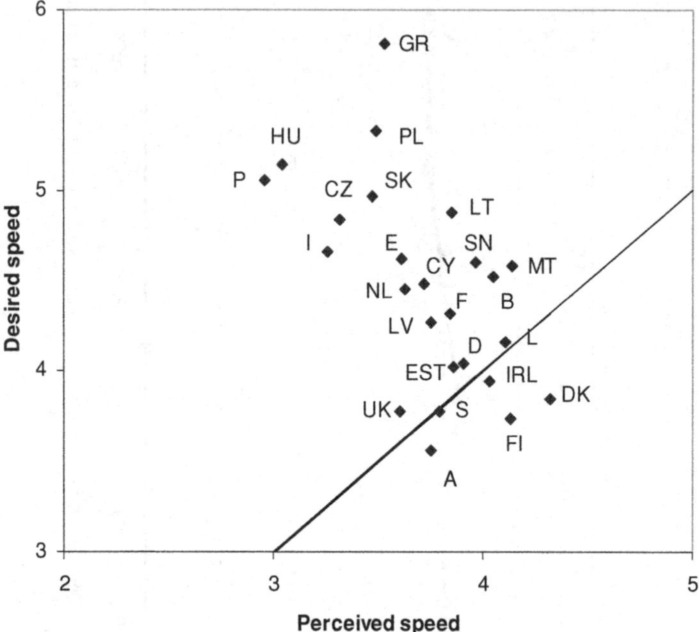

Chart 1.7. Actual and desired speeds of European integration, 2005. *Note*: For definition of scales, see Chart 1.6. *Source*: Eurobarometer 62.

There are few formal analyses of such clubs. One starting point could be the debates over the creation of a monetary union, since it was clear that not all EU countries would join at the outset. It was clear that some countries, such as the United Kingdom, would not be willing to give up their currencies. Others might not have been allowed to join because they were perceived as insufficiently prepared for macroeconomic policy discipline. In the end, twelve countries out of fifteen are now members of the euro area. At the time, some thought the single currency would enhance trade within the euro area while diminishing trade between the euro area and the rest of the EU. Preliminary theory and evidence shows that monetary unions increase trade among their members but do not result in trade diversion (Alesina and Barro, 2002; Frankel and Rose, 2002).

There is no reason the same results should apply to every club, and the article by Bordignon and Brusco (2003) seems to be the only one so far that addresses the issue. They show that clubs can indeed hurt nonparticipating members, but they derive a number of conditions under which clubs are welfare enhancing for all members. Some of these conditions – Pareto transfers, the possibility of renegotiating club rules when new members join – are not met by the enhanced cooperation clauses of the Nice Treaty. On the other hand, the authors note that these clauses provide a strong incentive for doubters to join in, if only to shape the rules.

There may be another argument from political economy considerations. Perhaps cohesion – commitment to the club's existence – among a sub-group of countries detracts from cohesion among the whole set. Here again, we don't know the answer. Even assuming the existence of a trade-off between partial and total cohesion, the proper policy response remains unclear. Clubs may have merits, but they are unlikely to be the best response to the policy failures that prevent better decision making.

Safer Centralization: Toward a Two-Way Street for the Acquis

EU decision making is characterized by polarization: QMV applies to domains of shared competency, unanimity to all other domains. QMV was meant to combine effectiveness and national representation in areas where national sovereignty had been transferred to the EU, while unanimity fully preserves each country's sovereignty. The gradual loss of effectiveness of QMV when enlargements have not been accompanied by adequate reforms (Chart 1.3) has blurred the distinction between the two decision processes.

Indeed, if the probability of making decisions under QMV declines too far, that is, if the number of blocking minorities increases sharply, QMV becomes less and less different from the unanimity voting rule. The lack of adequate reform of QMV decision making following enlargements becomes a source of paralysis. If, as argued above, this lack of reform is the manifestation of governments' resistance to their loss of power in spite of citizens' aspirations, the proper response is to deal with the political failure by better aligning governments' incentives with the wishes of their citizens. The evidence presented above suggests that this means making Europe work better and integrate further, not maintaining inefficient sacred cows such as the Common Agricultural Policy or the Structural Funds, which together represent the bulk of the Commission's budget.

The current principle is that the *acquis communautaire*, the decision to centralize some policies and transfer sovereignty, is permanent. This cannot be optimal since conditions may change. As previously argued, this considerably raises the stakes of the decision to centralize a domain. The result is a powerful incentive for governments to be very prudent in all potential new domains, which is bound to slow down integration. The justification for sheltering the *acquis* is to prevent disintegration. There is some merit to that view, but the EU must weigh the trade-off between the danger of backsliding and the deceleration of integration. This is indeed why national constitutions are sheltered from easy reform but not frozen forever. The EU approach is unique. Reducing the barrier between shared and national competences would lower the stakes and make it easier to reform the QMV process.

This suggests that it should be possible to move policy domains in both directions, from national sovereignty to shared competence, and the other way around. Such a change would lower the stakes of both centralization at the EU level and QMV voting. By making centralization safer, it would not only encourage experimentation – and thus speed up integration – but also make governments more willing to lower the hurdles in decision making.

There are many ways to proceed. One solution would be to make the street between shared and not-shared competences two-way. Unanimity rule would still prevail for any change of status, preventing the feared unraveling of Europe's prerogatives. Another, more radical solution would be to apply sunset clauses to some or all centralization decisions; only those domains for which centralization has proved to be desirable would remain shared competences.

More Power to the People

A different way of dealing with the governments' conflict of interest between preserving their own power and yielding to citizens' desire to speed up integration is to regulate their power. The traditional approach has been to build checks and balances. Europe has done this by vesting some power with the Commission, whose interest is to deepen integration. This is why the Commission has been given the right to set the agenda and the task of "guarding the Treaty." The limits of this approach have been obvious for many years. Since the end of the relatively powerful Delors Commission, governments have endeavored to re-establish a more favorable balance. They have done so by exploiting their democratic legitimacy to emphasize intergovernmentalism at the expense of the community method. The community method exploits the agenda-setting power of the Commission to advance proposals that can be adopted through QMV. Viewed this way, the erosion of the effectiveness of QMV can be interpreted less as the unwanted outcome of difficult intergovernmental negotiations than as the consequence of a gang-up coalition. This has led to a pause in the integration process and difficulties in adapting EU governance to enlargement. The feeling that Europe has lost its heart is partly related to this evolution.

The draft constitution's response was to widen the influence of the European Parliament, which is presented as closer to citizens' preferences.

Irrespective of whether this is true or not, the rising influence of the European Parliament comes more at the expense of the Commission than at the expense of national governments. Overall, this evolution is likely to slow down integration since the Commission is its main advocate. What are the other possibilities?

One way of redressing the current political failure and giving integration a chance is to enhance the European Parliament's influence relative to national governments, not the Commission, as proposed by the now-defunct draft Constitution. In contrast with – or in addition to – the draft Constitution, which focused on formal rights, the idea would be to emphasize the Parliament's legitimacy, which is currently no match for that of national governments. National governments enjoy strong legitimacy because they are democratically elected. In theory, the European Parliament, too, is democratically elected and should enjoy enough legitimacy to act effectively. In practice, however, the fact that elections to the European Parliament are conducted at the national level, and are mostly determined by domestic political issues, undermines the Parliament's legitimacy. It is also divided along both party and national lines, leading to significant fragmentation and decisions that citizens don't always understand or care about. Changing the way the European Parliament is elected could make a more decisive contribution than enhancing the co-decision process. The key here would be to make elections Europe-wide. This could be done in a variety of ways. Berglöf et al. (2003) discuss various possibilities: a single constituency with proportional voting, or the requirement that parties present candidates in a minimum number of countries. In any case, the aim should be pan-European parties whose electoral platforms deal with European, not national, issues. Only then would the European Parliament achieve sufficient legitimacy and cohesion to act as an effective counterpower to the Council.

An alternative would be to enhance the legitimacy of the European Commission. Currently, the Commission is a hybrid combining legislative and executive powers. It is subject only to the kind of limited democratic accountability that typically applies to bureaucracies. As guardian of the Treaty, it is meant to be nonpolitical, and indeed, it brings together Commissioners that are not jointly supported by any majority, either in the Council or in the European Parliament. Its legitimacy vis-à-vis the Council is therefore highly limited, which explains why governments can easily promote intergovernmentalism and bypass the Commission. There are two ways of giving the Commission more legitimacy. The first one is the parliamentary model: the Commission could be elected by the Parliament, where it would have to achieve majority support. The second one is the presidential model: the President of the Commission could be directly elected by all European citizens.[14] In both cases, the Commission would become more explicitly politicized. Politicization, of course, is a double-edged sword: it bestows legitimacy but it strengthens the risk of capture by organized interest groups. This is why a politicized Commission should surrender its purely technical missions to specially designed committees, which would be accountable to the European Parliament or to the Council. These committees would handle enforcement of the single market, including competition and trade.

Conclusions

This chapter has argued that there is no inherent trade-off between enlargement and deepening. Enlargement does not obviously dilute the Union, but it requires some adjustments, mainly in the decision-making process. The Nice Treaty's failure led to the Convention of 2002–2003, but the resulting draft treaty fell short of even modest expectations. Even if the Constitution had been ratified, the EU would have remained stuck because of its inability to deal with its success, the integration of most of the continent.

Contrary to many assertions, the EU is not being diluted nor is it becoming looser. Today's Union is considerably more structured than the old Community of Six, and there is no evidence it has become more heterogeneous. It faces three distinctive challenges.

First, the most obvious integration steps have been taken. Naturally, the next potential ones are more controversial. The easy answer, to stop here and limit the EU to a Common Market, is unsustainable. This chapter has argued that integration breeds the need for more integration, or at least for changing modes of integration. This is emphatically not an endorsement of the "bicycle theory," which holds that unless integration progresses it will unravel. It is an argument for continuing adjustments, in whichever direction is required to match citizens' aspirations.

Second, the difficulties in adjusting the decision-making procedure reflect the natural tension between national sovereignty and the collective interest. National governments are not well suited to deal with this problem, at least alone. They face a conflict of interest between their reluctance to give up power and the aspirations of their citizens. This is why the founding fathers have vested some executive and legislative power with the European Commission. Enlargement has diminished this power by making QMV decision

[14] For a discussion of the relative merits of the two systems, see Persson and Tabellini (2003). For an application to the EU, see Berglöf et al. (2003).

making highly inefficient and increasing the size of the Commission. Both problems can be fixed, but they require concessions that the national governments have been unable to make. Their reluctance is due not to popular resistance, but rather to a reluctance to give up power and influence.

Third, the irreversible increase in the range of domains subject to shared competences creates perverse incentives. It makes governments increasingly reluctant to make the decisions. It deters further transfers of competences, giving the impression of integration fatigue. It allows governments to use Europe as a scapegoat when implementing unpopular decisions that they supported behind the closed doors of the Council. It is largely responsible for the democratic deficit, the perception that more and more decisions are taken by unelected bureaucrats. The response must start with more democratic control at the EU level. This would mean the emergence of a European-level legitimacy, autonomous sources of power that would clash with the continuing predominance of the nation-state as locus of all legitimacy. The response must also include the option of renationalizing some shared competences if, with the benefit of experimentation, they prove to be poorly exercised or to go against citizens' wishes. The French and Dutch voters who rejected the Constitution were, in part, motivated by the fear of external encroachment into issues that they deeply care about. The EU must guarantee that such will not be the case.

The sense that Europe has lost its heart comes not from backsliding but from the contrast between the dramatic progress already achieved and the difficulties of dealing with its consequences. The European way has always been to deal with the requirements of deeper integration pragmatically, in small increments. There have been periods of slowdown followed by periods of acceleration. The last acceleration, the "re-launch of Europe" in the 1980s, led to the adoption of the Single European Act and the monetary union. The fifth enlargement of 2004 has given a false impression of acceleration, but it was widening, not deepening. Now Europe needs a new acceleration. Like the previous one, it needs to be carefully prepared. The next opportunity will be the preparation of a new agreement to replace the failed draft Constitution. The target date is 2009.

References

Alesina, Alberto, and Robert J. Barro. 2002. "Currency Unions." *Quarterly Journal of Economics* 117, no. 2: 409–436.

Baldwin, Richard, and Mika Widgrén. 2003. "Power and the Constitutional Treaty: Discard Giscard?" London: CEPR.

Baldwin, Richard, and Mika Widgrén. 2004. "Council Voting in the Constitutional Treaty: Devil in the Details." Unpublished paper, Graduate Institute of International Economics.

Baldwin, Richard, Erik Berglöf, Francesco Giavazzi, and Mika Widgrén. 2001. "Nice Try: Should the Treaty of Nice Be Ratified?" *Monitoring European Integration*, vol. 11. London: CEPR.

Berglöf, Erik, Barry Eichengreen, Gérard Roland, Guido Tabellini, and Charles Wyplosz. 2003. "Built to Last: A Political Architecture for Europe." *Monitoring European Integration*, vol. 12. London: CEPR.

Bordignon, Massimo, and Sandro Brusco. 2003. "On Enhanced Cooperation." Unpublished paper, Catholic University of Milan.

Bordignon, Massimo, Luca Colombo, and Umberto Galmarini. 2003. "Fiscal Federalism and Endogenous Lobbies' Formation." CESifo Working Paper 1017.

Buchanan, James, and Gordon Tullock. 1962. *The Calculus of Consent: Logical Foundations of Constitutional Democracy*. Ann Arbor: University of Michigan Press.

Frankel, Jeffrey A., and Andrew K. Rose. 2002. "An Estimate of the Effect of Currency Unions on Trade and Output." *Quarterly Journal of Economics* 117, no. 2: 437–466.

Gilbert, Mark. 2004. "A Fiasco but Not a Disaster: Europe's Search for a Constitution." *World Policy Journal* 21, no. 1: 50–59.

Grabbe, Heather. 2005. "The Constellations of Europe: How Enlargement Will Transform the EU." London: Centre for European Reform.

Haas, Ernst B. 1958. *The Uniting of Europe: Political, Social, and Economic Forces, 1950–1957*. Stanford: Stanford University Press.

Mitrany, David. 1975. *The Functional Theory of Politics*. New York: St. Martin's Press.

Moravcsik, Andrew, and Milada Anna Vachudova. 2003. "National Interests, State Power, and EU Enlargement." *East European Politics and Societies* 17, no. 1: 42–57.

Mundell, Robert. 1961. "A Theory of Optimum Currency Area." *American Economic Review* 51, no. 4: 657–665.

Persson, Torsten, and Guido Tabellini. 2000. *Political Economics*. Cambridge: MIT Press.

Persson, Torsten, and Guido Tabellini. 2003. *The Economic Effects of Constitutions*. Cambridge: MIT Press.

Tabellini, Guido, and Charles Wyplosz. 2003. *Réformes structurelles et coordination en Europe* (Structural Reforms and Coordination in Europe). Paris: La Documentation Française.

Wyplosz, Charles. 2004. "The Challenges of a Wider and Deeper Europe." In Klaus Liebscher, Josef Christl, Peter Mooslechner, and Doris Ritzberger-Grünwald, eds., *The Economic Potential of a Larger Europe*. Cheltenham: Edward Elgar.

TWO

Economic Implications of the Social Provisions of the Stalled EU Constitution

Georges de Ménil

Introduction

The growth of total factor productivity has been declining for several decades in the largest member states of the European Union. The program, which the EU announced at the Lisbon Summit in 2000 to reverse this trend, has so far failed. The passage of the halfway mark in the Lisbon Agenda calendar in 2005 was the occasion for numerous critical assessments and calls for renewed efforts to stimulate EU productivity.

In the midst of this productivity crisis, Europe is also constructing itself. In May 2004, it added ten new members. One month later, Valery Giscard d'Estaing handed a draft "Treaty Establishing a Constitution for the European Union" to the leaders of the expanded Union at a summit meeting in Thessaloniki. On May 29 and June 1, 2005, the electorates of France and the Netherlands rejected the Treaty in referenda and its ratification came to a halt. Will the Union eventually adopt principles and rules of governance that will allow it to function efficiently as a body of twenty-five? Will expansion continue? How will those processes affect the prospects for productivity and growth?

During the past two decades, the continuing development of the European Union has had an important liberalizing effect on its member states. The Single Market Act in 1986 and the implementation of the Economic and Monetary Union in 1999 have stimulated rationalization and restructuring.[1] A single, anti-inflationary currency has slowly made competition in

[1] Paradoxically, unemployment has grown and productivity growth slowed in spite of these liberalizing developments. The consensus among experts is that the market-friendly changes that have occurred in Europe have simply not gone far or fast enough. In the face

I have benefited from the comments of Anders Åslund and from discussions with Stephen Breyer and Jean-Claude Casanova. Any errors and all of the views expressed are mine.

financial markets, and even competition in the market for corporate control, progressively more intense. Enlargement has the potential to extend and intensify this process. The new member states, which were formerly in the Soviet sphere, have a labor force of high quality and low wages. Migration of labor and business will, over time, exert increasing pressure on public and private labor costs in the EU-15.[2]

But this dynamic of competition is coming into conflict with two political and institutional pressures. First, anxious electorates are increasingly attacking what they perceive to be the democratic deficit and the lack of transparency of European Union institutions. The accusation particularly singles out the European Commission. Since it is the Commission that has the primary responsibility for initiating and enforcing EU legislation, this challenge puts a brake on the Union's liberalizing agenda.[3]

Second, enlargement threatens to put decision making into deadlock. The highest political body of the Union is the Council of Ministers, in which each member state is equally represented. On many matters, the Council of Ministers must act unanimously. Though consensus was a feasible modus operandi when there were six member states, it became difficult when there were fifteen, and it risks becoming impossible with twenty-five or twenty-seven. Though that had been its principal purpose, the Nice Treaty (2000) failed to facilitate decision making in the enlarged EU. It extended Qualified Majority Voting (QMV) to the future new members, but simultaneously raised the threshold for the approval of legislation. Experts have estimated that under those rules only 3 percent of laws presented are likely to be approved. Clearly, new institutional rules are required for the enlarged Union to function effectively.

These two challenges have the capacity to quickly disrupt the Union's competitive dynamic. They also threaten its economic stability and growth in the longer run. In the countries that have adopted it, the euro is by and large

of increasing global competition, liberalizing changes have not kept up with the need to reduce regulatory rigidities. See Blanchard and Wolfers (2000) and Bertola et al. (2001).

2 Initially, the majority of the EU-15 chose the option provided by the Accession Treaties to impose transitional restrictions on the immigration of workers from the new member states. But immigration will in principle become free when those measures expire in 2011. In the meantime, Western businesses are increasingly investing in the new member states.

3 The recent travails of the Services Directive provide an important example. When in 2005 Commissioner Fritz Bolkestein published a draft of this directive, which was to be a key element of the Union's strategy to meet its Lisbon objectives, groups that felt threatened protested throughout the EU-15. One of the criticisms made was that an unelected Commissioner did not have the democratic legitimacy to initiate legislation that would so directly and importantly influence the citizens of member states. The intensity of the protest contributed to the rejection of the Constitutional Treaty by the French and the Dutch, and caused the directive to be both delayed and watered down.

popular. Politicians and economists tend to take its longevity for granted. But economic analysis tells us that prudent finance is a necessary concomitant of sound money. Whether the Stability and Growth Pact, which was intended to promote prudent finance, and its 2005 revision, were well conceived or ill conceived, it is clear that the Union still lacks an institution at the center with the legitimacy and the capacity to act on fiscal matters. The two key actors in excess deficit procedures are the Commission and the Council of Ministers, whose vulnerabilities I have just discussed. Should, one day, one of the Euroland countries be engulfed by a debt crisis, the Commission would lack the legitimacy and the Council of Ministers would lack the capacity to contribute to the resolution of the crisis. In this general sense, the necessity to ensure the longevity of the euro is another reason why both institutions must be strengthened.

The Treaty Establishing the Constitution for the European Union (henceforth Constitutional Treaty) attempted to address both of these problems. I argue below that it would have enhanced the democratic legitimacy of the Commission and strengthened the authority and ability to act of the Council of Ministers. Both developments would have reinforced the capacity of the EU to promote competition and stimulate productivity growth.

The Treaty also included social provisions whose importance was not always appreciated. Foremost among them was the elevation to Union-wide constitutional status of a number of social entitlements ranging from the right to be protected against "unfair" dismissal to the right to receive unemployment, health, and retirement benefits. I argue below that ratification of this "Solidarity " Title of the Charter of Fundamental Rights in the Constitutional Treaty would have, by increasing the uncertainties and the costs of structural change, reduced productivity growth.

In fact, the French and Dutch referenda halted the ratification of both the productivity-enhancing and the productivity-retarding features of the Constitutional Treaty. If and when the constitutional process is revived, pragmatic considerations may give priority to institutional changes affecting the Commission and the Council of Ministers. Enlargement has given these changes pressing urgency. Their more technical nature may also allow more easily for ratification by national Parliaments rather than by referenda. Giving constitutional status to a "Charter of Fundamental Rights" is more likely to require referenda, at least in some countries. In the current climate of economic frustration and euroskepticism, political leaders are likely to perceive new referenda as too risky to undertake.

This chapter focuses on the economic implications of the social entitlements in the Constitutional Treaty. It attempts to redress the gap between the potential importance of these constitutional, social issues and the paucity of attention they have received. I suggest that avoiding ratification of the "Solidarity" Title of the Charter of Fundamental Rights, in addition to being politically prudent, would also best serve the economic interests of the member states.

In a broad sense, the subject of this chapter is the relationship between EU institutions and the dynamism of the EU economy. This chapter is part of a growing literature on the relationship between economic performance and institutions, which traces its origins to Montesquieu, Adam Smith, and Hayek and has featured more recently the contributions of La Porta et al. (1998, 1999), Hall and Jones (1999), and Acemoglu et al. (2001).[4] The central question the chapter addresses is how different provisions of the Constitutional Treaty would have affected the general environment for private enterprise.[5]

The second section begins with a review of the medium-term economic record and the need for structural reform in Europe. The third section briefly describes the provisions of the Treaty, and identifies four as central: the clarification of the *acquis*, the increased authority of the Council, the increased authority of the democratically elected Parliament, and the scope of new social provisions. The remainder of the chapter focuses on the fourth of these, the social provisions. The fourth section describes the constitutionalization of social entitlements in the "Solidarity" Title in Part II of the Treaty. The fifth section discusses what could have been an alternative legislative option for addressing social issues at the Union level. The sixth section analyzes what the economic implications of the social entitlements in the "Solidarity" Title might have been had the Treaty been ratified. The seventh section concludes with an evaluation of where the emphasis should lie if the European constitutional process is revived.

[4] Recent econometric studies have examined the way in which the growth of onetime colonies has been influenced by differences in the institutions imported from the colonizing country. Whereas La Porta et al. (1998) suggest that Anglo-Saxon common law has been more conducive to development than Latin civil law, Acemoglu et al. (2001) claim instead that the determining difference is between colonies to which Europeans migrated, with their native institutions, and colonies in which the mother countries followed "exploitative" policies.

[5] This chapter does not address the questions that are treated in the very different and also growing literature on "the economic effects of constitutions." Persson and Tabellini (2003) and others focus on issues such as the way in which differences in the structure of government and in electoral rules from one democracy to another influence the efficiency of government. They ask, among other things, whether a presidential democracy is more or less likely to maintain balanced budgets than a parliamentary democracy.

Productivity and Structural Factors in Europe

Regulatory Burdens and Social Protection

A growing body of evidence suggests that excessive regulatory burdens and heavy costs of welfare entitlements are among the most important causes of both the sluggishness of productivity growth and the persistence of high unemployment rates in a number of EU member states. Since the unemployment effects are the most tangible and the most clearly documented, I shall discuss them first.

In the immediate aftermath of World War II, the governments of many Western European countries (responding among other things to the deprivations and destruction of the war and the internal and external threat of communism) instituted generous social programs. Many of them – some more than others – took advantage of the growth dividends of post-war expansion to increase these programs. By the time of the first oil shock in 1973, employment protection legislation was more stringent, unemployment compensation more generous, and social security taxes much higher in Europe than in the United States. High average levels coexisted with large country-to-country variations in Europe (Blanchard and Wolfers, 2000). The result was that the global, adverse supply shocks of the 1970s and 1980s caused unemployment rates to rise to dramatically new heights in Europe and stay there. In the United States, which experienced the same supply shocks, increases in unemployment were temporary. By the 1990s, the relationship between the two regions was the mirror image of what it had been a generation earlier. European rates of unemployment, which had been lower than those of the United States, had become much higher (see Table 2.1).

The consensus among analysts is that it was the higher degree of social protection in European countries, interacting with the global shocks, which was responsible for their transition to much higher unemployment rates. In the United States, real wages adjusted to the shocks and employment was restored. In Europe, rigid labor markets blocked the adjustment, real wages were maintained, and employment did not recover (Blanchard and Wolfers, 2000; Bertola et al., 2001). Heckman (2002) points out that the volatility of technological change and global competition in the 1990s has continued to interact in the same perverse manner with Europe's more rigid institutions.[6] The implication is that if unemployment is to be durably reduced in Europe, European institutions must move toward greater flexibility.

[6] Bertola et al. (2001) suggest that the counterpart of lower unemployment in the United States is a greater variability and inequality of real wage rates. Heckman (2002) cautions against extrapolating life-cycle inequality from observed cross-section inequality.

Table 2.1. *Overall Unemployment Rate (common definition), Selected Countries (percentage of active labor force)*

Country	Period 1970–1974	1995–1996
Australia	2.2	8.5
Belgium	2.2	14.2
Canada	5.8	9.6
Finland	2.2	16.7
France	2.7	11.5
Italy	4.3	12.0
Japan	1.3	3.2
Netherlands	1.8	7.1
New Zealand	0.2	6.2
Spain	3.0	23.0
Sweden	2.2	7.9
United Kingdom	2.5	7.9
Non-U.S. average (unweighted)	2.5	10.7
United States	5.4	5.5

Source: Blanchard and Wolfers (2000).

Europe's protective regulations have also contributed to slower productivity growth. The most visible manifestation of the relationship is the weakness of the high technology sector in the large, continental member states. Chart 2.1 suggests, for instance, that there is an inverse correlation in Europe between the intensity of labor market protection (expected cost of layoffs) and the use of the Internet, one of the central emphases of the Lisbon Agenda. A natural interpretation of this correlation is that countries and sectors where employment rationalization is constrained by protective regulations are discouraged from adopting new technologies, one of whose principal benefits is that they promise labor savings.

State control and product market regulations, particularly those which create administrative burdens and inhibit competition, have also been demonstrated to slow total factor productivity growth in Europe. Though privatization and regulatory reform have increased competitiveness in most EU countries over the 1980s and 1990s, the pace of these reforms has varied importantly from country to country. Nicoletti and Scarpetta (2003) show that the overall decline in productivity growth has persisted in countries and sectors that have been slow to reform and has been partly reversed where reform has proceeded more rapidly during this period.

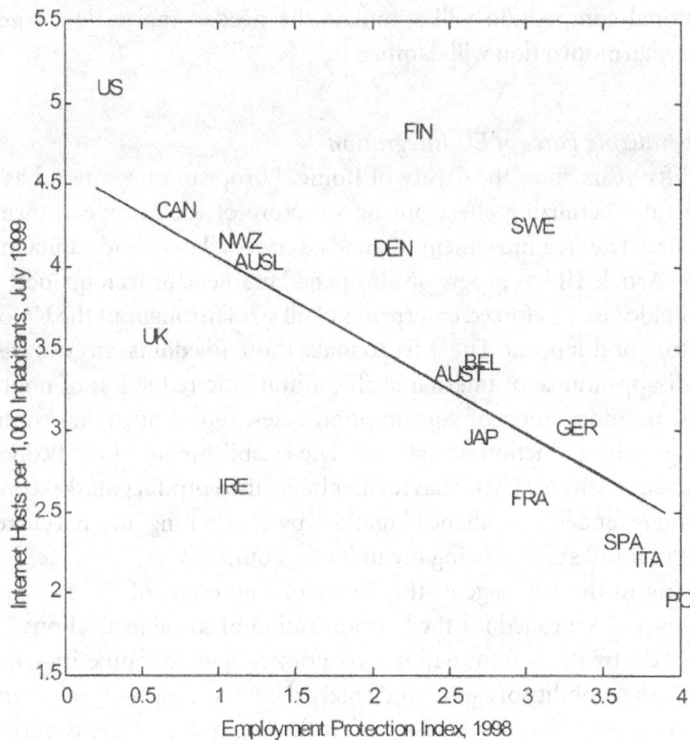

Chart 2.1. Internet usage and employment protection in OECD. *Source*: Samaniego (2006).

The differences in protection and its reform across countries within the Union are an important characteristic of the regulatory landscape in Europe. In Great Britain, state control and product and labor market regulations were dramatically reduced by Prime Minister Thatcher after 1979. Partly in response to budgetary pressures, the governments of Ireland and Denmark also initiated more market-friendly policies in the early 1980s. The Programme Commun in 1981 moved France, for a while, in the opposite direction. Member states differ in the form as well as the intensity of the protection they provide.

By the twenty-first century, the member states of the European Union faced a fundamental societal dilemma: how, particularly in the slower growing countries, could the institutions of social protection be adapted to create a context more favorable to economic growth? The challenge was and is clearly more than a quantitative challenge. What is needed above all is institutional innovation. A central hypothesis of this chapter is that institutional competition will stimulate the needed innovation, whereas statutory harmonization will dampen it.[7]

The Liberalizing Force of EU Integration

In the fifty years since the Treaty of Rome, European integration has had a powerful, liberalizing effect on the structure of the European member economies. The free movement of goods, services, labor, and capital mandated by Article III has progressively opened markets, broken up local economic fiefdoms, and forced enterprises of all sizes throughout the Union to restructure or disappear. The drive to make those freedoms effective has led to the disappearance of internal tariffs, a dramatic reduction of nontariff barriers, harmonization of consumption taxes, repeal of capital controls, and progressive reduction of state aid. The establishment of the Economic and Monetary Union (EMU) has further intensified product market competition and extended it to financial markets by eliminating internal currency fluctuations and standardizing the unit of account.

Nothing in the language of the Treaty of Rome nor of the subsequent Single Market Act called for the harmonization of social institutions.[8] The silence of the treaties left the national economies open to competition in this area. And the mobility of capital and enterprise has increasingly put pressure on the most generous social systems. At the beginning of the twenty-first century, a certain degree of institutional competition does exist between national systems of social protection. By its nature, it is unpredictable and slow. But it is real. The withdrawal at the beginning of 2005 of some of the thirty-five-hour work-week constraints in France, and the scaling back of unemployment compensation and sick leave in Germany in 2004, may be viewed in part as a response to these competitive pressures. As these examples suggest, these pressures have had a positive effect on productivity-enhancing

[7] A parallel can perhaps be drawn between this twenty-first-century challenge and the seventeenth- and eighteenth-century history of the emergence of the modern corporation and modern financial markets from the political competition for global dominance among Holland, England, Spain, and France. If any one of these powers had prevailed in an absolute sense early in the seventeenth century, the competition would have attenuated, and these institutional developments might have taken much longer to emerge (North and Weingast, 1989).

[8] Baldwin and Wyplosz (2004) suggest that this omission was logical. Their argument is that the aggregate labor supply is fixed in each country, and not in fact mobile across borders within the Union. Therefore, workers in each country must bear the full cost of cross-country differences in the social cost of labor, and these do not distort the economic structure of labor costs across countries. Consequently, they do not affect patterns of trade and do not distort the free movement of goods.

reform. The EU would benefit from more such institutional competition rather than less.

Highlights of the Constitutional Treaty

How would the Constitutional Treaty have influenced competition and structural change in the Union? The Treaty Establishing a Constitution for Europe was attacked by some for providing a death warrant to the nation-state, by others for enshrining laissez-faire liberalism, and by still others for laying the foundations of a monolithic federal welfare state. Almost everyone criticized it for being too long, at 230 pages. What were the changes that the leaders of the member states had agreed to but that the electorates in two key states rejected? I focus on the four features that were most important from an economic point of view.[9]

First, the Constitutional Treaty subsumed, rationalized, and simplified the three pre-existing founding treaties (Rome, Maastricht, and Amsterdam). Though seemingly a minor achievement, this would have been important in and of itself. It would have made executive and legislative procedures in the Union more legible and transparent. Second, the Treaty would have deepened the political integration of the member states. Paradoxically, institutional changes designed to enable the enlargement of the Union would have brought about increased deepening as well. The most fundamental of the measures proposed, the introduction of a double scale (number of states and size of population) for Qualified Majority Voting, was indeed intended to avoid a gridlock. By lowering the threshold for decision to 60 percent of the population of the Union, Giscard d'Estaing and the Constitutional Council have loosened the grip of sovereign obstruction left by Nice.[10] By the same token, it would also have increased the powers of the Union relative to those of the member states.

A similar reasoning applies to another, much discussed institutional change – the replacement of the rotating national President of the European Council with an individual President, named for two and a half to five years. By giving greater political authority to the center, this change would have facilitated cooperative resolution of potential conflicts between the member states, thus giving the Union greater political depth. To the degree that it

[9] I focus in what follows on the economic significance of the Treaty, and I therefore do not mention several innovations of substantial political importance, such as the creation of the office of Foreign Minister of the Union.

[10] Negotiations between the submission of the draft Treaty and its signature by heads of state and governments in June 2004 raised this legislative threshold to 65 percent.

would have facilitated the resolution of budgetary divergences, a nonrotating presidency would have indirectly strengthened the Monetary Union as well.[11]

Third, the Treaty would have increased the democratic legitimacy of Union legislative acts and of the EU executive branch, the Commission. Important changes in this regard were the proposal to expand powers of the European Parliament, which was to share the legislative authority with the Council, and, most importantly, which would be entrusted with approval of the nominations of the Council for the President of the Commission and for the Commission as a whole. Though the power simply to approve may not at first seem decisive, the example of the Revolution of 1688 in England shows that it is sufficient eventually to make a government (the Commission) responsible to Parliament.

The significance of these changes is not just that they would have enhanced the authority of the Parliament, but that they would have, thereby, increased the democratic legitimacy of the Commission and its President. Such legitimacy is of paramount importance in and of itself, but it is also significant from an economic point of view. It strengthens the capacity of the authorities to act; it provides a mechanism for the correction of errors; and it enhances the long-term viability of the institutions.

Fourth, the Constitutional Treaty would have given the European Court of Justice (ECJ) a new mandate to monitor social policies in the Union. It would have given constitutional status as "fundamental rights" to an important list of social entitlements, of which the ECJ would have become the guardian. It is to these constitutional social entitlements that I now turn.

Social Entitlements in the Constitutional Treaty

In fact, references to social objectives appeared throughout the Treaty.[12] Part I declared several of them to be among the central objectives of the Union. The third article of the Treaty, I-3.3, stated:

The Union shall work for a Europe of sustainable development based on balanced economic growth, a social market economy, highly competitive and aiming at full

[11] The Treaty also introduces several functional innovations, which could potentially have economic significance. "Enhanced Cooperation" could provide a vehicle for some member states to pursue closer budgetary and fiscal integration. The threat of "Suspension" may give more weight to functioning majorities. "Voluntary Withdrawal" may avoid a disorderly secession in a time of crisis.

[12] Article X, for instance, evokes as a desirable objective the creation of Union-wide collective bargaining procedures.

employment and social progress, and with a high level of protection and improvement of the quality of the environment.... It shall combat social exclusion and discrimination, and shall promote social justice and protection, equality between women and men, solidarity between generations and protection of children's rights.

The third article of Part III (III-117), which describes the "policies and functioning" of the Union in extensive detail, used similar language:

In defining and implementing the policies and actions referred to in this Part, the Union shall take into account requirements linked to the promotion of a high level of employment, the guarantee of adequate social protection, the fight against social exclusion, and a high level of education, training and protection of human health.[13]

The language in Parts I and III was, however, essentially rhetoric. It called on the institutions of the EU and the governments of the member states to pursue certain economic and social objectives, but it would not have created constitutional obligations with regard to specific undertakings. Part II of the Treaty, on the other hand, would have had more binding implications.

The "Solidarity" Title

Part II of the Constitutional Treaty integrates and elevates to constitutional status a previously non-binding Charter of Fundamental Rights of the Union, which includes, in Title IV ("Solidarity"), twelve articles that refer to conditions and procedures in the workplace and to numerous different benefits provided by the state.

These fundamental rights are not individual rights in the traditional liberal sense. An individual right (such as freedom of speech or equal protection under law) is a statement that enjoins government from infringing the stated liberty. Governmental authorities are not allowed to act in certain ways. Many of those traditional individual rights are restated and substantially expanded in Titles I–III and V–VII of Part II.[14]

The fundamental rights of Title IV are different. They oblige governments to provide certain protections and services (such as social security benefits or good health care). They are principles of social entitlement.[15] They are

[13] Article III-119 further mandates that "environmental protection requirements must be integrated into the definition and implementation of the policies and activities in this Part."

[14] Freedom of religion (II-70), freedom of expression (II-71), freedom of association (II-72), presumption of innocence (II-108), prohibition of ex post facto convictions (II-109), and so on.

[15] I choose to refer to the two concepts as "individual rights," on the one hand, and "principles of social entitlement," on the other, rather than to use the value-laden terminology, which is sometimes used, of "negative rights" and "positive rights."

new. Supporters of their inclusion in the Constitutional Treaty claimed that it would have been the first binding international agreement to include such principles of social entitlements.[16] Examples include:

- Social security benefits and services for maternity, sickness, accidents at work, old age, and unemployment (II-94);
- Good health care (II-95);
- A high level of environmental protection and improvement (II-97) and
- A high level of consumer protection (II-98).[17]

Other articles in Title IV confer constitutional status to workers' rights in the labor market, such as:

- the right not to be "unfairly" dismissed and
- the right to strike (including, without restrictions, for public employees).

Table 2.2 lists all of the entitlements covered by the "Solidarity" Title.[18]

Antecedents and Alternatives

Constitutionalization of social entitlements such as proposed by the "Solidarity" Title was not novel in the European Union in 2003, when Giscard d'Estaing submitted the draft treaty to its leaders. A strong tradition of constitutional jurisprudence on social matters already existed in many of the member states of the EU-15. In Germany, a single statement in the Basic Law of 1947 had been interpreted by a strong constitutional court as requiring that federal and *Laender* legislation provide minimum levels of social income and housing assistance.[19] The post-war constitution of Italy and the post-Franco and post-Salazar constitutions of Spain and Portugal include some twenty specific obligations of governments to provide social benefits.

However, the constitutionalization of social entitlements was not universal in the EU-15. England had, and still has, no written constitution. Individual liberties (freedom of speech, *habeas corpus*, right to trial by jury, etc.) have long been protected in England by common law tradition. But social benefits are not recognized in England as entitlements that a government is legally bound to provide. Ireland, Austria, and Luxemburg (the

[16] Duhamel (2003).

[17] Articles II-85 and II-86 in Title III ("Equality") recognize the right of the aged to "a dignified and independent life" and the right of the handicapped to "supportive measures."

[18] The distinction between the top and bottom and left and right of the table is discussed in the fifth section.

[19] "Human dignity shall be inviolable" (Article 2).

Table 2.2. *EU Constitution: Part II, Title IV "Solidarity"*

	"In accordance with Union Law and National Law and Practices"	No qualifier
"... has the right ..."	Worker's right to information (II-27)	Access to free placement service (II-29)
	Collective bargaining (II-28) Right against unjustified dismissal (II-30)	Working conditions that respect health, safety, dignity (II-31.1)
	Social security benefits and social advantages for all legal residents, including immigrants (II-34.2)	Limitation of maximum hours, rest periods, paid holiday (II-31.2)
	Right of access to preventative health care and right to benefit from medical treatment (II-35)	Prohibition of child labor (II-32)
		Family shall enjoy legal, economic, and social protection. Also maternity and paternity leave (II-33)
		A high level of environmental protection and the improvement of the quality of the environment must be integrated into the policies of the Union (II-37)
"the Union recognizes and respects (the right, the entitlement ...)"	Entitlement to social security benefits and social services (II-34.1)	Union policies shall ensure a high level of consumer protection (II-38)
	Social and housing assistance (II-34.3)	
	Access to service of general economic interest (II-36)	

latter two of which have constitutions shaped in the nineteenth century) also only recognize individual liberties, as does the constitution of the United States.[20]

In the member states in which social entitlements are not constitutionalized, social policies are the exclusive responsibility of legislatures. An advantage of the tradition that makes legislators rather than judges the arbiters of

[20] For the history and geography of individual constitutional rights and constitutional social entitlements in Europe, see de Ménil (forthcoming).

major societal choices is that it provides more leeway for the correction of errors. Legislators can, and not infrequently do, reverse themselves. Only thirty years, but a world of policy debate, separate the Great Society programs passed by the U.S. Congress when Lyndon Johnson was President from the repeal of many of them in the Welfare to Work reform passed by Congress when Bill Clinton was President. Other important instances of legislative reversal include the Hartz IV program, passed by the German legislature in 2004, and the loosening of France's thirty-five-hour work-week law, passed by its Parliament in 2005. Judges, particularly constitutional judges, have more difficulty reversing their decisions. As long as the constitution they are interpreting is not amended, they are reluctant to reverse precedents.[21]

An Alternative, Legislative Approach to Social Policy in the Union

An alternative approach to the treatment of social policy at the Union level would have been to enable the European Parliament and the European Council to take legislative action in these areas. The Constitutional Treaty did make some proposals in this direction, but they remained limited.

The Constitutional Treaty provided for social legislation at the Union level, in Articles III-207, III-210, III-234, and III-235. These articles authorized the Council and the Parliament, acting together in what the Treaty refers to as "ordinary legislative procedure," to pass binding laws concerning certain aspects of employment policies, social policies, environmental protection, and consumer protection.

Much but not all of this authority predates the Constitutional Treaty. Union legislation about working conditions was, for instance, already part of the *acquis communautaire*. Whether pre-existing or new, Union legislative authority would have been a far cry from the legislative authority of a full-fledged federal state. The total budget of the Union is a miniscule fraction of the budget of the German federal government or of the French government, and it will remain such for some time, since any expansion of the Union's revenues would require unanimous agreement of all member states. Therefore, in practical terms, the Union would have continued to be incapable of funding new social programs out of its own revenue or new revenues. What it can and could have done is to legislate unfunded mandates, that is, required member states to initiate programs that they have to fund with

[21] Amendment of the Constitutional Treaty of the Union would require unanimous ratification by all members.

their own resources.[22] The Union can also regulate the policies enacted by the member states, for instance, by setting minimum standards.

The most sensitive area, and the most important given the diversity of social regimes in Europe, is that of social policies. Article III-210 provided for Qualified Majority Voting concerning "improvement ... of the working environment," "working conditions," "the information and consultation of workers," and "the integration of persons excluded from the labor market." In those areas, some binding Union laws already existed, and others could have been passed.[23]

However, Article III-210 (and the predecessor provision in the Amsterdam Treaty) left many additional, important areas blocked by the requirement that Council approval must be given unanimously. The blocked areas include "social security and social protection," "the protection of workers where their employment contract is terminated," and "the conditions of employment for third-country nationals residing legally in the Union territory." A bridge provision (III-210.3) would have allowed the Council to decide by a unanimous vote that it might switch to QMV in the last two of these areas. The bridge was not tendered for "social security and social protection."

A special paragraph (III-210.6) stated explicitly that no aspect of the article was to apply to "pay, the right of association, the right to strike, or the right to lock out," topics considered off-bounds for Union legislation.

All in all, the Union's powers to legislate in social matters remained limited in the Constitutional Treaty. One can regret that the advocates of free market policies at the Convention did not endorse the extension of Qualified Majority Voting to social issues, and insist, in exchange, that the Charter of Fundamental Rights, particularly the "Solidarity" Title, retain its original precatory status. This would have entailed taking the risk that a European Qualified Majority might have undone some particularly liberal national statutes. But it would have avoided the burden and uncertainty of possible future litigation by the European Court of Justice over social entitlements. Moreover, in the context of current reform efforts, the risk that Union majorities might vote for more costly social provisions is not overwhelming.

[22] In the United States, Congress has legislated such unfunded mandates a number of times. One example is the requirement that local communities provide and fund special education for handicapped children.

[23] It would be theoretically possible, for instance, for a qualified majority of member states (with the Parliament) to pass legislation limiting work time to thirty-five hours a week in all member states.

The introduction of legislative authority to vote Union-wide social minima into the Constitutional Treaty would potentially have limited competition between national social systems. It would, nonetheless, have been preferable to their constitutionalization. It would have represented an important victory for democratic process, and the laws passed would have had the considerable benefit of being reversible.

Be that as it may, it was the interpretation of human rights as extending to social entitlements that prevailed at the Constitutional Convention. The alternative interpretation, focusing exclusively on individual liberties, failed.

What the Implications of the "Solidarity" Title Might Have Been

One Constitution for All

It takes time for the implications of constitutional provisions to become manifest. Nonetheless, it is clear that the inclusion of the "Solidarity" Title in Part II of the Treaty had the potential to affect the growth of productivity in all the member states.

The potential reach of the Constitutional Treaty with regard to social entitlements flows from two considerations. The first is that EU treaties take precedence over national statutes. This means that on any subject addressed, the Constitutional Treaty would have been binding for all member states. Even national constitutions could have done more – for instance, required more social protection – but could not have done less. The Constitutional Treaty would have become the binding minimum legal standard in the areas that it covered. In case of conflict, the European Court of Justice could potentially have declared conflicting language in the constitution of a member state to be non-operative. No member state would have been able to preserve statutes that conflicted with the Constitutional Treaty.

The second important consideration, which follows from the first, is that ratification of the Constitutional Treaty would have reduced the pre-existing constitutional diversity among the member states. In the long run, the scope for systems competition would have been seriously limited. If the Treaty had been ratified, the states that had not previously given social entitlements constitutional protection would have had to operate in a different legal framework. For instance, layoffs that had been legal under national law might have been challenged as "unfair" under European law.

The nation facing the greatest change in this regard would have been the United Kingdom, which has operated without any written constitution and has entrusted the defense of individual liberties to the common law jurisprudence of its civil courts and of the Law Lords. Not surprisingly, British representatives at the Constitutional Convention insisted on including safeguards in the text to protect the labor market reforms of the Thatcher Government against future challenges based on the "Solidarity" Title of Part II.[24]

Nations whose national constitutions did protect social entitlements, but whose courts had not actively defended these statutes, would perhaps have found the European Court of Justice to be stricter in its interpretations than their national courts had been. It is impossible to know now how the ECJ would have treated the "Solidarity" Title of Part II. But more than forty years of jurisprudence has shown it to be a strong court, which has not hesitated to uphold European treaties against the perceived national interests of member states.

Finally, all member states, even those with constitutional social entitlements actively defended by a strong constitutional court – of which Germany is an example – would have been influenced by the attenuation of competition between social systems across Europe. In time, the generalization of minimum social standards, which the Treaty implied, could have made it more difficult to reform social regulations throughout the EU.

Safeguards

Some analysts claim that representatives to the Constitutional Convention, notably the British, succeeded in including language in the Charter of Fundamental Rights (Part II), which would have limited its scope. Two different safeguards have been inserted.

The first would have limited appeal to the ECJ on the basis of the Charter to matters involving Union actions and laws and their implementation. Article II-112.5 stated, "The provisions of this Charter . . . shall be judicially cognizable only in the interpretation of acts . . . taken by institutions . . . of the Union [and by] member states when they are implementing Union Law."

This limitation would effectively have "grandfathered" existing national legislation that might otherwise be challenged under the Charter. In that sense, the British representatives were successful in their effort to guarantee that the Thatcher labor market reforms could not have been overturned by the ECJ.

24 See notably the affirmation of an unqualified right to strike, in both the public and private sectors, in II-88.

Going forward, it is less obvious that the exemption from Charter control of strictly national legislation would have remained a significant exemption. Experts have estimated that 70 percent of national legislation in most member states will soon consist essentially of the implementation of Union laws. Any law whose direct or indirect implications were deemed to violate the Charter would have been subject to challenge.

An example is useful. Suppose that British authorities, implementing a Union law on environmental protection, were to order the closure of a polluting plant in the Midlands, and that workers were to be laid off. Had the Constitutional Treaty been ratified, the workers could have appealed to British courts to enjoin the closure on the grounds that their dismissal was "unjustified" and that the Constitutional Treaty entitled them to be protected against it. They would simply have had to argue, on technical grounds, that other environmental solutions could have been found that would have avoided closure and preserved employment. In the end, they might not have prevailed, but nothing in Article II-112.5 would seem to have foreclosed such a procedure.

The second safeguard was supposed to exempt member states, which had not yet themselves passed protective legislation, from the reach of certain articles in the Charter. Eight of the articles of the Charter (all of them in the "Solidarity" Title) declared certain social entitlements to be fundamental rights "in accordance with Union Law and national law and practices." That qualifying phrase was not included in the statement of other fundamental rights (social and otherwise) (see Table 2.2).

It is possible to interpret the "in accordance" phrase as meaning that the Union right in question would not have existed in states that had no pre-existing national law or practice to that effect. This would have implied, for instance, that the Court could not uphold the right to "protection against unfair dismissal" (Article II-90) in states that had no similar, pre-existing law or practice. It also could not have obliged a state with no pre-existing statute mandating employer-employee concertation (Article II-87) to create such a statute *de novo*. The official comments of the Presidium of the Convention, annexed to the Constitutional Treaty, confirm that this was indeed the intention of the language, at least in regard to social security provisions.[25]

The limiting powers of the language would, nonetheless, only have applied to entitlements that were totally absent in certain member states. What is more important is that attempts by a member state to cut back on an existing

[25] See Comments of the Presidium of the Convention.

social entitlement would have been subject to a legal challenge involving the ECJ, if the Constitutional Treaty had been ratified.

Commenting on the "Solidarity" Title, a Socialist delegate to the Convention, who was a strong supporter of its inclusion in the Treaty, wrote, "The debate (about social security at the Convention) brings out the fundamental judicial nature of constitutionally guaranteed social rights. They do not create the obligation for any State to institute new forms of social payment, but they do guarantee the preservation of forms of payment which have been created. In this sense, the Charter is more of a protection against reductions than an assurance of increases."[26]

Conclusion

The enlargement of the European Union, and the accompanying deepening that it requires, and that the Treaty Establishing a Constitution for the European Union would have provided, have the unquestionable potential to stimulate much needed productivity growth in the Union. In the first half of the twenty-first century, economic competition between the new member states and the old member states may well be the most important stimulus for productivity growth in the region. For the benefits of that competition to accrue, the Union must endure and the region must enjoy reasonable macroeconomic stability. That, in turn, requires that the European Commission and the European Council have the authority and legitimacy to promote competition and reduce major tensions between the budgetary policies of member states when they occur. The Constitutional Treaty would have been a step on the road toward the necessary institutional framework.

This being said, the social provisions of the Treaty – most notably the social entitlements given constitutional status in the "Solidarity" Title of the Charter of Fundamental Rights of the Union – would not have been favorable to productivity growth. They would have tended, other things being equal, to slow down the structural reforms that are an urgent priority in many member states. The problem in Europe is not that there has been too little social policy, but that there has been too much. The challenge in each country is to find an appropriate balance between the necessity to compete in an open and changing world and legitimate desires to limit the social costs of risk and change. The "Solidarity" Title of the Charter would have tended to slow down that process, by limiting competition between the member

[26] Duhamel (2003), p. 283, author's translation.

states and displacing resolution of these societal issues from the legislative arena toward the European Court of Justice.

By halting the ratification of the Constitutional Treaty process, the French and Dutch referenda of 2005 have deprived the EU of necessary institutional advances but have avoided the economic uncertainties its "Solidarity" Title would have generated. If the constitutional process were to be revived, political prudence and the necessity of economic growth would argue that it focus on strengthening Union institutions and continue to treat social entitlements as aspirations rather than constitutional obligations.

References

Acemoglu, Daron, Simon Johnson, and James A. Robinson. 2001. "The Colonial Origins of Comparative Development: An Empirical Investigation." *American Economic Review* 91, no. 5: 1369–1401.

Badinter, Robert, and Stephen Breyer. 2003. *Les entretiens de Provence (The Provence Talks)*. Paris: Fayard.

Badinter, Robert, and Stephen Breyer. 2004. *Judges in Contemporary Democracy*. New York: New York University Press.

Baldwin, Richard, and Charles Wyplosz. 2004. *The Economics of European Integration*. London: McGraw-Hill.

Bertola, Guiseppe, Francine D. Blau, and Lawrence M. Kahn. 2001. "Comparative Analyses of Labor Market Outcomes: Lessons for the U.S. from International Long-Run Evidence," NBER, Working Paper 8526. Cambridge, Mass.: National Bureau of Economic Research.

Blanchard, Olivier, and Justin Wolfers. 2000. "The Role of Shocks and Institutions in the Rise of European Unemployment: The Aggregate Evidence." *Economic Journal* 110, no. 462: c1–c33.

Burgorgue-Larsen, Laurence, Anne Levade, and Fabrice Picod. 2005. *La Constitution Européenne expliquée au Citoyen (The European Constitution Explained to the Citizen)*. Paris: Hachette Littératures.

de Ménil, Georges. (forthcoming). "Social Entitlements in European Constitutions." *Journal of Law and Economics*.

Duhamel, Olivier. 2003. *Pour l'Europe (For Europe)*. Paris: Le Seuil.

Giscard d'Estaing, Valery. 2003. *La Constitution pour l'Europe (A Constitution for Europe)*. Paris: Albin Michel.

Hall, Robert E., and Charles I. Jones. 1999. "Why Do Some Countries Produce so Much More Output per Worker Than Others?" *Quarterly Journal of Economics* 114, no. 1: 83–116.

Hayek, Friedrich A. von. 1960. *The Constitution of Liberty*. Chicago: University of Chicago Press.

Heckman, James J. 2002. "Flexibility and Job Creation: Lessons for Germany." NBER, Working Paper 9194. Cambridge, Mass.: National Bureau of Economic Research.

La Porta, Rafael, Florencio Lopez-de-Silanes, Andrei Shleifer, and Robert W. Vishny. 1998. "Law and Finance." *Journal of Political Economy* 106, no. 6: 1113–1155.

La Porta, Rafael, Florencio Lopez-de-Silanes, Andrei Shleifer, and Robert W. Vishny. 1999. "The Quality of Government." *Journal of Law, Economics & Organization* 15, no. 1: 222–279.

Lamassoure, Alain. 2004. *Histoire secrète (Secret History)*. Paris: Albin Michel.

Nicoletti, Guiseppe, and Stefano Scarpetta. 2003. "Regulation, Productivity and Growth: OECD Evidence." *Economic Policy* 18, no. 36: 9–73.

North, Douglass C., and Barry R. Weingast. 1989. "Constitutions and Commitment: The Evolution of Institutions Governing Public Choice in Seventeenth-Century England." *Journal of Economic History* 49, no. 4: 803–832.

Persson, Torsten, and Guido Tabellini. 2003. *The Economic Effects of Constitutions*. Cambridge: MIT Press.

Samaniego, Roberto. 2006. "Employment Protection and High-Tech Aversion." *Review of Economic Dynamics* 9, no. 2: 224–241.

Traité établissant une constitution pour l'Europe (Treaty Establishing a Constitution for Europe). 2004. Paris: La Documentation Française.

THREE

Fiscal Policy and Fiscal Rules in the European Union

Vito Tanzi

Introduction

In his revolutionary work, the godfather of modern fiscal policy Lord Maynard Keynes gave a central role to discretion in fiscal policy. Thus, in some ways, he, and even more his followers, who probably pushed his ideas beyond where he would have liked, gave policy makers what many of them had always wanted: a justification for spending more or, in particular cases, for reducing taxes without cutting public spending. A correct or effective discretionary fiscal policy is, however, difficult to pursue because it requires information and attitudes that are often in short supply. When countries try to fine-tune their fiscal policy, they often end up making mistakes. This chapter focuses on those difficulties within the European context. It discusses problems that have not received the attention that they deserve.[1]

Since it was first proposed, and then endorsed by the Keynesians, with a revolutionary fervor that at times paralleled that of true religious believers, countercyclical fiscal policy has been subjected to occasional criticism. Three major lines of criticism can be distinguished.

First is the existence of various lags. It was noticed from the beginning that there are likely to be lags in (1) the recognition that fiscal action is needed, (2) the taking of the action, and (3) the time that passes between when the action is taken and when the economy begins to feel its effects. These lags reduce the effectiveness of countercyclical policy. This criticism was frequently heard in the 1950s and the early 1960s, but although it is certainly valid and important, it seems to have largely disappeared from recent writings. A good discussion of the early criticism can be found in Stein (1969).

[1] Some of the issues discussed in this chapter have been dealt with in some detail. For the Italian context, see Tanzi (2005).

The existence of lags may help to explain why empirical studies of fiscal policy often find it to be pro-cyclical rather than countercyclical (see, e.g., OECD, 2004, and International Monetary Fund (IMF), 2004). It may be worthwhile to cite the IMF study: "Discretionary fiscal policies in euro area countries over the past three decades have generally been pro-cyclical – that is, expansionary in good times, contractionary in bad times – thereby undermining the role of automatic stabilizers" (IMF, 2004, p. 111). This was a concern of those who stressed the significance of these lags. For other groups of countries, fiscal policy has also been found to be pro-cyclical. For example, a study of 104 countries found that fiscal policy is pro-cyclical, that is, government spending increases in good times and falls in bad times (Kaminsky et al., 2004). Gavin and Perotti (1997) found pro-cyclical fiscal policies for Latin American countries, and Talvi and Vegh (2000) found pro-cyclical fiscal policy for the whole developing world.

Thus, the problem of pro-cyclicality seems to be rule rather than exception. However, that problem has not been related, in recent writings, to the existence of these lags. It has not reduced the policy makers' and economists' enthusiasm for fiscal discretion and for countercyclical fiscal policy. This enthusiasm is largely at the base of the attacks against the Maastricht rules, which are accused of impeding such a policy.

Second is the criticism associated with the so-called Ricardian equivalence. This criticism was often heard in the late 1970s and in the 1980s after Robert Barro reformulated and publicized a theory (first advanced by Ricardo) that had been well known in the Italian literature on public finance for a very long time (Barro, 1974). This theory assumes that individuals react to government deficits and public debt by increasing their own savings in anticipation of higher future taxes to repay the debt. By so doing, they may neutralize fully, or at least to some extent, the potential effect on the economy of the fiscal policy action.

There has been considerable controversy about the extent of this presumed reaction or compensation on the part of individuals. Some, including Vilfredo Pareto almost a century ago, have been skeptical about the ability of individuals to anticipate future tax increases. However, while many economists have rejected the notion of a *full* compensation, many would agree that there is some compensation. This is more likely to happen now, when the information about the existence of fiscal deficits and public debts is more generally available than in Ricardo's times. A recent analysis, conducted by the OECD, has concluded that in OECD countries, "[t]he evidence of partial, yet substantial, direct offsetting movements in private saving is strong. The aggregate initial offset is about half in the short term ... rising to around 70 percent in the long run" (OECD, 2004, p. 143).

The third line of criticism can be based on the observation that it is easier to find countries whose economies have grown faster after fiscal contractions than after fiscal expansions. It is, in fact, hard to find specific countries where a countercyclical fiscal policy led to a fast recovery from a cyclical downturn. Some would point to the United States after 2001, when record expansionary measures were taken by the Bush administration that, in the view of some observers and claims from the Bush administration, pulled the country out of the downturn. However, in 1993 the country came out of an even steeper downturn while contractionary fiscal measures were being taken, and even so, the expansion of the 1990s became one of the longest in U.S. history. Furthermore, in 2001–2002, the U.S. Federal Reserve took extraordinary measures by reducing interest rates to historically low levels. Work by Giavazzi and Pagano (1996), followed by works by Alesina et al. (1998), Schuknecht and Tanzi (2005), and others, have shown that fiscal contractions can be expansionary for a variety of reasons, but mainly because they reduce the worries about future fiscal developments, thus helping to change the psychology of economic agents and investors.

I would like to add one additional difficulty encountered in the pursuit of countercyclical fiscal policies. It is a difficulty, or criticism, based on public choice considerations. An implicit and fundamental assumption of countercyclical fiscal policy is that taxes and public spending can be changed with the same facility *in both directions*. Thus, there is no bias in the application of Keynesian policies. However, in reality, there is often asymmetry in the use of fiscal instruments, because it is generally far easier, politically, for governments to cut taxes and raise spending than to do the reverse. This asymmetry tends to lead to structural fiscal deficits and to high debts even in normal periods, as the European experience indicates (Tanzi, 2004).

The above criticisms should have reduced the enthusiasm of many for the possibility of using countercyclical policy in the real world. But apparently they have not, because the enthusiasm for discretionary fiscal policy remains strong. In this chapter, I do not elaborate on the above criticisms. Rather, I deal with issues that, though important, have received far less attention, perhaps because they require a kind of insider's knowledge not easily available to many economists who write papers on fiscal policy. These are issues of particular importance for European countries and especially for the application of the Stability and Growth Pact.

The rest of the chapter is organized as follows. The second section describes the process by which fiscal rules have become progressively more relaxed over the years. They have lost their bite. The third section discusses problems of a practical nature that arise in the real-life implementation of countercyclical fiscal policy. The fourth section discusses briefly fiscal policy in the European Union. The final section summarizes the arguments and draws some conclusions.

The Progressive Relaxation of Fiscal Rules

As a consequence of the Keynesian "revolution," fiscal rules that had traditionally guided fiscal actions were dismissed as archaic or reflecting the views of "dead economists." The proponents of the Keynesian revolution were very critical, especially in the formative years of the 1950s and 1960s, when the "revolution" was in full swing, vis-à-vis these rules and the policy makers who still abided by them. For example, in 1958, James Tobin stated, "Orthodox fiscal doctrines have . . . dominated our policies . . . and . . . have brought the nation to the brink of catastrophe" (Tobin, 1966, p. 57).

The "orthodox fiscal doctrines" alluded to by Tobin, which had guided fiscal policy at least since Cicero's time, were the "balanced budget rule" and the belief that the level of public spending and taxes should be as low as possible (Tobin, 1966). These doctrines collided with the Keynesian view that the public sector should be larger and the budget did not need to be in balance.[2] Of course, it had always been recognized that when exceptional events occur, such as wars, major catastrophes, or major public works, the balanced budget rule could be broken. Over the centuries, these events had occasionally led to (temporary) tax increases and to debt accumulation. But once normal times returned, the governments were expected to fully repay the debts they had accumulated by running fiscal surpluses, to reduce the exceptional spending and taxes, and, as soon as feasible, to return to the balanced budget rule. This "tax smoothing" was consistent with a rule that required zero debt and balanced accounts in normal times.

Keynes added the business cycle to the reasons that justify violation of the balanced budget rule. It should be noted, however, that he was writing during the Great Depression, an event that surely qualified as exceptional.[3]

[2] Again quoting Tobin, "Increased taxation is the price of growth" (1966, p. 87); and quoting Galbraith, "The conventional insistence on the balanced budget under all circumstances and at all levels of economic activity was in retreat. Keynes, as we shall see presently, was also on his way to constructing a new body of conventional wisdom, the obsolescence of some parts of which, in its turn, is now well advanced" (1958, p. 18).

[3] During the Great Depression, 25 percent of the American labor force was unemployed. GDP fell from \$97 billion in 1930 to \$58 billion in 1933. Between 1930 and 1941 when the United States entered the war, the fiscal deficit of the U.S. government fluctuated between

The Keynesians added the normal business cycle (as distinguished from a depression) to the list of events that required the abandonment of the balanced budget rule. More recently, the policy makers who met in Brussels in March 2005 and modified the Maastricht arrangements on fiscal policy added, implicitly, a slowdown in economic growth (which is different from a cycle) to the list of events that can justify the abandonment of fiscal rules.[4]

Some policy makers have been arguing for special treatment, in the fiscal accounts, for a whole range of categories of public spending (public investment, R&D, defense, contributions to the EU, expenditures for structural reforms) or even for reductions in public revenue due to tax cuts. They have argued that these expenditure increases or revenue reductions would justify larger fiscal imbalances. In their view, the measure of the fiscal deficit that should determine whether a country is in compliance with the general Maastricht rules should be corrected to reflect these fiscal actions. Thus, we have been witnessing a progressive slackening of the discipline that used to guide the policy makers in charge of fiscal policy. We seem to have gone from a straitjacket to one that may approach complete laxity. According to this thinking, the relevant gauge for assessing fiscal policy must be adjusted for the effect of the cycle *and* for that of particular expenditures or even particular tax cuts.

The recent relaxation of the Maastricht rules is an almost natural extension of the relaxation of the balanced budget rule that started with the Keynesian revolution. In the early 1960s, a sophisticated version of the Keynesian countercyclical fiscal policy introduced the theoretically important distinction between actual revenue and expenditure and their cyclically adjusted counterparts (Council of Economic Advisors, 1962). According to this version, the actual budgetary outcomes could be compared with the counterfactual or virtual budgetary outcomes that would have occurred if the economy had been at its "potential." The differences between these variables would indicate whether current fiscal policy provided the needed stimulus or whether it was "deflationary" or "expansionary." It would thus signal whether some restrictive or stimulative policy action was needed. The theory assumed that potential income was a variable that could be estimated objectively (even though it existed only in its virtual form) and that its future growth could be forecast. One could project with some confidence, using past trends, how

a surplus of 0.8 percent of GDP in 1930 and a deficit of 5.9 percent of GDP in 1934. For other years, it was generally around 4 percent of GDP.

4 In this case the rule that would be compromised would be the one that constrains the deficit to 3 percent of actual domestic product.

potential income would evolve in future years and use this projection for determining the needed discretionary fiscal action.[5]

A fiscal policy judged to be sound required the balance between the cyclically adjusted revenue and the cyclically adjusted public expenditure. In other words, it required a balanced budget rule applied to (unobservable) virtual variables.[6] If these cyclically adjusted variables were not in balance, policy action was required. This policy could be used to stimulate the economy or to slow it down.[7] If cyclically adjusted revenue exceeded cyclically adjusted expenditure, fiscal policy would justify more spending or less taxation. If the reverse were true, fiscal action would promote less spending or higher taxes. A cyclically adjusted budget that was balanced would, thus, be consistent with an (actual) fiscal deficit in a recession (when "potential" income fell below actual income) and a fiscal surplus during a boom (when actual income exceeded "potential" income).

Built-in stabilizers would make the response of fiscal variables to the cycle more accentuated. They would create larger surpluses in boom times and larger deficits in recessions and help to reduce the amplitude of the cycles. There was a push in the 1960s to make income taxes more progressive and the taxes on corporations more important because these taxes reacted more to fluctuations in income, helping to stabilize the economy. The sensitivity of the tax system to changes in income was a variable that received much attention in the 1960s and 1970s (Tanzi, 1969; Tanzi and Hart, 1972). Flat rate taxes and low taxes on enterprises now in fashion, especially in the new market economies of Europe, would reduce the built-in stabilizing properties of the fiscal variables and require larger discretionary actions during business cycles.

A "cyclically neutral" fiscal policy, applied faithfully and correctly, would produce a zero fiscal deficit over the cycle and, thus, would not lead to long-term debt accumulation. The debt accumulated during a recession should be repaid during the upswing. However, with rare exceptions (Luxemburg, Norway, and Estonia), countries have ended up with large public debts, even in periods when no major wars, depressions, catastrophes, or big pushes in public works have occurred. This is evidence that more constraining fiscal rules are needed. Large public debts divert valuable tax resources toward

5 At that time American economists believed that business cycles were well behaved. There were courses on business cycles in universities and these courses explained the average length of cycles and their average amplitude. Also, productivity growth was assumed to be largely a constant.

6 That is, it required fiscal balance at potential income.

7 The role of monetary policy in this context was always vague.

the servicing of the debt and make it more difficult for countries to have their fiscal accounts in balance. There is some empirical evidence that interest payments on public debts reduce public investment (Tanzi and Chalk, 2000).

Some European countries' authorities have, on one hand, argued that the high public debt makes it difficult for the country to have good fiscal accounts. On the other hand, they have supported the push toward more fiscal relaxation that could easily lead to the further accumulation of public debt. Furthermore, when public debt is owed to foreigners, the cost of servicing it becomes higher and the potential danger associated with it also grows. For economies that had been centrally planned, the public debt is often foreign debt, because they have not developed domestic financial markets. For these countries the sustainable public debt is likely to be lower than in more advanced countries with more developed financial institutions (Coricelli, 2005).

Pitfalls in the Implementation of Discretionary Policy

Surprisingly, while the theory of countercyclical fiscal policy has received a lot of attention over the years and is routinely taught in many economics courses, its implementation has received very little attention. The view must be that what is true in theory must be correct and feasible in practice. Or, alternatively, it is possible that those who teach the theory are not fully aware of the many difficulties faced in its implementation.[8] In the rest of this chapter, I focus on the practical implementation of the theory. I have little difficulties with the theory itself. In a perfect world, I would want to follow it. But then a perfect world would not have economic fluctuations.

Cyclically adjusted fiscal policy compares actual variables (revenue, expenditure, fiscal deficits, and even public debt) with counterfactual variables, that is, with variables that are not observed and that must, somehow, be estimated as if they existed. This is far more difficult than is assumed. In this process, mistakes tend to creep in, and they may not always be honest or random errors. Furthermore, even the measurement of actual current fiscal variables has proven to be difficult, as Eurostat and the IMF, over

[8] Once again, I am ignoring here the difficulties connected with lags that did receive attention. I am also ignoring the theoretical criticism associated with the so-called Ricardian equivalence. This criticism dominated the economic literature in the 1980s, but it seems to have almost disappeared from recent discussions.

many years, have found out.[9] Thus, it is easy to imagine the difficulties that exist in estimating counterfactual variables. The issues discussed below are complex. They deserve a more extensive treatment. But I hope to convey a sense of the difficulties. I first discuss the technical requirements for adopting a countercyclical fiscal policy and then focus briefly on political difficulties.

Consider first the technical requirements. First, a countercyclical policy requires the estimates of "potential" income for the current and relevant future periods. How much does actual income vary from potential income? The theoretical literature assumes that the question can be answered easily. Unfortunately, this is not the case. Business cycles are not well behaved, and it is difficult or impossible to determine whether current changes in the growth of income reflect the effect of a genuine business cycle or a change in trend caused by structural obstacles. A good example of this difficulty is provided by Japan. A decade or so ago, when the Japanese economy slowed down, the IMF and the OECD mistook the change in that country's income for a cyclical slowdown, rather than a change in trend. Thus, these organizations strongly and vocally recommended expansionary fiscal policies to inject additional demand. After some hesitation, the Japanese endorsed the recommendation. The result has been that a country that in the early 1990s had by far the best fiscal accounts among OECD countries now has the worst, with a public debt that is 170 percent of GDP and a gaping fiscal deficit that shows no sign of shrinking. This sharp deterioration in the fiscal accounts (1) did not produce any positive effects on the real economy and (2) is likely to constitute a major obstacle to the future growth of that economy.[10] Are we confident that the recent slowdown in several European countries, and especially in the large ones, is part of a cycle and not the beginning of a new slower growth trend? And are we confident that a relaxation of the Maastricht constraints will stimulate growth and not repeat the Japanese mistake?

Second, the pursuit of a correct countercyclical policy requires that the effect of the cycle on the fiscal accounts can be isolated from the effect of discretionary changes on the revenue and the expenditure sides of the budget. Most economists do not appreciate how difficult it is to isolate changes in

[9] Eurostat has recently made embarrassingly large revisions to the deficit estimates for some countries (Greece, Italy) for past years. The IMF has often discovered that the deficits reported for some countries were substantially wrong.

[10] Also, the emphasis on fiscal expansion and the pressure on the Japanese coming from the international organizations and from the G7 countries distracted the Japanese authorities from the major obstacles to growth that were structural in nature. The statements of the G7 always emphasized the need for a fiscal expansion over the need for structural reforms.

fiscal variables due to discretionary measures (including those of an administrative character) from those due to the cycle. In many countries, this separation is impossible to make, but it is still reported. In many countries, discretionary changes, either of a policy type or, more often, of an administrative type, take place all the time. In particular, tax administrations are very active and their activities can have significant effects on tax revenue.

This is an area where the U.S. experience has influenced thinking. In the United States, until recent years, and especially on the tax side, there were few if any discretionary changes in most years. Only infrequent tax reforms introduced such changes. The Internal Revenue Service is required to administer the taxes in a consistent way. The policy changes come at discrete times and are highly advertised. Thus, cyclical adjustments that might have had some justification when applied to the United States have been applied to countries with very different situations. In the footnote to the table that reports the output gap relative to potential GDP, the European Commission cautions that "[o]utput gaps are often non-observable concepts and can be measured in different ways. Analysis based on them should be treated with prudence." The IMF warns that "[e]stimates of the output gap and of the structural balance are subject to significant margins of uncertainty" (IMF, 2004, p. 188). Unfortunately, they do not seem to be treated with "prudence," and the "significant margins of uncertainty" are ignored.

Third, the pursuit of a correct countercyclical policy requires the availability of well-established and robust quantitative relationships between public revenue or public spending, on one side, and national income, on the other. These relationships must have been estimated for long periods of time by netting out the effects of discretionary actions, which, as already stated, is often almost impossible to do. These relationships have proven unstable in various situations as, for example, in the later years of the Clinton administration when the profits from the "new economy" distorted tax revenues. Recently, they have also proven unstable in the United Kingdom and Germany. Therefore, past relationships may be poor predictors of future relationships even in the absence of discretionary changes. When these estimates of past relationships are based on only a few years, as must be the case for new members of the European Union, they would be particularly suspect.

Finally, the pursuit of countercyclical fiscal policy requires a precise determination of where a country is at a given moment. What is its true current fiscal situation?[11] Unfortunately, as strange as it may sound, definitive,

[11] The fact that this question is now being asked almost daily in countries such as the United States, Italy, and Germany indicates that the question is not rhetorical.

objective measures of current revenue, spending, fiscal deficit, and even income are often not available. There are practical or even conceptual difficulties in providing these measures, and ex post facto changes in the measures are common and at times embarrassingly large.

Estimates of the fiscal deficit were traditionally based on cash payments to and from the government. These are the easiest to calculate when all the flows can be controlled, that is, when there are no extra budgetary flows. However, they lend themselves to maneuvers aimed at making the deficits look smaller for given periods, and at times do not cover the whole public sector, but only a part of it. Partly for the first of these reasons and partly because "accrual" concepts are supposed to better reflect the time when the measures have an impact on the real economy, statisticians tend to prefer measures based on accrual concepts. Eurostat has favored accrual measures. These, however, are not easy to determine and often can be determined only with considerable lags.[12] Also, there remain several gray areas in the Eurostat methodology that create debates and invite interpretation on the part of the countries' experts.[13] A consequence has been that large "revisions" to the estimates are often made years after governments provided the data. In particular cases (Greece and Italy), these revisions have amounted to several percentage points of GDP. Unfortunately, the revisions are in one direction. They all raise the size of the fiscal deficit, suggesting that the errors may not have been purely random. Because of political pressures, the incentives for the national experts have been to interpret the Eurostat rules in ways that tend to reduce the size of the fiscal deficits.

A related point is that in some cases, as in Italy, there have been uncomfortably wide differences between the cash measure of the fiscal deficit and the accrual or, better, Eurostat measure. Furthermore, there have been differences even between supposedly conceptually identical definitions, but measured by different institutions. This raises two questions. First, which measure of the deficit is the correct one? Second, which is the one relevant for the pursuit of a countercyclical policy? When one measure gives a deficit of, say, 2 percent of GDP and another a deficit of, say, 4 or 5 percent of GDP, which measure should drive countercyclical fiscal policy? Unfortunately, economists have largely ignored these questions, even though they are fundamental to the conduct of countercyclical policy.

Consider now the political requirements of an effective countercyclical policy. Political cycles must not be present, elections must not influence

[12] This, for example, is the case regarding health expenditures in Italy.

[13] The Eurostat methodology is still partly dependent on cash flows and thus is not purely accrual.

the fiscal decisions of governments, there must be no incentive to present biased data, and there must not be any incentive to manipulate the data through "financial engineering" or through once-for-all measures. Unfortunately, tax amnesties, sales of public assets, creation (à la Enron) of extra budgetary accounts to which some debt is shifted, the assumption of contingent liabilities on the part of the government not shown in the accounts, attempts to push some institutions outside the budget, postponement of some payments, as, for example, tax refunds, to creditors, anticipation of some future revenue, for example, by pressuring some enterprises in which the government has a controlling interest to anticipate the distribution of dividends, and so on, are too frequent occurrences, as various papers and the events have shown (Brixi, 2005; Koen and van den Noord, 2005). "Financial engineering" has come to influence fiscal policy strongly. In the ministries of finance of some countries, "financial engineers" have replaced, in influence at least, traditional fiscal experts. Their role is to "package" the financial accounts to make them look better than they are. Unfortunately, some policy makers seem to be more interested in making the accounts look good than in genuinely improving them. At times, they lose the ability to distinguish the genuine accounts from the "packaged" ones.

Add to all of this the view, now popular with some policy makers, that fiscal deficits are good for growth (and not just to help a country get out of a temporary recession), and it is easy to see the potential problems encountered when a broadly defined "balanced budget rule" is abandoned. The problems mentioned above become greater when flexibility is introduced in a rule that already allows fiscal deficits of 3 percent of GDP and public debts of 60 percent or more of GDP. It would be better if the rule required a zero fiscal deficit and a zero public debt as the normal objective, recognizing that this objective could not be achieved every year or immediately by countries that started their membership in the European Union by being far from it. The flexibility should be in the speed of transition toward a zero deficit and a near zero public debt and not vis-à-vis much less ambitious goals. When a 3 percent deficit and a 60 percent debt, as proportions of GDP, are allowed, these tend to become the minimum, as has happened recently.

Fiscal Policy in the EU

The abandonment of a strict interpretation of the whole package of Maastricht rules (excessive deficit provision and procedure plus the Stability and Growth Pact proper) signals a worrisome trend. A few years from now we may be lamenting the recent decisions by the Council of Ministers.

But by that time other ministers would be on the scene and would suffer the consequences of the March 2005 decision taken by their predecessors.

The pre-Maastricht period was fiscally friendly. There were no wars, no major catastrophes, and no major depressions in EU countries. There was yet no fiscally unfriendly aging of the population and no, or little, negative impact on tax revenue coming from tax competition and globalization. The economic competition from lower spending and lower taxing countries (China, India, Mexico, other countries from Southeast Asia) was still very limited. Therefore, in this fiscally friendly, pre-Maastricht period one would have expected healthy fiscal outcomes for European countries. One statistic is sufficient to convey a sense of fiscal developments in that period. For the twelve EU countries combined, the share of public debt to GDP rose from 31 percent in 1977 to 75 percent in 1997. This was a phenomenal change that took place in a fiscally friendly period.[14] With all its faults and possible tricks, Maastricht brought that growth to a temporary stop. Before Maastricht, some among the twelve EU countries were risking to go the Argentine way. The growth in public debt seems to have started again and from a much higher level. Such growth, combined with, or promoted by, higher interest rates, could create a truly worrisome debt dynamic.

The bad experiences of many countries with fiscal outcomes, both within and outside Europe, have brought back some interest in fiscal rules. Many different rules have been proposed, and some have been introduced into the laws or the constitutions of some countries, including the Netherlands and Poland. But these rules remain controversial because they go against the political and short-run interests of policy makers, who worry about the next elections, and against the entrenched intellectual beliefs of many economists, who have spent too little time in the real world and too much time in the Keynesian world. As Milton Friedman once remarked, at some point, we all became Keynesians. This often means that, when we come to fiscal policy, we pay little attention to structural impediments to growth and we put our faith in an active fiscal policy. Unfortunately, this policy is often implemented from a position when the fiscal accounts are already in difficulty and are already sending worrisome signals to the public. At this point, countercyclical fiscal policy is not likely to do much good because whatever stimulative effect it may have on consumers is balanced by the negative effects on investors and economic agents that originate from and

[14] In the three largest countries of the EU, the debt as a share of GDP rose as follows: from 27 to 61 percent in Germany; from 20 to 59 percent in France; and from 56 to 120 percent in Italy.

accompany deteriorating fiscal accounts. When, for example, a government wants to stimulate an economy by spending more or taxing less, but the message that economic agents receive daily is that the discretionary action will make precarious fiscal accounts even more precarious, why should we expect a positive impact from the fiscal action?

The introduction of fiscal rules runs, of course, into the problem of different initial positions. Two countries that have very different fiscal situations cannot be expected, overnight, to move to identical fiscal outcomes. This was, especially, the situation on the public debt in 1997 because of the high debts of Italy, Belgium, and Greece. It may be the situation with the fiscal deficit today for Poland, Hungary, and some other countries, which start with higher fiscal deficits. Thus, flexibility is required as to the time needed to conform to the rule, but the rule should not be relaxed to the point of making sinning more acceptable for everyone.

Concluding Remarks

Theories may experience cycles just as economies do. They may be popular at some point in time, then lose their popularity to regain it once again. This seems to have happened to countercyclical fiscal policy. The theory became popular in the 1950s and especially in the 1960s. It started to lose some popularity in the 1970s, because of stagflation and the various intellectual attacks on it that came with the Ricardian equivalence, with rational expectation theories, with the implication of the permanent income hypothesis, with technologically based real business cycles, and so on. By the 1980s, that theory seemed to be in retreat. More recently, however, it has made a comeback, especially, but not only, at the political level. Political figures have used it to justify more spending, or even cutting of taxes, on the grounds that these actions would stimulate growth. The attacks against the Stability and Growth Pact have been justified largely on Keynesian grounds.

The new popularity of this theory is puzzling mainly because it is difficult to find countries where it has clearly worked. In fact, it is easier to find countries where fiscal consolidation seems to have promoted healthier economic performance. Fiscal consolidation may reduce worries and concerns about the future and may stimulate economic decisions that promote growth. However, the promotion of fiscal stimuli, through increases in public spending or cuts in taxes, in situations when the fiscal accounts are already in a precarious state (with high public debts and large fiscal deficits), is likely to produce negative reactions from investors and the public in general. This is especially the case in a world where fiscal policy is continually discussed in the media so that the worries of experts become general worries.

This chapter has discussed some of these issues. However, the main focus has been to show that the pursuit of countercyclical fiscal policy is, on technical or practical grounds, much more difficult than is normally assumed, even by economists. Often, the needed information is not available and the variables often used (potential income, structural balance, fiscal reaction functions, etc.) depend on assumptions that are often wrong.

Countercyclical fiscal policy should not be abandoned in depressions and it could be tried in milder slowdowns when the fiscal accounts of a country are in good condition (deficit close to balance, debt close to zero). However, it is doubtful whether it should be tried by countries whose fiscal accounts are in a precarious condition. In the view of this writer, fiscal accounts with public debts of 60 percent of GDP and fiscal deficits at 3 percent of GDP are in a precarious stage.

The implications of this conclusion for the Stability and Growth Pact are obvious. But the problem remains of how to introduce more conservative fiscal rules in a situation where the initial conditions are widely divergent and the political decision is to encourage countries to join a monetary union and not wait until their accounts are under control. Countries should be given more time to converge rather than to relax the long-term standards, as was done in the March meeting of European ministers. But how this is to be done needs much more consideration.

References

Alesina, Alberto, Silvia Ardagna, and Jodi Gali. 1998. "Tales of Fiscal Adjustment," *Economic Policy* 13, no. 27: 487–545.

Barro, Robert. 1974. "Are Government Bonds Net Wealth?" *Journal of Political Economy* 82, no. 6: 1095–1117.

Brixi, Hana Polackova. 2005. "Contingent Liabilities in New Member States." Mimeo.

Coricelli, Fabrizio. 2005. "Fiscal Policy and the Adoption of the Euro for New EU Members." Mimeo.

Council of Economic Advisors. 1962. *Economic Report of the President.* Washington, D.C.: United States Government Printing Office.

Galbraith, John Kenneth. 1958. *The Affluent Society*. Boston: Houghton Mifflin.

Gavin, Michael, and Roberto Perotti. 1997. "Fiscal Policy in Latin America." NBER, *Macroeconomics Annual 1997*. Cambridge, Mass.: National Bureau of Economic Research.

Giavazzi, Francesco, and Marco Pagano. 1996. "Non-Keynesian Effects of Fiscal Policy Changes: International Evidence and Swedish Experience." *Swedish Economic Policy Review* 3, no. 1: 67–103.

International Monetary Fund. 2004. *World Economic Outlook.* Washington, D.C.: IMF, October.

Kaminsky, Graciela L., Carmen M. Reinhart, and Carlos A. Vegh. 2004. "When It Rains, It Pours: Procyclical Capital Flows and Macroeconomic Policies." Mimeo.

Koen, Vincent, and Paul van den Noord. 2005. "Fiscal Gimmickery in Europe: One-off Measures and Creative Accounting." Economics Department Working Paper 416. Paris: OECD.

Kopits, George. 2001. "Fiscal Rules: Useful Policy Framework or Unnecessary Ornaments?" IMF Working Paper 01/145. Washington, D.C.: IMF.

OECD. 2004. *Economic Outlook.* Vol. 2, no. 76. Paris: OECD.

Schuknecht, Ludger, and Vito Tanzi. 2005. "Reforming Public Expenditure in Industrialized Countries: Are There Trade-offs?" European Central Bank Working Paper Series 435. Frankfurt: ECB.

Stein, Herbert. 1969. *The Fiscal Revolution in America.* Chicago: University of Chicago Press.

Talvi, Ernesto, and Carlos A. Vegh. 2000. "Tax Base Variability and Procyclical Fiscal Policy." NBER Working Paper 7499. Cambridge, Mass.: National Bureau of Economic Research.

Tanzi, Vito. 1969. "Measuring the Sensitivity of the Federal Income Tax from Cross-Section Data." *Review of Economics and Statistics* 54, no. 2: 206–209.

Tanzi, Vito. 2004. "The Stability and Growth Pact: Its Role and Future." *Cato Journal* 24: 1–2.

Tanzi, Vito. 2005. "Fiscal Policy: When Theory Meets Reality." Mimeo.

Tanzi, Vito, and Nigel Chalk. 2000. "Impact of Large Debt on Growth in the EU: A Discussion of Potential Channels." *European Economy* 2: 23–43.

Tanzi, Vito, and Thomas Hart. 1972. "The Effect of the 1964 Tax Reform on the Sensitivity of the U.S. Individual Income Tax." *Review of Economics and Statistics* 54, no. 3: 326–328.

Tobin, James. 1966. *National Economic Policy: Essays.* New Haven: Yale University Press.

FOUR

Design and Implementation of the Stability and Growth Pact

The Perspective of New Member States

Fabrizio Coricelli

Introduction

Since their entry into the European Union in May 2004, the larger new member states (Czech Republic, Poland, Hungary, and Slovakia) have been subjected to the Excessive Deficit Procedure (EDP) of the Stability and Growth Pact (SGP) (Box 4.1). Subsequently, the EU has even declared Hungary in a state of excessive deficit. This pattern contrasts with the EU's prior experience. In the past, entry into the European Monetary Union (EMU) was a powerful mechanism to induce EU members, such as Italy, to adjust fiscal policies. In the last few years, however, the SGP has ceased to be an effective constraint on fiscal policy in EU countries.

The decision of the European Council of Economic Ministers (ECOFIN) to halt the EDP for France and Germany has weakened the credibility of EU fiscal rules. The reform of the SGP introduced in March 2005 further worsened the situation by expanding the list of circumstances that allows countries to breach the deficit ceiling of 3 percent of GDP. Countries are now excused not only for exceptional circumstances, such as a decline in output of 2 percent or more, but also for persistent economic slowdowns or for reforms, such as pension reform, that adversely affect the budget. The horizon for adjusting the budget deficit has been lengthened. The special treatment of France and Germany and the SGP reform have sharply increased the arbitrariness in the evaluation of fiscal policy and in the implementation of the SGP. The clear targets and constraints that acceptance to the Eurozone and the SGP once provided for the ten new member states (NMS) have become elusive and "flexible."

I wish to thank, without implicating, Anders Åslund, Jean Pisani-Ferry, and Vito Tanzi for very useful comments on an earlier draft of this chapter.

Box 4.1. Stability and Growth Pact

The Stability and Growth Pact (SGP) is the EU's answer to concerns regarding budgetary discipline in the Economic and Monetary Union (EMU). Adopted in 1997, the SGP strengthened the EMU treaty provisions on fiscal discipline described in Articles 99 and 104. The SGP took full effect when the euro was launched on January 1, 1999. In March 2005, ECOFIN approved several modifications, especially in the implementation of the SGP.

The principal purpose of the SGP was to enforce fiscal discipline, which was meant to be a permanent feature of the EMU. By safeguarding sound government finances, the SGP would ensure price stability and thus establish conditions for strong and sustainable growth. However, it was also recognized that with the loss of the exchange rate instrument, the automatic fiscal stabilizers at the national level would need to play a larger role to help economies adjust to asymmetric shocks, making it "necessary to ensure that national budgetary policies support stability oriented monetary policies." This is the rationale behind the core commitment of the SGP, that is, to set the "medium-term objective of budgetary positions close to balance or in surplus," which "will allow all Member States to deal with normal cyclical fluctuations while keeping the government deficit within the reference value of 3 percent of GDP."

Formally, the SGP consists of three elements:

- *A political commitment* by all parties involved in the SGP (Commission, member states, and the Council) to the full and timely implementation of the budget oversight process, contained in a resolution passed by the Amsterdam European Council on June 17, 1997. This political commitment ensures that effective peer pressure is exerted on a member state failing to live up to its commitments.
- *Preventive elements* that through regular oversight aim at precluding the budget deficits from exceeding the 3 percent reference value. To this end, Council Regulation 1466/97 reinforces the multilateral oversight of budget positions and the coordination of economic policies. It foresees the submission by all member states of stability and convergence programs, which are examined by the Council. This regulation also includes an early warning mechanism to be activated in the event of a significant slippage in the budgetary position of a member state.

- *Dissuasive elements* that require member states to take immediate corrective action if the 3 percent reference value is breached and allow for sanctions if necessary. These elements are contained in Council Regulation 1467/97 On Speeding Up and Clarifying the Implementation of the Excessive Deficit Procedure.

Besides these legal means, the Code of Conduct on the content and format of the stability and convergence programs, endorsed by the ECOFIN Council on July 10, 2001, incorporates the essential elements of Council Regulation 1466/97 into guidelines to assist the member states in drawing up their programs. It also aims at facilitating the examination of the programs by the Commission, the Economic and Financial Committee, and the Council.

Source: European Commission Web site.

In this chapter, we argue that an effective implementation of the SGP is crucial for the new member states, perhaps even more than for the "old" EU members. The NMS are still emerging markets that are characterized by dependence on foreign finance, large current account deficits, and weak financial markets. While their potential for output growth is higher, the volatility of their main macroeconomic variables is also greater.

Interestingly, one of the official justifications for the reform of the SGP has been the enlargement of the EU: "The Stability and Growth Pact needs to be strengthened and its implementation to be clarified, with the aim of improving the coordination and monitoring of economic policies. In doing so, due account should be taken of changing circumstances, in particular the increased economic heterogeneity in the Community of 25 Members and the prospects of demographic changes" (European Commission, 2005). Although some new features of the SGP represent improvements, namely, consideration of different output growth potentials, initial debt levels, and fiscal impacts of growth-enhancing reforms, other modifications reduced clarity and increased risk. Arbitrary implementation of the SGP is the most worrying aspect of recent developments. To pay more attention to debt sustainability, rather than to budget deficits, might create the wrong incentives for the NMS, since most of them have low levels of debt. The peculiar features of the NMS, their underdeveloped financial sectors and high volatility of output and fiscal revenues, call for a careful definition of safe debt-to-GDP ratios. We argue that there is little room for increasing debt ratios in the NMS, and we suggest complementing the SGP framework with national expenditure rules, which should serve as a more effective reference for evaluating policies.

This chapter is structured as follows. In the second section, we argue that during the transition to the euro, especially during the Exchange Rate Mechanism-II (ERM-II) period, the NMS have to rely on tight fiscal policies in order to avoid sizable output costs, which could cause them to fail to transition to the euro. In the third section, we discuss the main trends of fiscal policy in the NMS, highlighting the presence of two distinct patterns: low deficits in small countries and high deficits in larger countries. In the fourth section, we consider some features of the SGP and its revisions from the perspective of the NMS. The final section concludes the chapter.

Fiscal Policy and the Pace of Transition to the Euro

The prospect of EMU membership fostered fiscal adjustment in several EU countries during the 1990s (Gali and Perotti, 2003). It could potentially have a positive effect on the new EU members as well. However, the NMS can be divided into two groups with distinct patterns of behavior. One group, comprised of the smaller countries, has embarked on prudent fiscal policy that is facilitating their fast entry into the Eurozone. The other group, which consists of the larger countries, entered the EU with high and growing budget deficits and has opted for a much slower path toward the euro.

The procedures leading to EU accession did not involve any conditionality on macroeconomic indicators for the candidate countries. In several of the NMS, the fiscal accounts deteriorated considerably during the run-up to their EU entry. Apparently, the NMS did not anticipate they would be subject to tight fiscal constraints on entry, although the 3 percent budget deficit ceiling and the SGP apply to every member of the EU. There was a strange, perhaps accidental, convergence between the positions of "populist" forces within the NMS, which pushed for higher deficits, and the EU Commission and the European Central Bank (ECB), which explicitly favored a slow process of entry into the Eurozone. In a nutshell, the idea was that there was a trade-off between "real" and "nominal" convergence. Budget deficits could be tolerated, as they were considered instruments for stimulating growth.

Fiscal Policy in the NMS: A Heterogeneous Picture

The first problem of public finances in the NMS is that the "size of government" (measured as the ratio of government revenue or expenditure to GDP) in these countries is high for their level of development (approximated by income per capita).

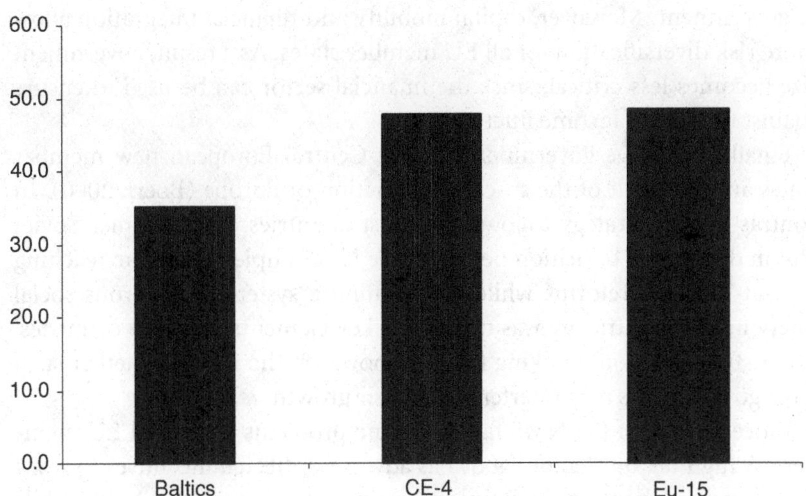

Chart 4.1. Size of government in the new member states in 2003 (total expenditure of government to GDP). *Source*: Eurostat.

Size of the Government

Chart 4.1 shows that the size of government in the NMS, except for the Baltics, is not far from the EU average, although the average GDP per capita in the NMS is less than half of the EU average. One could conclude that the governments are too large for their countries' level of development and argue that they have prematurely adopted the "European model." GDP per capita, however, is only one of the variables affecting the "natural" size of the government. The demographic structure is another factor, and the demographics in the NMS are similar to those of the "old" EU members. A third factor, recently emphasized by Rodrik (1998), is an economy's degree of openness to foreign trade. According to Rodrik, trade openness increases the risk of output fluctuations in an economy due to fluctuations in the terms of trade. Indeed, the effect on income from changes in the terms of trade is determined by multiplying the change by the share of trade in GDP. If the latter rises, the impact on income from changes in the terms of trade also increases. An increase in the size of the government can compensate for such fluctuations, reducing output fluctuation.

Although this view might have some relevance for evaluating the size of NMS's governments, for the NMS the increase in openness goes hand-in-hand with EU integration, which implies integration not only of trade flows, but also of factors of production and financial sectors. Free capital mobility generates tax competition, which induces pressure to reduce the size of government. Moreover, capital mobility and financial integration allow more risk diversification for all EU member states. As a result, government size becomes less critical, since the financial sector can be used to ensure against the risk of income fluctuations.

Finally, the large governments of the Central European new member states are the result of the so-called attraction of Europe (Boeri, 2000). In contrast to the strategy followed in most countries of the former Soviet Union during the transition period, these NMS implemented far-reaching market-oriented reforms while maintaining a system of generous social safety nets. This strategy was one of the key elements for these countries' successful transition. Looking forward, however, the issue is whether such large governments may interfere with their growth.

Indeed, most of the NMS face the same problems as the old EU members. A high tax burden on labor has adversely affected incentives to work and thus the labor supply. Employment rates are low in the NMS, while unemployment rates are generally high and the underground economy is very large.[1]

Deficits

The experience of the NMS has been highly heterogeneous: one can identify two distinct groups of countries, following different fiscal strategies. In Central Europe, average budget deficits have hovered well above the 3 percent ceiling, in contrast to the Baltics and Slovenia. Country size appears to influence fiscal policy. But low-deficit countries, especially the Baltics, also use currency boards or fixed exchange rate regimes.

A comparison of the Baltics and Slovenia with Central Europe (Poland, the Czech Republic, Slovakia, and Hungary) suggests that high budget deficits cannot be attributed to special factors associated with transition and EU accession. The difference in size of the countries suggests the importance of political economy factors. In small and more homogeneous countries there is less pressure to use the budgetary process to win elections. Unfortunately, it is difficult to separate the effects of such political factors from economic factors, such as the greater constraints for small and highly open economies.

Nevertheless, it is interesting to contrast the superior growth performance of the Baltic countries with that of the Central Europe-4 (CE-4) countries (Poland, Czech Republic, Slovak Republic, and Hungary; see Chart 4.2). Chart 4.3 shows the Baltic states' prudent fiscal policy in contrast to the

[1] For these reasons, several NMS have opted for low income and corporate taxes. This strategy has led Estonia, Lithuania, and Slovakia to adopt flat tax systems, which are currently under attack by several old EU government officials.

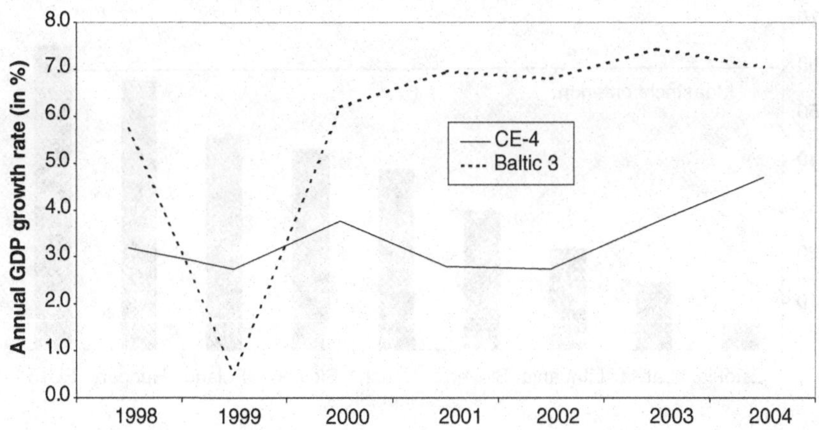

Chart 4.2. Growth in the new EU members, 1998–2004. *Source*: Eurostat.

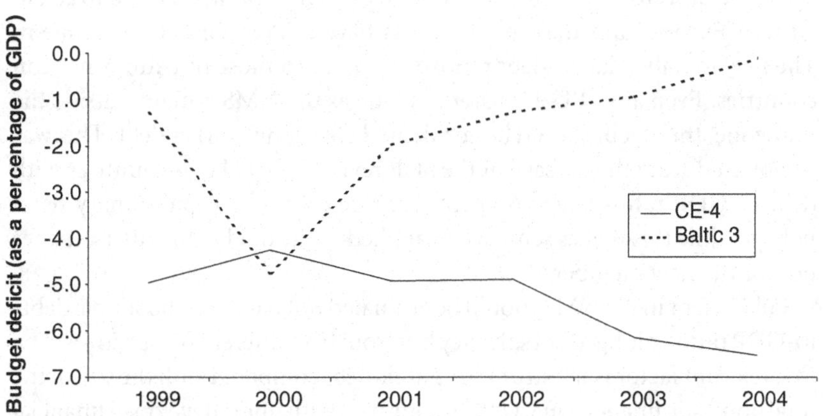

Chart 4.3. Budget deficits in the new member states, 1999–2004. *Source*: Eurostat.

CE-4. No clear correlation exists between the size of the budget deficit and public investment – contrary to what is often said to justify high deficits in the NMS. It seems the large NMS simply anticipated no binding constraints on their fiscal accounts during their EU entry process.

Debt

On average, the NMS display debt-to-GDP ratios well below those of old EU members. However, such comparisons are flawed, because the NMS are emerging markets rather than advanced economies (see Chart 4.4).

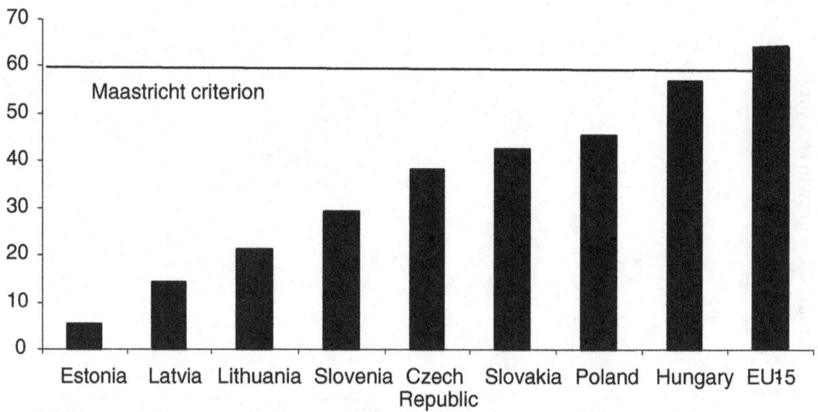

Chart 4.4. Debt to GDP ratios in 2003. *Source*: Eurostat.

Financial sectors are still underdeveloped in the countries of Central and Eastern Europe, and their public debts have a large foreign component. The new member states' debt ratios are similar to those of Latin American countries. Even after EU accession, as long as the NMS remain outside the Eurozone, their debt should be considered emerging market debt. This was forgotten during the passage of the SGP revision that allows countries with debt-to-GDP ratios below 60 percent more room for expansionary fiscal policy. While this makes sense when applied to the old EU members, it does not for the new members.

Public debt in the NMS should be evaluated not based on the simple debt-to-GDP ratio or long-term solvency but from two different perspectives. The first relevant factor is the size of the public debt compared with the size of the total domestic financial markets. In countries with underdeveloped financial sectors, the crowding-out effect of public debt can be very serious. Chart 4.5 compares debt-to-M2 ratios in the NMS with those of old EU countries. The striking result is that debt ratios in the NMS are close to those in old EU member states and in some cases even higher.

The second relevant criterion is the "natural debt limit," which takes into account the uncertainty associated with high revenue volatility and expenditure rigidity for countries that might face severe constraints on foreign borrowing (Mendoza and Oviedo, 2004). Emerging economies do not have the same ability as advanced economies to use international financial markets to counter large shocks. In crisis situations, emerging economies find it very hard to borrow abroad at reasonable rates. This phenomenon has been defined as a "sudden stop" in recent literature (Calvo et al., 2003). Given that emerging markets have accumulated public debts that are largely owed

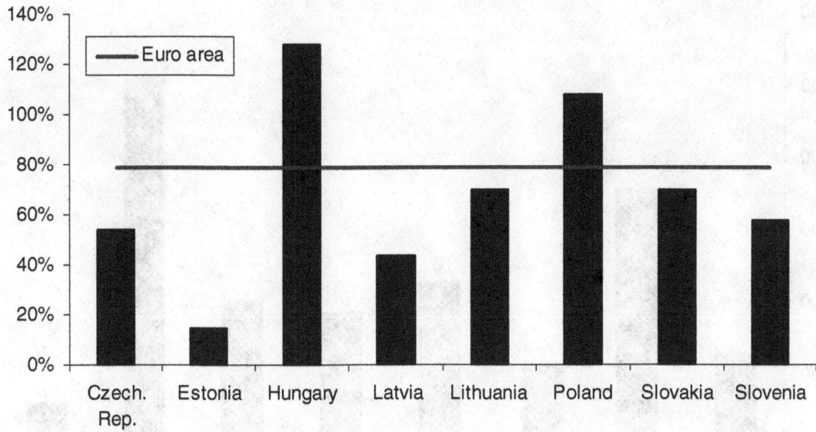

Chart 4.5. Debt to M2 ratios in various countries. *Source*: Eurostat and EBRD.

to foreigners, the question is whether in the event of a sudden stop these countries can service their debt, taking into account their limited ability to raise revenues and compress expenditures.

This perspective offers a much more accurate evaluation of new member states' debt sustainability than long-run solvency, because emerging economies display much greater revenue volatility than advanced economies. In emerging economies, an adverse situation may result in a sharp drop in the revenue-to-GDP ratio, but public expenditure cannot be compressed to zero. The degree of expenditure rigidity depends on the structure of expenditures and the national political process. For expenditures, we can assess the rigidity by observing the minimum ratio in recent years; for revenues, we can use the difference between the mean and the standard deviation of the revenue-to-GDP ratio.

Like other emerging economies, the new member states have highly volatile revenue-to-GDP ratios (Chart 4.6). We select Estonia to compute the "natural debt limit" (NDL), because it has the lowest debt-to-GDP ratio and the fastest real GDP growth rate, so a debt solvency approach would yield a very high equilibrium debt-to-GDP ratio. As a result, one would be tempted to advise Estonia to rapidly increase its public debt in order to exploit the room between its current debt level and the Maastricht debt ceiling of 60 percent of GDP. Computing the natural debt limit for Estonia is instructive, because its current debt level is not far from such a "natural limit."

The definition of NDL is

$$\text{NDL} = \frac{T_m - G_m}{R - \gamma},$$

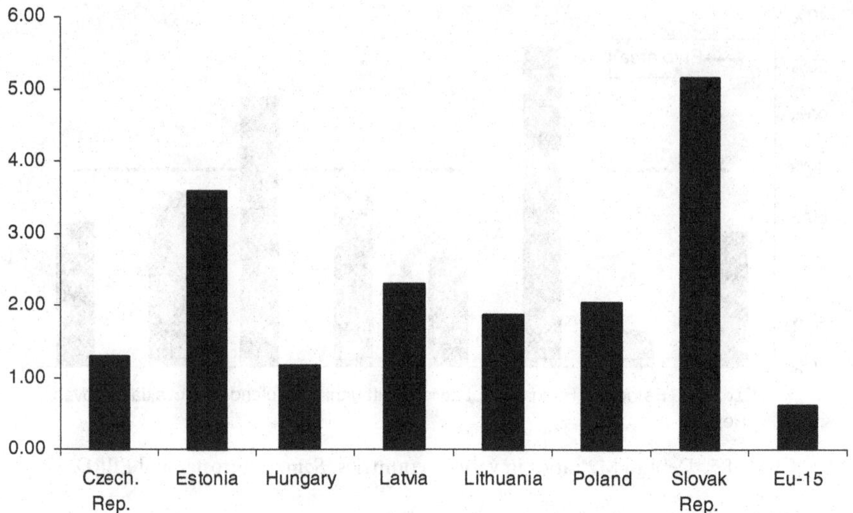

Chart 4.6. Revenue volatility, 1995–2004 (standard deviation of revenues to GDP). *Note*: For Hungary, data are for the period 2001–2004. *Source*: Author's calculations based on data from Eurostat.

with T_m = "worst case" realization of revenue-to-GDP ratio, G_m = minimum level of expenditure, R = real interest rate, and γ = rate of growth of real GDP. It is useful to compare such a definition with the level consistent with long-run solvency

$$D = \frac{T - G}{R - \gamma},$$

where the value of the numerator indicates the current level of primary surplus.

We compute the worst case level of revenue-to-GDP ratio for Estonia as the difference between the average ratio and twice its standard deviation. We use the same formula for minimum expenditure. We use a real interest rate differential with respect to real growth of 1.6. Interestingly, the NDL is equal to 20 percent of GDP. Of course, such a calculation is only illustrative; however, it is useful to compare it to the traditional level computed based on long-run solvency. Using the same numbers for the real interest rate and the real rate of growth produces a level of 66 percent. The huge discrepancy between the two measures of equilibrium debt level indicates the importance of revenue volatility in emerging economies, and suggests that for the NMS it is advisable to give larger weight to deficit indicators, rather than the Maastricht debt ratio. Of course, this implies that NMS approaching 60 percent are a fortiori in a risky zone.

The emphasis on deficits rather than debts would seem questionable for countries that are characterized by much higher rates of output growth (Buiter, 2004). As shown in the next section, our approach can be reconciled with Buiter's, by taking seriously the full-cycle close-to-balanced budget requirement – the cornerstone of the Stability and Growth Pact. Our view might seem overly restrictive for NMS, but in fact, it only suggests that during the period of transition to the euro, the debt of NMS carries a much higher risk than that of the old EU members. Such risk is unlikely to be incorporated into the risk premium by the market because it is associated with a low probability event (the worst case scenario).

The NMS should be advised to adopt medium-term fiscal frameworks that imply a close-to-balanced budget over the cycle, and thus stable debt-to-GDP ratio over the same horizon. Unfortunately, the current approach to SGP implementation has several drawbacks, especially if viewed from the perspective of the NMS.

Shortcomings of the Existing Framework for New Members

The EU fiscal framework is based on three main assumptions:

(1) For EU member states, the 3 percent of GDP limit on the budget deficit provides a sufficient margin to absorb the "normal" cyclical fluctuations caused by GDP volatility. During "exceptional times" the 3 percent ceiling can be breached without penalties. This implies that in "normal" and "bad" times there is no pro-cyclical bias. The issue of incentives to avoid pro-cyclicality during "good" times remains open. The SGP offers a solution by indicating that countries should ensure convergence to a balanced structural position over the medium term. Accordingly, in periods of favorable cycles governments should run budget surpluses, matched by deficits during downturns. Since, on average, the budget is balanced, the 3 percent ceiling will be breached only in exceptional circumstances.

(2) The European Commission (EC) estimates that in most EU countries the budget balance to output gap elasticity is between 0.5 and 0.6. This means that one should observe a cyclical deficit of roughly half of the output gap. To pass the 3 percent ceiling (assuming the budget is initially balanced), a country must experience a negative output gap of roughly 6 percentage points of potential output. This is rather

unusual; for instance, in France during the period 1980–2002 the largest negative output gap was 2.6 percent in 1985, while in Germany it never exceeded 1.6 percent.

(3) The cyclically adjusted balance provides a good measure of the national government's discretionary policy.

Summing up, a country that behaves well should have countercyclical deficits due to the functioning of automatic stabilizers. Their functioning is fully consistent with the 3 percent limit for well-behaved countries. We in turn discuss the three elements of the EU fiscal framework and highlight their limitations. We begin by showing that the foundations for the 3 percent ceiling and the cyclical safety margin are rather weak, especially for the NMS. Then, we emphasize the drawbacks of the evaluation and monitoring procedures of the EC, which are not solved by looking at the cyclically adjusted budget.

GDP Volatility and the 3 Percent Ceiling

The 3 percent deficit ceiling was designed for countries with projected annual GDP growth of about 2 percent. Taking the EC budget balance to output gap elasticity estimate of 0.5, a country in which a 2 percent GDP growth projection becomes a 2 percent GDP drop would also suffer a shortfall in the budget equal to 2 percent of GDP. If such countries maintained a close-to-balanced budget over the cycle, they would risk hitting the 3 percent ceiling only in exceptionally rare cases; however, this is not true for countries that are characterized by much higher rates of growth and are exposed to much wider GDP oscillations. A negative GDP change of 2 percent from a potential growth path of 5 percent would imply a 7 percentage point change. The elasticities of the budget-to-GDP and revenue-to-GDP ratios in the NMS are of the same magnitude as in the EU-15 countries. Thus the NMS can easily hit the 3 percent ceiling even in a normal cycle.[2]

Per capita income levels (in purchasing power parities) in the NMS are on average 40 percent of those of the old EU countries. Convergence of the GDP per capita levels in the EU is going to be a long-term phenomenon. Therefore, in the next few decades, the NMS should display higher rates of growth than the old EU members. Assuming the well-known Barro's rule of thumb on convergence, the NMS growth rate should be 2 points higher than

[2] As shown by the EC (2003), the GDP elasticity of the budget is dominated by the revenue effects. Indeed, Coricelli and Ercolani (2004) find the output-gap budget elasticity for NMS only slightly lower, at around 0.45, than those of EU-15 countries.

the average EU growth rate. Studies on the EU, and on monetary unions in general, suggest that an even higher difference in rates, close to 3 percent, is needed for convergence. As the average rate of potential output growth is around 2 percent in the old EU, potential output in acceding countries can be expected to grow between 4 and 5 percent per annum. The volatility of GDP growth is also likely to be much higher in the NMS. This implies that with neutral fiscal policy, fluctuations in the cyclical budget balances should display much larger amplitude. This can be observed in the data. Looking at the period from 1996 to mid-2002, a recent paper by the European Central Bank (ECB) finds that the NMS posted an average GDP growth rate of about 4 percent against 2.2 percent for the Eurozone countries. Volatility was much higher in the NMS, with a standard deviation of output growth almost three times higher than in the euro area (Süppel, 2003). The study concludes that since higher growth and higher volatility of growth reflect a catching up process, they are going to persist in the medium run.

Given these structural features, the 3 percent budget deficit limit does not provide a margin wide enough to absorb cyclical fluctuations in the budget deficits for the NMS. For the old EU members, however, with an estimated budget balance to output gap elasticity of around 0.5, the 3 percent budget deficit limit might represent a wide enough margin to absorb regular cyclical fluctuations in the budget.

Pro-Cyclical Bias

A second possible drawback of the existing rules is the pro-cyclical bias associated with recessionary growth of budget deficits, which, if they approach the 3 percent ceiling, force governments to undertake adjustments during "bad" times. According to Gali and Perotti (2003), the Maastricht criterion on the budget deficit has not been a constraint on the use of countercyclical policies by the EMU countries. This study compared the impact the output gap had on cyclically adjusted deficits in the pre- and post-Maastricht phases. The authors found no effect of a pro-cyclical bias after the introduction of fiscal constraints. A recent report by CEPR (Buiter, 2004) broadly confirms this result. It found that only in the cases of Portugal and Italy have there been tightenings of fiscal policy during a downturn. However, it could be argued that a similar effect would have occurred in Germany and France had the Excessive Deficit Procedure been approved by the Council of Economics and Finance Ministers of the European Union (ECOFIN). This would have implied a pro-cyclical stance in four members of the EMU during the most important downturn in the post-Maastricht period. Thus, although there is no strong evidence of a pro-cyclical bias in the existing fiscal rules, it is

Table 4.1. *Correlation Between Cyclical Variations of Government Consumption and GDP, 1995–2003 (cyclical variations are computed as percentage deviations from trend, computed with Hodrik-Prescott filter)*

Czech Republic	Estonia	Hungary	Latvia	Lithuania	Poland	Slovakia	Slovenia
0.80	0.03	−0.06	0.30	0.63	0.84	0.34	−0.58

Source: Author's calculations based on data from Eurostat.

clear that a sizable slowdown in the rate of GDP growth sharply increases the probability of hitting the 3 percent ceiling, a problem that is bound to be much more serious for the NMS.

Furthermore, looking at correlations between cyclical variations in government consumption and GDP, we found that the NMS, like other emerging markets, display a pro-cyclical fiscal policy (Fiorito, 1997; Talvi and Vegh, 2000). Considering that government consumption does not vary automatically with the cycle, it can be used as a proxy for the discretionary component of fiscal policy. A positive correlation between the cyclical components of government consumption and GDP is a measure of the pro-cyclicality of fiscal policy (see Table 4.1). Indeed, for several NMS, that correlation was positive or close to zero during the period 1995–2003 (Coricelli and Eianchovina, 2004). This indicates that countercyclical fiscal policy in the NMS has had a limited role. EU fiscal rules do not provide effective disincentives for pro-cyclical policies, and this could be a serious drawback for NMS that tend to have pro-cyclical fiscal policies.

Evaluating Policies, Not Just Outcomes

Rules are important because they can strengthen the credibility of policies. The current crisis of the SGP illustrates the distinction between the credibility of policies and that of policy makers. There is indeed an inconsistency in the current framework.

The task of the European Commission is to monitor fiscal accounts and to evaluate the Stability and Convergence Programs of national governments. When the structural (or cyclically adjusted) balance is in danger of breaching the 3 percent ceiling, governments are invited to adopt an adjustment plan. On this basis, national governments and the EC discuss budgetary plans. If the government follows those plans, it should be defined as a "dependable" government, and thus a credible policy maker. However, if a government behaves according to the stated plans and ex post facto the EC identifies the government as breaking the rules, there is an obvious problem. Unexpected outcomes, unrelated to policy actions, cannot be used to evaluate policy makers. The conceptual underpinning of the 3 percent ceiling is flawed.

Consider this example. In year *t*, country A had a balanced budget. In the following three years, it planned to increase expenditures in line with its expected rate of GDP growth. With no adjustment in tax rates, no change in tax collection, and a unitary elasticity of revenue with respect to GDP, the budget was expected to remain balanced. The country grew at 3 percent in the year $t - 1$, and the GDP was projected to continue growing at 3 percent a year for the three years considered. But in reality, GDP growth declined to 1 percent per annum. The output gap may have remained positive (actual output less than potential); nevertheless, the deficit has grown, approaching the 3 percent ceiling. From an ex ante point of view, the government has maintained its promises. The deficit was caused by a forecast error and was completely structural. The government did not switch to a looser fiscal policy through discretionary measures.

The first conclusion to draw is that the current framework for evaluating fiscal policy in the EU is misleading. A proper definition of discretionary policy should take into account the fact that the actual budgetary process is based on expected output (Buti and van den Noord, 2003; Larch and Salto, 2003).

If governments were welfare maximizers, they would generally follow a fiscal rule consistent with tax smoothing: set expenditures according to the expected growth of potential output.[3] Abstracting from measurement errors of potential output, this rule would imply a structurally balanced budget and cyclical budget balances proportional to the deviation of the real rate of growth from potential growth. Actual developments of GDP would determine movements in the budget balance, but not the output gap. Expenditures would be countercyclical by construction, with a unitary elasticity of expenditure-to-GDP ratio with respect to the deviation of actual from potential growth. Although this cyclical movement of expenditures is different from what is commonly defined as automatic stabilizers, it works in a similar fashion.

Of course, if potential growth is tenaciously overestimated, a deficit will persist. For this reason, a confidence interval should be applied when calculating potential growth, and the lower end of the expected band should be chosen, ensuring a prudent management of expenditures. The ensuing error is likely to be much smaller than the forecast error in the actual GDP. Neutral fiscal policy can be defined as consistent with the above rule (Buti and van den Noord, 2003; Buiter, 2004). The difference between actual and

[3] See Coricelli and Ercolani (2004) for a discussion of this rule.

neutral policy can be defined as discretionary policy. Moreover, from this discretionary policy one should subtract the effect of actual GDP forecast error to obtain what Buti and van den Noord define as "genuine" discretionary policy, as expenditure is planned ex ante on the basis of expected output. Thus, even with the amendments introduced in the SGP, the current framework is affected by ambiguity of interpretation on fiscal stance, leaving room for political influence.

The Stability and Growth Pact and the 3 percent budget deficit limit are examples of how rules can be simple but at the same time highly ambiguous – especially within the new SGP. ECOFIN has the final word on whether the excessive deficit procedure should be adopted. The use of controversial measures, such as the cyclically adjusted balance, to evaluate fiscal stance reduces the credibility of EU fiscal rules and makes their implementation subject to decisive political interference.

The first conclusion is that the indicators used by the EC to evaluate the fiscal policy of EU governments are misleading.[4] Governments' forecasts, however, are also likely to be inaccurate, as they tend to overestimate growth for political reasons (Larch and Salto, 2003). Interestingly, in the main episode of the SGP crisis, associated with the early warning to Germany and France, the forecast error in the EC data was as large as in the national data. Without denying the relevance of political considerations, it is apparent that the EU's current framework for fiscal policy evaluation leaves ample room for arbitrary interpretations and endless debate between national authorities and the EC. The result is a loss of credibility for the entire fiscal framework in the EU. On the one hand, the behavior of ECOFIN damages the credibility of the EC; on the other, the application of the procedure of the SGP damages the credibility of national fiscal authorities, providing an improper assessment of their discretionary policy.

Therefore, there is a need to move toward monitoring policies and not exclusively their results (a point also stressed by Annett et al., 2005). The problem of time inconsistency in policies can be reduced by acting on the predictable part of policy, not on unforeseen events (Drazen, 2004). All these issues are more relevant in an enlarged EU, as forecast errors for the NMS are bound to be even larger given their higher standard deviation of GDP growth.

Alas, the current debate on reform of the SGP is unlikely to produce any fundamental change in EU fiscal rules. In the summer of 2003, the EC put

[4] This is recognized in two papers written by EC economists: Buti and van den Noord (2003) and Larch and Salto (2003).

forward a proposal for some modifications of the SGP; unfortunately, it did not tackle the main issues discussed above. Sensible reform can be achieved by complementing the SGP with an expenditure rule that is easy to monitor, allows governments to own their policies, and allows the EU Commission to act as an outside monitoring body. It would be even better if independent national technical bodies were established to provide a complementary view on the computation of potential growth rates and the assessment of government policies.

In Coricelli and Ercolani (2004), we argue that a more suitable rule for an enlarged and more heterogeneous EU would be a simple expenditure rule, according to which expenditures would grow at the same rate as that of potential output (Box 4.2). Interestingly, the Czech Republic has introduced a medium-term fiscal program with an expenditure rule.

Box 4.2. A Medium-Term Framework with an Expenditure Rule

Primary expenditures grow in line with the growth rate of potential output, while target revenues, at unchanged tax rates, grow in line with actual output. Denoting with* the target variables, with y the real GDP growth, and with π the inflation rate, we can write the rule as follows:

Target expenditure:

$$g^* = g_{t-1}\left[\frac{1+y_t^*+\pi_t^*}{1+y_t+\pi_t}\right]$$

Target revenues:

$$\tau^* = \tau_{t-1}\left[\frac{1+y_t^*+\pi_t^*}{1+y_t+\pi_t}\right]$$

where we have assumed that the output elasticity of revenues is equal to one.

Target budget deficit:

$$d^* = g^* - \tau^*$$

Estimating potential output so that deviations of actual output from potential have a mean of zero (for instance, by applying the Hodrick-Prescott filter used until recently by the EU Commission), on average actual output will be equal to its potential level. As a result, on average, the actual deficit will be equal to the target deficit. Actual expenditure is a function of expected output, inflation, and a discretionary component, while actual revenue follows the behavior of output, inflation, and the discretionary changes in tax rates. Thus, actual expenditures and revenues are as follows:

$$\tau^* = \tau_{t-1}\left[\frac{1+y_t+\pi_t+\tau_t^d}{1+y_t+\pi_t}\right]$$

$$g = g_{t-1}\left[\frac{1+y_t^e+\pi_t^e+g_t^d}{1+y_t+\pi_t}\right]$$

where *e* stands for expected values and *d* for discretionary.

The budget deficit, in terms of actual GDP, equals:

$$d = g - t$$

One can identify a measure of discretionary fiscal policy as the difference between the actual and the target budget deficits:

$$DP_t = \left[\frac{(g_{t-1}g_t^d - \tau_{t-1}\tau_t^d) + g_{t-1}(y_t^e - y^* + \pi_t^e - \pi^*)}{1+y_t+\pi_t}\right]$$

The "true" discretionary policy is obtained by subtracting from the *DP* the effects of forecast errors:

$$DP_t^{true} = DP_t - \left[\frac{g_{t-1}(y_t^e - y^* + \pi_t^e - \pi^*)}{1+y_t+\pi_t}\right] = \frac{(g_{t-1}g_t^d - \tau_{t-1}\tau_t^d)}{1+y_t+\pi_t}$$

From the rule described in Box 4.2, it is apparent that when real GDP growth equals potential GDP growth, and inflation equals its target (that could be the ECB target rate when a country is a member of the Eurozone), the actual deficit equals its target value. When actual output growth falls short of potential growth, a budget deficit results, while a surplus will emerge when actual output growth exceeds potential growth. The rule embodies an automatic "growth dividend": in good times the country accumulates surpluses that can be spent in bad times, ensuring a stable average level of debt-to-GDP ratio. Whether the rule is consistent with the 3 percent Maastricht ceiling on budget deficit depends on the magnitude of the deviations of output growth from its potential rate. What is more important is that if the country follows the above rule, it cannot be blamed for lax fiscal policy. The worsening of budget deficits will result entirely from a downturn in the economy and not from a discretionary loosening of fiscal policy. It would be simple to monitor fiscal policy, because the rule implies specific nominal values for expenditure. In summary, the framework proposed allows for an evaluation of fiscal stance that is superior to alternative indicators such as the cyclically adjusted budget deficit. The proposed measure of discretionary fiscal policy better illuminates discretionary policy decisions by the government.

Conclusions

In this chapter, we add the dimension of enlargement to the already heated debate on EU fiscal rules. By analyzing the main drawbacks of such rules from the perspective of the NMS, the fundamental shortcomings of the EU fiscal framework became apparent. More important, however, is that fiscal discipline is the key to a successful and fast convergence of the NMS to the income levels of the EU-15 countries. Such discipline ultimately rests on a credible commitment from national authorities. Indeed, the heterogeneous experience of the NMS, resulting in the emergence of two distinct groups, is telling. The Baltic states have followed prudent fiscal policies and reduced government size. This policy has yielded high rates of economic growth and macroeconomic stability, which have allowed them to enter the fast track to Eurozone accession. Slovenia has followed a similar path, although it is still in the middle of an internal debate on tax reform and on the role of the state in the economy. By contrast, the Central European countries have let their budget deficits surge and their debt levels rise. Starting with an oversized government, these countries must struggle to adjust their fiscal accounts in the near future, not only as a precondition for entry into the Eurozone, but also to support faster economic growth.

References

Annett, Anthony, Jörg Decressin, and Michael Deppler. 2005. “Reforming the Stability and Growth Pact.” IMF Policy Discussion Paper 05/2. Washington, D.C.: IMF.

Boeri, Tito. 2000. *Structural Change, Welfare Systems, and Labour Reallocation.* Oxford and New York: Oxford University Press.

Buiter, Willem H. 2004. “To Purgatory and Beyond: When and How Should the Accession Countries from Central and Eastern Europe Become Full Members of EMU?” CEPR Discussion Paper 4342.

Buiter, Willem H., and Clemens Grafe. 2004. “Patching up the Pact.” *The Economics of Transition* 12, no. 1: 67–102.

Buti, Marco, and Paul van den Noord. 2003. “Discretionary Fiscal Policy and Elections: The Experience of the Early Years of EMU.” OECD Working Paper 351. Paris: OECD.

Calvo, Guillermo, Alejandro Izquierdo, and Ernesto Talvi. 2003. “Sudden Stops, the Real Exchange Rate and Fiscal Sustainability: Argentina’s Lessons.” NBER Working Paper 9828. Cambridge, Mass.: National Bureau of Economic Research.

Coricelli, Fabrizio. 2002. "Exchange Rate Policy During the Transition to the European Monetary Union: The Option of Euroization." *The Economics of Transition* 10, no. 2: 405–417.

Coricelli, Fabrizio, and E. Eianchovina. 2004. "Shocks and Volatility in Accession Countries of Central-Eastern Europe." Mimeo, the World Bank.

Coricelli, Fabrizio, and Valerio Ercolani. 2004. "Cyclical and Structural Deficits on the Road to Accession: Fiscal Rules for an Enlarged European Union." In George Kopits, ed., *Rules-Based Fiscal Policy in Emerging Markets*. Houndmills, Basingstoke, Hampshire, and New York: Palgrave-Macmillan.

Creel, Jerome. 2003. "Ranking Fiscal Policy Rules: The Golden Rule of Public Finance vs. the Stability and Growth Pact." OFCE 2003–04. Paris: OFCE.

Drazen, Allan. 2004. "Fiscal Rules from a Political Economy Perspective." In George Kopits, ed., *Rules-Based Fiscal Policy in Emerging Markets*. Houndmills, Basingstoke, Hampshire, and New York: Palgrave-Macmillan.

European Commission. 2003. *Public Finances in EMU*. Directorate-General for Economic and Financial Affairs, Brussels.

European Commission. 2005. *Proposal for a Council Regulation*. April 20.

Fatas, Antonio, Andrew Hughes Hallett, Anne Sibert, Rolf Strauch, and Jurgen von Hagen. 2003. *Stability and Growth in Europe: Towards a Better Pact*. Monitoring European Integration 13. London: CEPR.

Fiorito, Riccardo. 1997. "Stylized Facts of Government Finance in the G-7." IMF Working Paper 97/142. Washington, D.C.: IMF.

Gali, Jordi, and Roberto Perotti. 2003. "Fiscal Policy and Monetary Integration in Europe." *Economic Policy* 18, no. 37: 533–572.

Gros, Daniel, Massimiliano Castinelli, Juan Jimeno, Thomas Mayer, and Niels Thygesen. 2002. *The Euro at 25: A Special Report on Enlargement*. CEPS Macroeconomic Policy Group. Brussels: CEPS.

Kopits, George, and Steven A. Symansky. 1998. "Fiscal Policy Rules." IMF Occasional Paper 162. Washington, D.C.: IMF.

Kopits, George, and Istvan P. Székely. 2002. "Fiscal Policy Challenges of EU Accession for Central European Economies." Mimeo, IMF.

Larch, Martin, and Matteo Salto. 2003. "Fiscal Rules, Inertia and Discretionary Fiscal Policy." European Economy Economic Papers 194. European Commission.

Mendoza, Enrique, and P. Marcelo Oviedo. 2004. "Fiscal Solvency and Macroeconomic Uncertainty in Emerging Markets: The Tale of the Tormented Insurer." Mimeo, University of Maryland.

Rodrik, Dani. 1998. "Why Do More Open Economies Have Bigger Governments?" *Journal of Political Economy* 106, no. 5: 997–1032.

Süppel, Ralph. 2003. "Comparing Economic Dynamics in the EU and CEE Accession Countries." European Central Bank Working Paper No. 267. Frankfurt: European Central Bank.

Talvi, Ernesto, and Carlos Vegh. 2000. "Tax Base Variability and Procyclical Fiscal Policy." NBER Working Paper 7499. Cambridge, Mass.: National Bureau of Economic Research.

FIVE

Perspectives on the Lisbon Strategy

How to Increase European Competitiveness

Daniel Gros

Introduction

This contribution focuses on the plight of (most of) the old member states, as the new member states are unlikely to face the same problems. The latter are growing faster than the old EU-15. They are likely to continue to benefit from their low production costs, a production base with a relatively well-educated work force, an improving policy framework, and their proximity to the biggest market in the world.

By contrast, the main theme of the Euroland economy continues to be weakness of both demand and supply.[1] And it is not only the economy that is weak, but also the economic policy making. Fiscal policy plans go awry all the time; the Lisbon Agenda is constantly invoked but no action is taken; and so on. This disarray results from the assumptions underlying existing policies: they are geared for a growing economy in which every year growth allows for some redistribution. Growth prospects are now rather dim throughout most of Euroland due to lower productivity growth and, particularly in Germany, due to demographic developments. Economic policy making is squeezed from both sides.

The low growth diminishes the potential for redistribution, which has an impact on both fiscal and monetary policy. Fiscal policy is deteriorating as finance ministers try to save, and then discover every year that despite their attempts at cutting expenditures, the ratio of public expenditure to GDP does not go down. Year after year, deficits are higher than expected. Finance ministers fail to understand that measures that would have redressed fiscal imbalance ten years ago are now barely sufficient to avoid even larger deficits.

The slowdown in growth and the vanishing room for redistribution affect monetary policy less directly. Judging from its own predictions, the

[1] "Euroland" refers to countries that have adopted the euro as their currency.

European Central Bank (ECB) has also been slow to recognize the fall in potential growth and has thus regularly overestimated growth prospects and underestimated inflation. However, the magnitude of the error (about 0.5 percent per annum) has not endangered price stability. This might change when the pressure on economic policy increases. Experience shows that price stability cannot be maintained when there is extreme pressure on public finances as, for example, during wars. This is where the danger lies. The long-run impact of aging on public finance in Europe is actually comparable to the cost of a major war (Deutsche Bank, 2004).

The short-term impact of demographic developments is less well known, and it is examined first. The slowdown in productivity is analyzed in more detail next.

From Demographic Bonus to Malus

That the European population is aging rapidly is widely known. What is not widely known is that not only will the impact of aging be felt in twenty to thirty years, but it has a major impact on the economies of some member countries already today.

The word "aging" does not describe adequately the problem Europe is facing. True, average life expectancy is increasing continuously in all developed countries. But the main reason why the proportion of the elderly in the population is expected to almost double over the next fifty years is fertility. On average, fertility has fallen so much below replacement levels that natural population growth has turned negative, and it will stay negative for the foreseeable future. With lower birth rates the average age of the population increases. Such low birth rates are characteristic of Europe (and Japan) but not of the United States, as shown by the demographic projections presented in Table 5.1.[2]

This table concentrates on old-age dependency ratios, which measure the consequences of aging for public finances (since an increasing proportion of elderly implies higher pension and health expenditures). It shows that for the EU-15, old-age dependency will, on average, double by the year 2050 to reach over 50 percent. By contrast, the dependency ratio of the United States will increase much less and will remain about a third lower than that of Europe. Among the major member countries, Germany stands out as having to face a considerably faster aging process than France, for example.

[2] These projections are based on the assumption that fertility in Europe will recover somewhat and that the increase in life expectancy will slow down.

Table 5.1. *Old-Age Dependency Projections for 2000, 2025, and 2050 (percentage of old age pensioners in relation to labor force)*

	2000	2025	2050
Japan	25.1	47.0	64.6
United States	18.8	29.3	34.6
France	24.5	36.0	45.9
Germany	24.2	39.4	52.9
EU-15	24.4	36.1	51.0
EU-28	21.5	31.9	48.5

Source: U.S. Census, author's calculations.

There is little difference between the EU-15 and a larger EU-28.[3] Even the inclusion of Turkey would not change the average much. In relative terms the deterioration expected would be even bigger for the EU-28 than for the EU-15. The dependency ratio of the EU-15 will likely increase to "only" 2.1 times its 2000 level by 2050, while that of the EU-28 will increase to 2.25 times its 2000 level.

The old-age dependency ratio is widely used to illustrate the pressure on pension systems. However, the ratio of the working-age population to overall population better indicates the overall impact of demographic factors on the economy (and economic policy). In a certain sense, this ratio measures potential GDP per capita. Changes in this ratio show, *ceteris paribus*, how demography affects the room for re-distribution. For example, if this ratio increases by 1 percent, potential GDP per capita should go up by 1 percent *ceteris paribus*, that is, holding constant productivity, employment rates, and so on. A fall in this ratio indicates the opposite. Potential GDP per capita falls, implying there is less to re-distribute to pensioners and other interest groups.

The history of this indicator for Germany shows why the "redistribution struggle" has become much tougher over the last few years. During the five years preceding reunification, demographic factors provided a strong tail-wind for economic policy, as the ratio of working-age population to total population was increasing by about 0.8 percent per annum. By contrast, during the five years up to 2005, demographic factors generated a head-wind for economic policy. The ratio, which had begun falling rapidly after 1995, deteriorated by about 0.54 percent per annum. The total deterioration

[3] Including also Bulgaria, Romania, and Croatia.

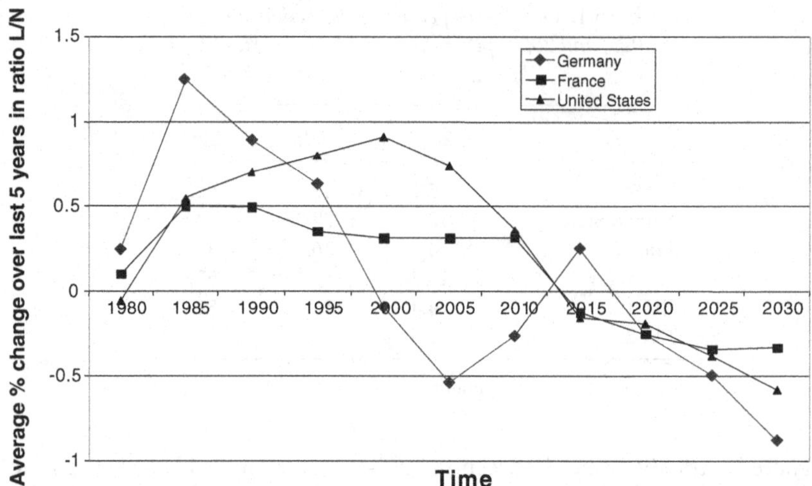

Chart 5.1. Change in demographic potential GDP, 1980–2030. *Source*: U.S. Census.

between the late 1980s and now amounts to almost 1.5 percent per annum. The German economic system, which until the end of the 1990s could count on a demographic bonus every year, was not prepared for this change.

Interestingly, France is in quite a different position: its demographic situation is evolving more slowly, and the main deterioration will occur only during the next decade. The United States shows a similar pattern, but with a somewhat more pronounced deterioration over the next ten years. In the United States, the trend will change from plus 0.7 percent per annum now, to around minus 0.2 percent in the five years up to 2015, which is equivalent to a negative change of over 0.8 percent per annum over the next ten years (just when the budget is supposed to be brought under control) (see Chart 5.1).

The data for Germany, which remains the largest Euroland economy, represent the worst case: rapidly worsening demographics and lower productivity growth. This combination, which lies behind the German loss of control over fiscal policy, explains why the half-hearted reforms undertaken so far have not turned the economy around. Other member countries face less extreme pressure because their demography is evolving more smoothly, but few member countries will be able to escape the twin pressures of worsening demography and productivity. To provide a comparison, Chart 5.2 shows the same demographic data for the largest new member state, Poland, some of the old EU-15 "cohesion countries," and Turkey.

Turkey constitutes an interesting case, as it is in the midst of a demographic transition. Its population, which expanded by 2.5 to 3.0 percent a year in

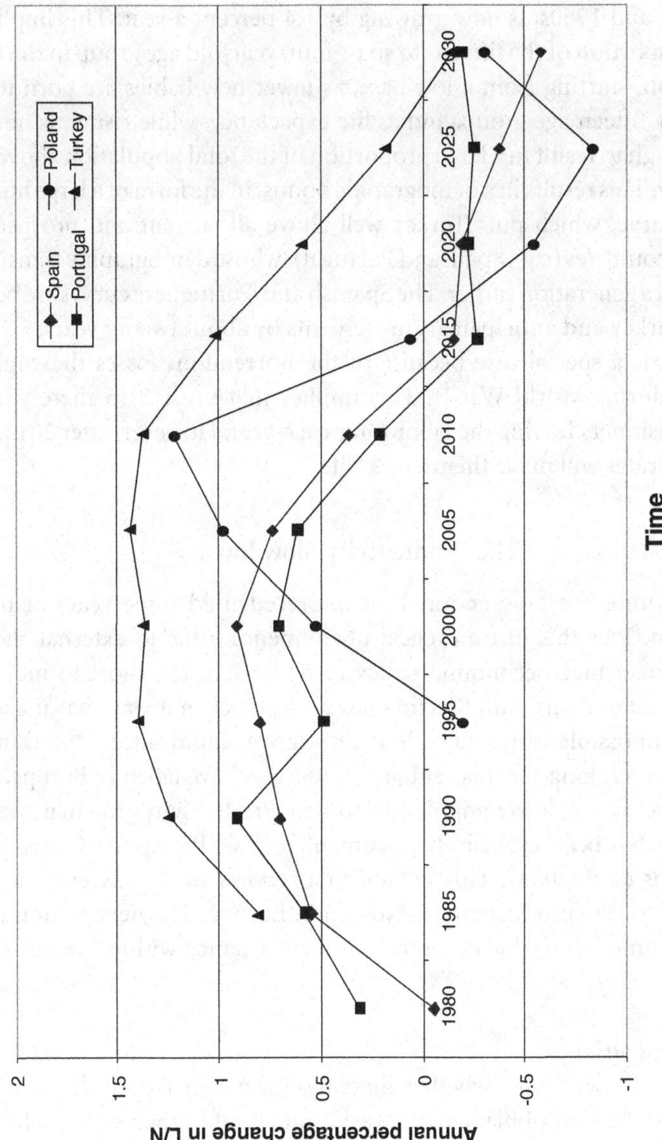

Chart 5.2. Demographic bonus: change in labor force to total population ratio, 1980–2030. *Source:* U.S. Census.

the 1950s and 1960s, is now growing by 1.4 percent a year. This implies a rising proportion of the fifteen- to sixty-four-year-old age group in the total population, starting from a low base, as fewer new babies are born to fill the under-fifteen age group, and as life expectancy, while rising, is not yet long enough to result in a large proportion of the total population above age sixty-four. This results in a demographic bonus, in the form of a large hump-shaped curve, which puts Turkey well above all current and prospective member countries (e.g., Spain and Portugal), whose demographic transition happened a generation earlier. The Spanish and Portuguese curves are below that of Turkey and anticipate its movements by about twenty years.

Poland is a special case because of the horrendous losses the country suffered during World War II. This implies that until 2015 there will be fewer pensioners leaving the labor force each year. However, after 2015, the low birth rates will make themselves felt.

The Productivity Slowdown

The Eurozone has now endured an unprecedented three years of near-stagnation. Was this just a cyclical phenomenon, due to external shocks and incorrect macroeconomic policy responses? In the short to medium run, cyclical and structural factors always interact in a way that makes it next to impossible to disentangle their relative significance. One thing is clear, however: long-term potential growth rates have fallen in Europe, and not only because of lower population growth. Productivity growth has fallen as well, as has been extensively documented in CEPS reports (Gros 2001, 2002; Gros et al. 2003). This section first reports some new evidence on the causes of the productivity slowdown in Europe. The next section then turns to some interesting differences in performance within the Euroland economy.

Growth Potential

How can one determine whether there has been a structural slowdown in Europe? In the view of Blanchard (2004), one should concentrate on hourly productivity. Blanchard has pointed out that the level of output per man-hour in some important member countries is close to the U.S. level. Table 5.2 shows how the growth rate of GDP per hour worked has fallen from around 2.6 percent per annum during the first half of the 1990s to less than 1.5 percent per annum from 1995. This fall was not cyclical. The period since 1995, which until 2002 generally saw positive GDP growth, was not worse

Table 5.2. *Growth of GDP per hour worked in the EU and the United States, 1970–2002*

Total economy, OECD data	1970–1980	1980–1990	1990–1995	1995–2002	(1995–2002) minus (1990–1995)
EU-11	3.6	2.3	2.6	1.4	– 1.2
United States	1.6	1.4	1.2	2.0	+0.8
EU-11 minus United States	+2.0	+0.9	+1.4	– 0.6	– 2.0

Note: EU-11 = EU-15 excluding Austria, Greece, Luxemburg, and Portugal because of limited data availability. *Source*: Daveri, 2004.

in terms of the business cycle than the period 1990–1995, which contained a recession.

Table 5.2 shows that productivity as measured by GDP per hour fell by 1.2 percentage points at a time when the opposite happened in the United States, where hourly productivity growth increased by 0.8 percentage points. Given this discrepancy between the European and American data, the dismal performance of the European economy in recent years is not just the result of a negative shock coming from the U.S.-driven global business cycle.

Why did productivity growth fall in the EU? It is often argued that the EU-U.S. difference can be explained by the advantage of the United States in new technologies, mainly information technologies (IT). However, the IT gap between the EU and the United States cannot explain why Europe's performance deteriorated when measured against its own past. One reason for the productivity slowdown in Europe might be quite simple: total factor productivity (TFP) growth might have declined.

One cannot yet say whether capital or TFP was behind the EU productivity slowdown of the 1990s. Any answer is still tentative because the necessary data are available only for a subset of EU countries. The limited available information suggests, however, that a slowdown in capital deepening – rather than diminished TFP growth – is the main culprit behind the European slowdown.

This conclusion emerges when one decomposes the growth rates of value added per hour worked into their capital deepening, TFP growth, and labor quality growth components for the United States and the aggregate EU-4 (France, Germany, Italy, and the United Kingdom). The capital deepening component is further split into an IT capital component and a non-IT capital component.

Table 5.3. *Decomposing Aggregate Labor Productivity Growth in the Business Sector, 1979–2000*

	United States		EU-4	
Business sector	1979–1995	1995–2000	1979–1995	1995–2000
Labor productivity growth	1.21	2.46	2.30	2.02
Contributions to labor productivity growth from:				
IT capital	0.46	0.86	0.33	0.53
Non-IT capital	0.35	0.43	0.70	0.25
TFP growth	0.26	1.05	0.94	1.07
Labor quality	0.13	0.13	0.33	0.18

Source: Daveri, 2004.

The results tabulated in Table 5.3 suggest the European productivity slowdown is mostly due to diminished capital deepening from non-IT capital. TFP growth has not changed much, continuing at respectable rates of about 1 percentage point. The slowdown in productivity growth for the EU aggregate – milder for the four countries considered here than for the EU-15 – is more than accounted for by the diminished contribution of non-IT capital (minus 0.45 percentage points) and the decline in labor quality, which has contributed another minus 0.15 percentage points.

On the positive side, productivity has benefited from an increase in the already positive contribution from IT capital (up from 0.3 to 0.5 percentage points) and from the slight increase in TFP growth (from 0.9 to 1.05 percentage points). At least for the overall business sector, one has to concur with Jorgenson (2003) that TFP and IT capital are unrelated to the European productivity slowdown. This contrasts with the United States, where TFP growth accelerated from 0.25 to more than 1 percentage point per year and the contribution of IT capital jumped almost half a percentage point (from 0.4 to 0.8 percentage points).

Recent evidence essentially confirms the findings in Daveri (2000, 2002) and Gros (2001, 2002), where rough overall measures of IT capital and TFP were employed. Other sources report a small decline in TFP, which appears inconsistent with the data reported here. However, the data available for the EU-15 do not account for changes in labor quality, whose effects are thus attributed to TFP. The more detailed data on labor quality, available only for the EU-4, suggest that part of the apparent decline of TFP might have been due to deterioration in labor quality. How could labor quality diminish when the general level of education was constantly increasing? During the late 1990s the share of the lower-skilled labor in the work force increased. This was the aim of many labor market reforms, but it had the side-effect of reducing average labor quality and overall productivity.

The more detailed data necessary to distinguish between TFP and labor quality are available only up to 2000. So the period covered by Table 5.3 comprises just the upswing following the 1995 recession. These data are likely to overestimate productivity growth, particularly in TFP. If one compares periods that are similar in business cycle terms, as done above (i.e., using the 1995–2002 period), the fall in overall productivity would probably be much larger, and the performance of TFP would probably be much worse. But the detailed data to perform this exercise are not yet available.

Will productivity growth improve over the next few years? One way of addressing this question is to start with the official Lisbon employment goal, which is to raise the EU-15 employment rate – the ratio of total employment over total working-age population – to 70 percent by 2010. Given the 2003 EU-15 employment rate of 63 percent, this implies an increment of about one percentage point per year until 2010. In turn, if the working-age population keeps growing at about 0.5 percentage points per year – an average of 0.3 percentage points for the native population and 1.2 percentage points for immigrants – total employment has to go up by 1.5 percent per year until 2010 to meet the Lisbon employment goal. This is a bit higher than 1.25 percent, the 1995–2002 average growth rate of total employment in the EU-15, but it is not unfeasible. If coupled with a continuation of the long-run trend toward a reduction of average hours worked (about half a percentage point per year), this translates into an expected increase in labor input of about 1 percent per year from now to 2010.

What does this imply in terms of capital deepening, that is, the contribution of capital to productivity growth? To come up with an educated guess, one must project past growth rates of the capital stock for the whole economy (e.g., for 1996–2000) into the future. Based on the data in Inklaar, O'Mahony, and Timmer (2005), one can get estimates ranging between 0.8 percent per year for France and 4.2 percent per year for the United Kingdom, with Germany and the Netherlands in between (but much closer to the United Kingdom). Hence, a simple continuation of past accumulation rates would imply a growth rate of the capital stock of about 3 percent per year for these four countries. The corresponding growth rate of the capital stock per hour worked would be 2 percent per year, and the growth contribution from capital deepening would be equal to two-thirds of a percentage point

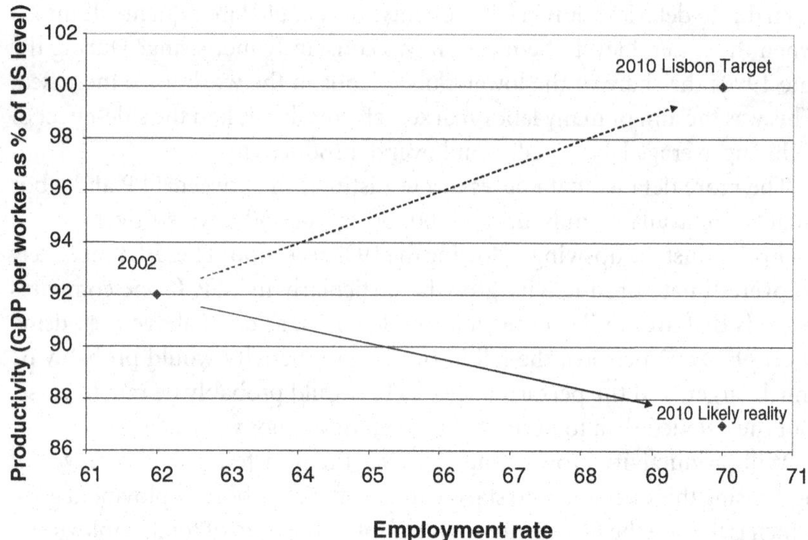

Chart 5.3. Lisbon: employment versus productivity?

per year (at least as long as the value-added share of capital stays unchanged at one-third). This compares with 0.78 percentage points computed for the EU-4 in 1995–2000.

If the Lisbon employment goal is taken seriously, it will require a much greater investment effort for capital deepening to take off again and contribute more to productivity growth through 2010. If capital accumulation stays constant, the contribution from capital deepening will fall even more, implying that at unchanged rates of TFP growth, overall productivity might actually fall (or at least not recover noticeably).

There will be an adverse impact on labor quality as the additional employment will have to come from that part of the labor force that is at present unemployed, that is, the lower skilled. The data reported above suggest that this could lead to a further loss of productivity growth of ten to twenty basis points. Hence one would need a considerable increase in capital deepening just to keep productivity from falling.

Under unchanged rates of capital accumulation there is thus a clear contradiction between two Lisbon goals: increased productivity and increased employment. Chart 5.3 shows this in terms of the two headline goals: reaching an employment rate of 70 percent (more or less the U.S. value) and reaching a productivity level equal to that of the United States.

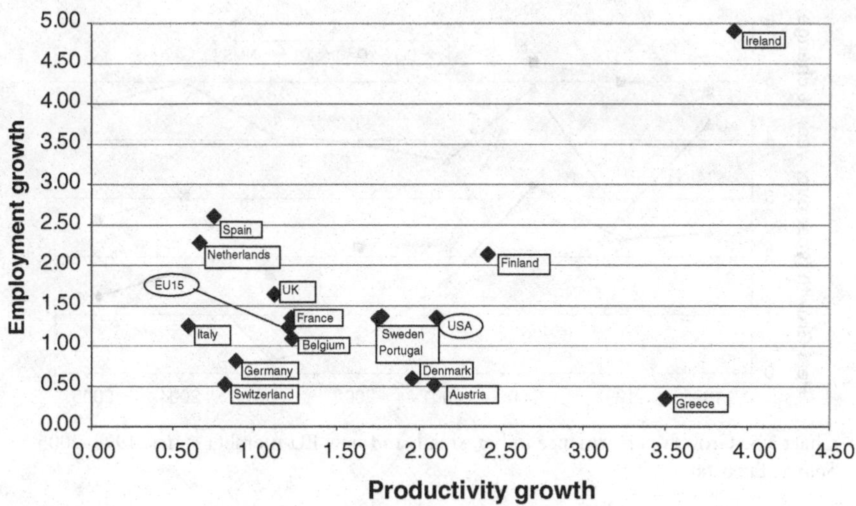

Chart 5.4. Productivity growth and employment growth in Europe and the United States, 1995–2002. *Notes*: "Employment growth" is the growth rate of total employment; "productivity growth" is the growth rate of GDP per employed person. *Source*: OECD Economic Outlook.

Big and Small: Lessons for a More Flexible Europe?

The growth performance of the Eurozone has been disappointing, at least if one looks at the average. But this average hides considerable variation. Can one discern any systematic pattern? The answer seems to be yes if one compares the performance of the large and the small European Monetary Union (EMU) states. Since the start of the EMU the three largest member states (France, and particularly Germany and Italy) have consistently underperformed. As together they represent three-quarters of Eurozone GDP, their sluggishness is behind the underperformance of the Eurozone (and of the EU) relative to the United States and the EU's own past performance.

Since 1999 the growth rates of the three "Euro-dinosaurs" have been 1.6 percentage points lower on average than those of the eight small member countries (Chart 5.5). This implies a total underperformance of 10 percent over this six-year period (the new member states have performed even better, but this is natural because they are still in a catch-up process).

Since monetary policy has been the same for all members of the Eurozone, it is unlikely that an overly tight monetary policy was responsible for the poor growth performance of the Eurozone.

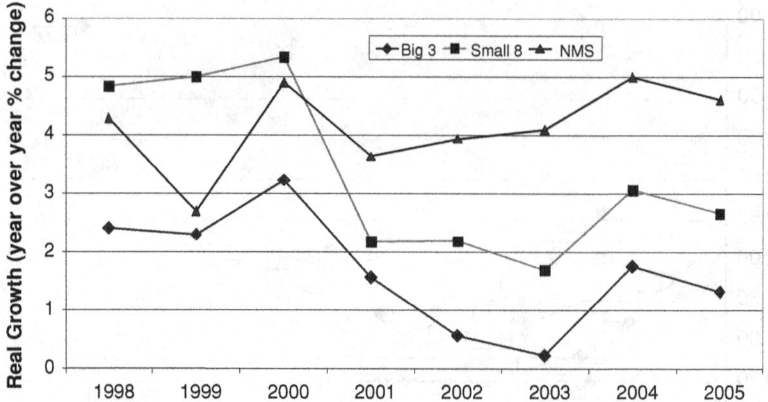

Chart 5.5. Growth performance in big, small, and new EU member states, 1998–2005. *Source*: Eurostat.

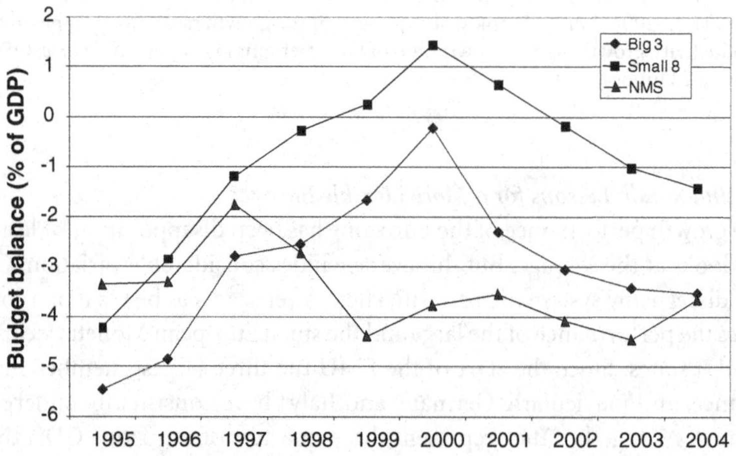

Chart 5.6. Budget balances in big, small, and new EU member states, 1995–2004. *Source*: Eurostat.

Interestingly, the much better growth performance of the smaller countries has been accompanied by much healthier public finances. Chart 5.6 shows that the eight smaller member countries have on average run a budget "close to balance," as required by the Stability Pact. Did their better growth performance come in spite of or because of this fiscal strictness? The facts suggest the latter explanation, since over the last few years the smaller countries have maintained their lead in terms of growth, while the difference in fiscal policy has increased. Maybe the leaders of the big three should

Table 5.4. *Large Versus Small Countries*

Averages 1998–2004	Big 3	Small 8	France	Germany	Italy	NMS	United States
Real GDP growth	1.3	2.7	2.0	0.8	1.2	4.6	4.4
Fiscal balance	−2.4	0.0	−2.6	−2.4	−2.10	−4.0	−1.8
Labor productivity growth	0.7	1.7	1.0	0.9	0.3	3.9	2.3
Share of industry	20.5	17.6	16.2	21.8	23.3	24.6	12.3

Source: Author's calculations based on AMECO data.

reflect more on the long-term benefits of strong fiscal policy, rather than band together to bend the rules against excessive deficits according to their short-term political preferences.

The much tighter fiscal policy pursued by the smaller euro area countries did not reduce their growth, but it did have a strong impact on their debt levels. A decade ago the smaller euro area countries had a slightly higher debt ratio than the big three (France, Germany, and Italy). This changed radically over the last ten years. The smaller countries now have a debt ratio (in percent of GDP) about twenty points lower than that of the big three. The big three debt ratio increased over the last decade and has stagnated at a high level since the start of the EMU. The smaller countries are much better prepared for the fiscal implications of population aging and the possibility of higher future interest rates.

Why do smaller countries perform better? Inflation was somewhat higher in the smaller countries, so they faced lower real interest rates. But this factor alone cannot explain a growth differential of this size. Perhaps the "big three" need more structural adjustments. Table 5.4 provides some summary data on the big-small divide. The relatively high weight of industry in the larger countries may have become a handicap. As long as markets were separated, the larger member countries offered a larger home market and were thus a better location for industry than their smaller EU partners. With the single market and the euro, this comparative advantage has disappeared. At the same time the competitive pressure on industry is increasing, not only because of globalization, but also because of enlargement. In the past, the rather high share of industry in employment in the big three (21 percent of the work force, compared with 15 percent in the smaller countries) might have been a source of strength. Today it is a problem that might explain part of their underperformance relative to the smaller member countries (not to speak of the United States, where the share of industry is even lower). The new member countries also have a rather large share of industry. But

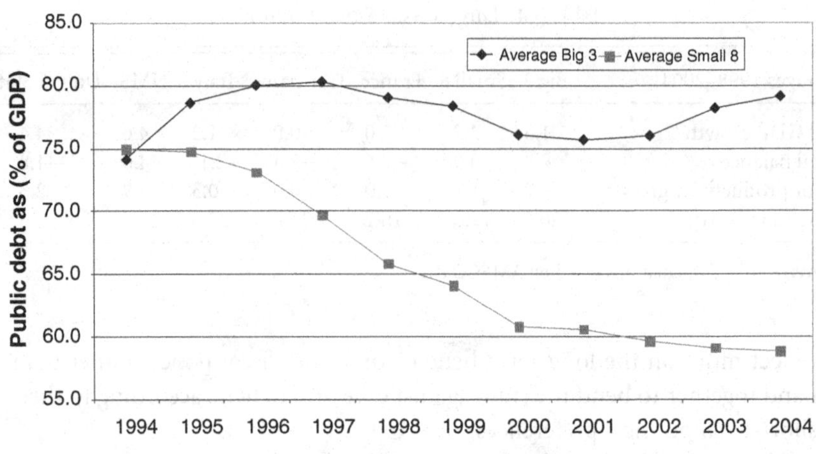

Chart 5.7. Public debt ratios compared, 1994–2004. *Source*: Eurostat.

given that exporting industrial goods is the only way they can export their relatively abundant supply of labor, this is not a handicap for the time being.

France has a lower share of its population in industry than Germany and Italy. This might explain why France performs somewhat better on productivity.

Smaller member countries are not just lucky in that they happen to have less of a problem with de-industrialization. They have also been able to react much better to economic shocks. External shocks, such as the 9/11 terrorist attacks or the Iraq war, are routinely used as an excuse for European economic weakness. This assertion can be tested. If it were true, one would expect the small countries to suffer more than the large countries, because the smaller member countries have a much larger exposure to the rest of the world. However, the data indicate the opposite. As Chart 5.7 shows, the small euro area countries have continued to outperform the "big three" even during the turbulent period since 2001.

Does Weak Supply Lead to Weak Policies?

A negative supply shock can lead to negative secondary effects due to the stress it puts on macroeconomic policy. In this section I discuss how this has happened in fiscal and structural policy.

The Crumbling of Fiscal Policy Discipline

To safeguard against a relapse into fiscal profligacy, EU governments concluded the Stability and Growth Pact (SGP) in 1997. Its purpose was to provide a framework for the operation of the excessive deficit procedure, enshrined in the Maastricht Treaty, within the EMU. Fiscal discipline remains indispensable to ensure long-run government solvency against the background of an aging population. The Stability and Growth Pact, albeit far from perfect, remains the best available instrument for trying to enforce discipline.

Unfortunately, during the first few years of the EMU, when growth was strong, poor implementation of the Pact allowed countries to run structural deficits (partially because the ongoing slowdown in potential growth was ignored). This set the stage for trouble during more recent economic weakness. As economic growth dropped close to stagnation in 2001–2003, pressure on budget deficits rose, forcing governments to choose between tough (and possibly pro-cyclical) spending cuts to meet the requirements of the Stability and Growth Pact and a weakening of the budget constraints. With both Germany and France – the heavyweights in the EU and the EMU – having difficulties adhering to fiscal discipline, it is no surprise that the Council of Ministers opted for softening of the budget constraint.

In the March 2005 "reform" of the Pact, the Council made the exceptions in case of a violation of the 3 percent deficit limit more generous and lengthened the periods within which excessive deficits have to be slashed (Box 5.1). As a result, the threat of sanctions for running an "excessive deficit" has faded, and fiscal discipline is being eroded. In its fiscal projections from April 2005, the EU Commission expected no further reduction in budget deficits at the Euroland level and forecast that France, Italy, Portugal, and Greece will run deficits in excess of 3 percent of GDP by 2006. The ratio of government debt to GDP, which fell from 76.1 percent for the euro area as a whole in 1996 to 69.4 percent in 2001–2002, increased again in 2003–2004. The risk is now high that it will continue to increase in the medium term. With the inevitable rise in age-related public spending coming in the next decade, a serious crisis of government finances in many Euroland countries within the next ten to fifteen years is now a distinct possibility.

The standard defense of this weakening of the SGP has been that countries should not be forced into an overly hasty fiscal adjustment. However, there is a clear long-term cost associated with allowing countries to run larger fiscal deficits: public dissavings tend to crowd out private investment. There is a large literature on this phenomenon. One could argue that in an area that has access to the world capital market, it does not really matter how much the government dissaves, since private investment can still be financed by capital imports, if needed.

Box 5.1. Key Points of the Stability and Growth Pact – Old and New

	Old	New
Small overshoot of deficit permitted if	• Exceptional event (natural disaster) • Recession with GDP falling by more than 2%	In addition if there are structural reforms or spending on • research and development • European political goals • international solidarity • investment • pension reform • EU contributions
Excessive deficit possible if	• Drop of GDP by more than 2% • Drop of GDP by more than 0.75% if downturn is sudden, the output gap is positive, or there are exceptional circumstances	In addition if economy is stagnating or growing very slowly
Time to correct excessive deficits	One year after establishment	Additional time when growth is slow
Implementation of fiscal adjustment program	Within four months	Within six months
Medium-term fiscal policy goals	Balanced budget or surplus	1% deficit if low debt or high potential growth, balanced budget, or surplus otherwise
Fiscal policy in good times		• 0.5% per year deficit reduction • exceptional revenue earmarked for debt reduction • early warning

Source: The amendments were declared in European Council Presidency Conclusions on March 22 and 23, 2005, in Brussels. Buti (2006) is one of the most recent references to show the differences between the old and the new pacts.

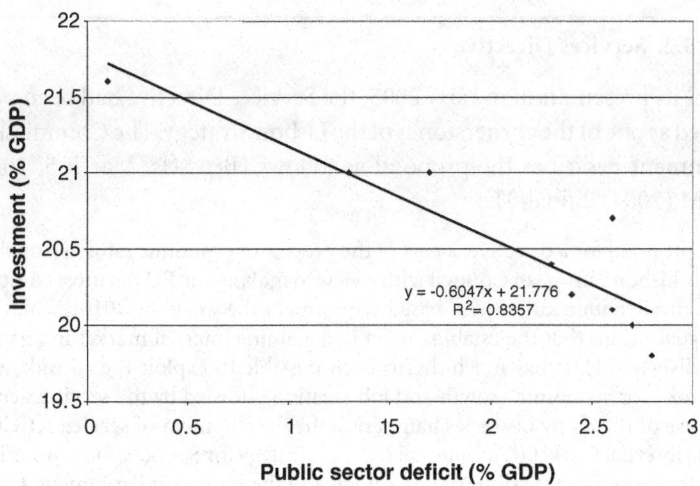

Chart 5.8. Eurozone investment and government savings, 1998–2004. *Source*: Eurostat.

We do not wish to review this complex of arguments in detail here. We simply point out that, in reality, larger deficits have been associated with lower investment in recent years. Chart 5.8 shows this close relationship. If this relationship were stable, one could conclude that an elimination of the structural deficits, which now are over 2 percent of GDP, should increase investment by about 1 percentage point of GDP. As we showed above, declining capital deepening is one of the causes of the productivity slowdown, which means that the abandonment of fiscal discipline will lead to lower future growth.

The Unraveling of Structural Reform

The Lisbon Agenda was Europe's answer to competitive challenges from low-cost, high-quality suppliers from abroad. Key to this agenda was the completion of the internal market, especially for services. This was expected to inject new dynamism into the European economy through greater competition in a sector accounting for about 70 percent of employment and GDP (Box 5.2). Member countries were supposed to complement the Lisbon Agenda with structural reform, especially in the areas of tax, labor market, and regulatory policy.

Five years on, the achievements have been truly disappointing. At the EU level, the European Council dealt a major and perhaps fatal blow to the Lisbon Agenda in March 2005, sending the Services Directive back to the

Box 5.2. Services Directive

Until its presentation in early 2005, the Services Directive had been portrayed as one of the cornerstones of the Lisbon Strategy. The Commission document describes the proposal as follows (Brussels, March 5, 2004, COM (2004) 2 final/3):

This proposal for a directive is part of the process of economic reform launched by the Lisbon European Council with a view to making the EU the most competitive and dynamic knowledge-based economy in the world by 2010. Achieving this goal means that the establishment of a genuine internal market in services is indispensable. It has not hitherto been possible to exploit the considerable potential for economic growth and job creation afforded by the services sector because of the many obstacles hampering the development of service activities in the internal market ("An Internal Market Strategy for Services," Communication from the Commission to the Council and the European Parliament, COM (2000) 888 final, December 29, 2000). This proposal forms part of the strategy adopted by the Commission to eliminate these obstacles and follows on from the Report on the State of the Internal Market for Services, which revealed their extent and significance (Report from the Commission to the Council and the European Parliament on "The State of the Internal Market for Services," COM (2002) 441 final, July 7, 2002).

The Commission underscores the importance of the Services Directive:

Services are omnipresent in today's economy, generating almost 70 percent of GNP and jobs and offering considerable potential for growth and job creation. Realizing this potential is at the heart of the process of economic reform launched by the Lisbon European Council and aimed at making the EU the most competitive and dynamic knowledge-based economy in the world by 2010. It has not so far been possible to exploit fully the growth potential of services because of the many obstacles hampering the development of services activities between the Member states.

The Commission proposal is also part of the Lisbon Agenda:

In March 2000, the Lisbon European Council adopted a programme of economic reform aimed at making the EU the most competitive and dynamic knowledge-based economy in the world by 2010. In this context, the EU Heads of State and Government invited the Commission and the Member states to devise a strategy aimed at eliminating the obstacles to the free movement of services. (Presidency Conclusions, Lisbon European Council, March 24, 2000, paragraph 17. The need to take action in these fields was also highlighted at the Stockholm and Barcelona Summits in 2001 and 2002.)

Commission for a comprehensive overhaul. Most important, the critics of the Commission's draft have questioned the country-of-origin principle in the mutual recognition of regulations, which is at the heart of the single market. According to the critics, this principle, which allows providers to offer their services within the EU under home regulations, leads to unfair competition and "social dumping." These critics claim that as suppliers based in high-cost, densely regulated countries were pushed out of the market, there would be a "race to the bottom" in regulations and social protection. To safeguard against this, they want to adopt the country-of-destination principle, where service providers have to observe the rules in the consuming country. The result would be protection of high-cost service suppliers and the continuing fragmentation of the European services market.

National governments' structural reform efforts have also run out of steam. Politicians have taken a cautious approach, fearing the ire of their electorates. In the last few years, euro area governments have eased tax burdens somewhat, reduced regulations to a certain extent, and eased restrictions in certain segments of the labor market. All these were steps in the right direction, but the measures were not comprehensive enough to engineer a clear turnaround in the labor market and to boost GDP growth. With the results of reforms disappointing, electorates are increasingly leaning toward backward-looking protectionist policies. Politicians eager to disguise their own failings are catering to these sentiments by questioning the rationale of an open, market-oriented economy. This political backlash may well lead to protectionist policies in Euroland, dampening economic growth even more.

Toward the end of the last millennium, some observers wondered whether the first ten years of the new millennium would become the decade of Europe. The Lisbon Agenda, launched in 2000 to create "the most dynamic knowledge-based economy of the world by the end of this decade," reflected these hopes for a European revival. With only five more years left to meet this goal, the current decade is very unlikely to be Europe's. In fact, future economic historians may well conclude that this decade confirmed the decline of Europe. The fall of the Berlin Wall at the end of the 1980s appeared to open a new future for Europe, but the 1990s consolidated the political and economic weight of the United States in the world. At the beginning of the decade, Europe set itself high political and economic goals. But it will probably miss both. With the rise of Asian countries in recent years, Europe will probably end the decade as a shrinking political and economic power, continuing the trend that began with World War I.

Concluding Remarks

This contribution has documented the structural weakness of the Eurozone, or rather its largest member countries (France, Germany, and Italy). Even the best structural reforms cannot change some fundamental parameters, including negative demographic trends and a declining capital-labor ratio. But reform can help. The smaller euro member countries show that better performance is possible. However, the rejection of the draft directive on liberalizing trade in services suggests that some countries are resisting this reform.

Why has policy not improved? The key reason is that policy decisions are determined by short-term considerations. This applies in particular to fiscal policy, which is now governed by a mix of political expediency and some primitive Keynesian ideas. In this context, the long-term objectives and issues are often forgotten. Two of these long-term considerations are particularly germane for Europe today: aging makes surpluses desirable, and deficits crowd out investment.

A fiscal policy oriented toward the long run could produce a "double dividend": it would prepare governments for aging and crowd in investment, making it easier to maintain the capital-to-labor ratio, and hence productivity growth. Europe needs not only structural economic reforms, but also a structural reform of fiscal policy. The reform of the Stability and Growth Pact, initiated by France and Germany but passed with almost unanimous support, unfortunately suggests that policy makers are going in the opposite direction. They are looking for excuses to continue a policy that emphasizes short-term expediency at the expense of long-term gains.

References

Blanchard, Olivier. 2004. "The Economic Future of Europe." *Journal of Economic Perspectives* 18, no. 4: 3–26.

Buti, Marco. 2006. "Will the New Stability and Growth Pact Succeed? An Economic and Political Perspective." European Directorate General for Economic and Financial Affairs Economic Paper 241.

Daveri, Francesco. 2000. "Is Growth an Information Technology Story in Europe Too?" IGIER Working Paper 168.

Daveri, Francesco. 2002. "The New Economy in Europe, 1992–2001." *Oxford Review of Economic Policy* 18, no. 3: 345–362.

Daveri, Francesco. 2004. "Why Is There a Productivity Problem in Europe?" Centre for European Policy Studies Working Document 205. Brussels: CEPS.

Deutsche Bank. 2004. "Inflation Is Dead, Long Live Inflation." Deutsche Bank Global Markets Research.

Gros, Daniel, ed. 2001. *Testing the Speed Limit for Europe.* 3rd Macroeconomic Policy Group Report. Brussels: CEPS.

Gros, Daniel, ed. 2002. *Fiscal and Monetary Policy for a Low-Speed Europe.* 4th Macroeconomic Policy Group Report. Brussels: CEPS.

Gros, Daniel, Juan Jimeno, Thomas Mayer, Niels Thygesen, and Angel Ubide. 2003. *Adjusting to Leaner Times*. 5th Macroeconomic Policy Group Report. Brussels: CEPS.

Inklaar, Robert, Mary O'Mahony, and Marcel P. Timmer. 2005. "ICT and Europe's Productivity Performance: Industry-Level Growth Account Comparisons with the United States." *Review of Income and Wealth* 51, no. 5: 505–536.

Jorgenson, Dale W. 2003. *Economic Growth in the Information Age*. Cambridge: MIT Press.

SIX

Is Europe Reforming?

Evidence from Cross-Country Structural Indicators

Patrick Lenain

Introduction

In March 2000, the EU established the ambitious goal of becoming the most dynamic and competitive economy in the world by 2010. A variety of measurable targets were set accordingly, from increases in employment to higher spending on research and development. Despite initial optimism, the first half of the decade has been dispiriting and the EU is unlikely to achieve the objectives of the Lisbon Strategy. Over the last five years output has moved in fits and starts, without embarking on a sustained expansion, at a time when other OECD economies, notably the United States, were enjoying a strong recovery from the post-bubble recession. In the labor market, high unemployment has persisted in a number of EU countries. Trend labor productivity growth has declined toward the lowest pace ever recorded during the post-war period. Many observers have concluded that governments have failed to implement much-needed policies required to achieve the Lisbon targets and that, without radical changes, the strategy will fail to deliver on its promises (IMF, 2004; Kok, 2004). While this has been true for a long time, the lack of structural reform has become all the more problematic following the May 2004 enlargement, which brought into the EU ten countries with a total of 4.8 million job seekers.[1] As more countries with large numbers of unemployed workers are knocking on the door, Europe must accelerate the pace of reform if it is to rise to the challenge.

[1] In this chapter, the European Union refers to the group of fifteen countries that constituted the EU before the 2004 enlargement. An overall assessment of the EU-25 is not possible at this stage due to the lack of OECD data on new member countries.

The views presented in this chapter are those of the author and should not be construed as representing official views of the OECD.

Nonetheless, it would be wrong to say that structural policies have been standing still. Using cross-country indicators compiled by the OECD, the present chapter shows that signs of changes have emerged since the start of the decade. For instance, several countries have introduced pro-employment policy reforms, so as to increase demand for low-skilled workers and incite older workers to retire at a later age. This has been associated with a somewhat better labor market performance, notably higher employment rates. Regulatory policies have been eased, following the opening of markets to competition, pressuring firms to invest and innovate. While this is welcome, the EU needs more comprehensive labor and product market reforms to mobilize unused labor resources, put productivity growth on a faster trend, and accelerate the growth of GDP per capita. Recent labor market reforms, such as those enacted in Germany under the Agenda 2010 program, could have a positive impact during the second half of the Lisbon Strategy.

This chapter describes changes in structural indicators relevant to the Lisbon Strategy. No attempt is made here to link changes in structural policy indicators to economic outcomes. But a large body of academic and institutional analyses has shown that the indicators presented in this chapter have a significant economic impact. The first part of the chapter addresses the Lisbon goal of fostering employment by reviewing recent developments in indicators of labor market performance and labor market policies. The second part addresses the Lisbon goal of fostering productivity. Rather than covering the many policies that affect productivity, the chapter focuses on one particular area where the EU has a specific interest, namely, the regulatory policies influencing competition on product markets. The final part takes stock of this overview and raises some political economy issues related to the method of coordination adopted by the Lisbon Agenda. The EU should see the new Lisbon Strategy for Growth and Jobs, together with its periodic National Reform Programs, as an opportunity to go beyond initial steps to a path of fast output and employment growth.

Recent Changes in European Labor Markets

Fostering the use of potential labor resources is one of the main goals of the Lisbon Strategy. The strategy aims to increase the overall EU employment rate from 64 percent to 70 percent by 2010, with subtargets for older and female workers. Although the EU will probably not meet the midterm targets set for 2005, there are signs that employment trends are changing. The EU employment rate has risen by 4.5 percentage points since the mid-1990s

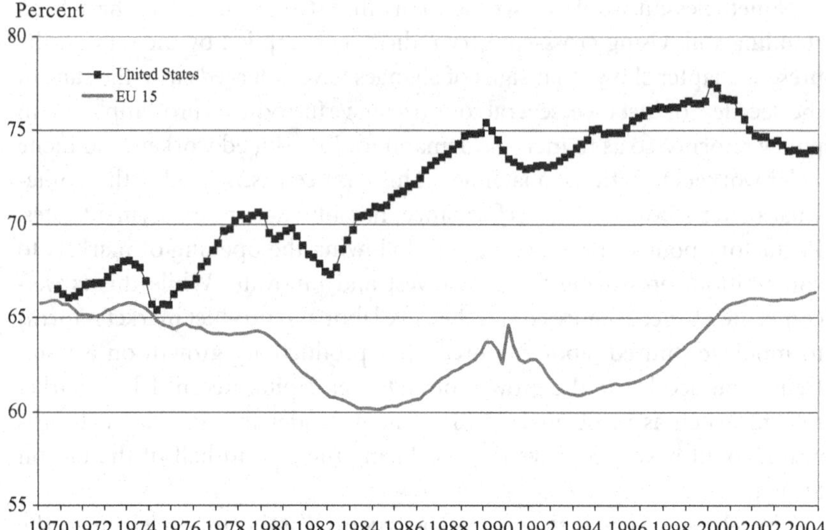

Chart 6.1. Diverging trends in employment rates, 1970–2004 (percent). *Source*: OECD (differs from employment rate calculated by Eurostat).

(Chart 6.1). This increase partly reflects a cyclical bounce-back from the severe downturn in the first half of the past decade, but there are also signs that a structural change may be under way. The recent slowdown in output had scarcely any effect on EU employment, whereas previous downturns saw large job losses, and unemployment has increased only moderately since the last peak of activity (European Commission, 2004a). This resiliency contrasts with the sharp decline of U.S. employment, which has declined more than 3 percentage points since 2000, as discouraged workers have exited the labor market and young people have prolonged their transition from school to the job market (Table 6.1). Although a large gap still prevails between the employment rates of Europe and the United States, this gap may be slowly narrowing.

A possible structural change can also be seen in the relation between activity and labor input. Chart 6.2 shows the relation between real GDP growth and total hours worked during the last three decades. In the early 1970s, high annual GDP growth rates of 4 percent were associated with a trend decline in hours worked. Robust activity growth did not prevent a decline in labor input. This relation gradually changed, and, since the mid-1990s, real GDP growth of 2 percent has been associated with an increase in hours worked of about 1 percent per year. Recent work by the European Central

Table 6.1. *Employment Rates by Groups of Workers, 1992–2010 (share of employed persons of working age, in percent)*

	1992	1995	2000	2003	Lisbon targets 2005	2010
European Union						
Total employment rate, of which	61.2	60.1	63.4	64.4	67	70
– Male workers	72.8	70.5	72.8	72.7	–	–
– Female workers	49.7	49.7	54.1	56.1	57.0	60.0
Older workers (55–64)	36.3	36.0	37.8	41.7	–	50
United States						
Total employment rate, of which	70.8	72.5	74.1	71.2		
– Male workers	78.3	79.5	80.6	76.9		
– Female workers	44.6	47.5	50.6	54.5		
– Older workers (55–64)	53.4	55.1	57.8	59.9		

Source: EU structural indicator.

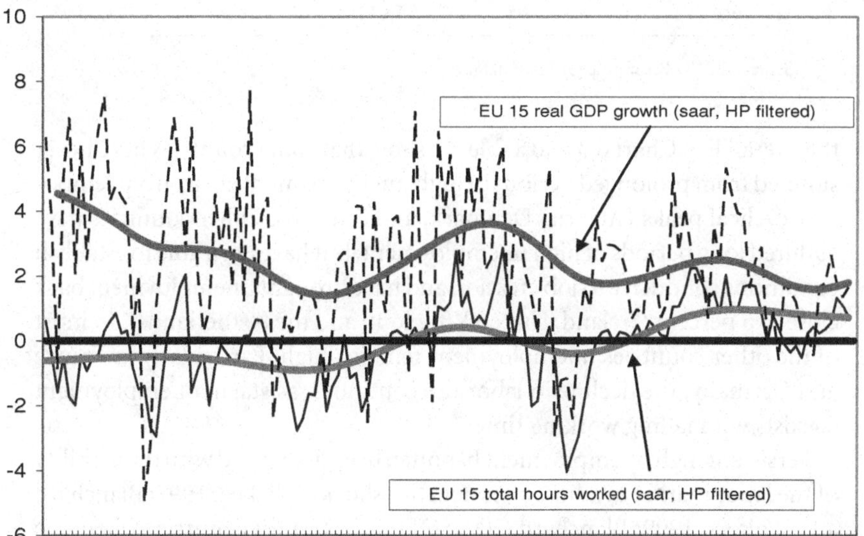

Chart 6.2. Growth has become more labor-intensive, 1970–2004. *Source*: Eurostat.

Bank (Mourre, 2004) has identified a structural break in the relation between GDP growth and employment around 1997.

While aggregate labor market conditions have changed in the EU, significant disparity continues to prevail across countries. Thus it is preferable to talk about labor market conditions in individual countries, rather than in

Table 6.2. *Unemployment Rates in EU Countries, 1970s–2004*

	1970s	1980s	1990s	2004
Luxemburg	0.3	1.4	2.5	4.3
Ireland	7.4	13.9	11.8	4.5
United Kingdom	3.3	9.2	7.9	4.7
Netherlands	2.7	7.6	5.6	5.0
Sweden	2.1	2.5	6.2	5.5
Austria	1.3	3.3	5.2	5.5
Denmark	3.0	6.6	6.9	5.8
Portugal	4.9	7.7	5.6	6.7
Belgium	3.4	9.3	8.5	7.8
Italy	4.7	8.4	10.7	8.0
Finland	3.6	4.9	11.9	8.9
Germany	1.4	5.2	7.3	9.3
France	3.9	9.1	11.0	9.8
Spain	3.4	13.8	15.1	10.8
Greece	1.8	6.6	9.5	11.0
Variance	*3.05*	*13.11*	*10.83*	*5.54*

Source: OECD Economic Outlook database.

the overall EU. Chart 6.3 and Table 6.2 show that some countries have never suffered from prolonged periods of high unemployment, apart from temporary cyclical peaks (Austria, Denmark, and Sweden). Other countries have endured long periods of high unemployment, but have been able to establish conditions conducive to job creation and have brought unemployment back close to 5 percent (Ireland, United Kingdom, and the Netherlands). In most of the other countries unemployment remains high. Particularly in France and Germany, the decline in labor use continues, as stagnant employment coexists with falling working time.

Persistent high unemployment has often been associated with the inability of the labor market to adjust after negative shocks (Nickell, 1997; Blanchard and Wolfers, 1999; Blanchard, 2004; OECD, 2005). In countries where the labor market does not adjust rapidly, temporary spells of unemployment tend to persist and result in high long-term unemployment. In countries where labor markets function well, unemployment does not last long, as self-correcting mechanisms, notably lower wages, help to restore the equilibrium. Long-term unemployment does not exercise the same type of pressure on the wage level as short-term unemployment because workers tend to lose their skills and become less employable over time. Insiders don't see them as serious competitors. In several EU countries, notably Germany and

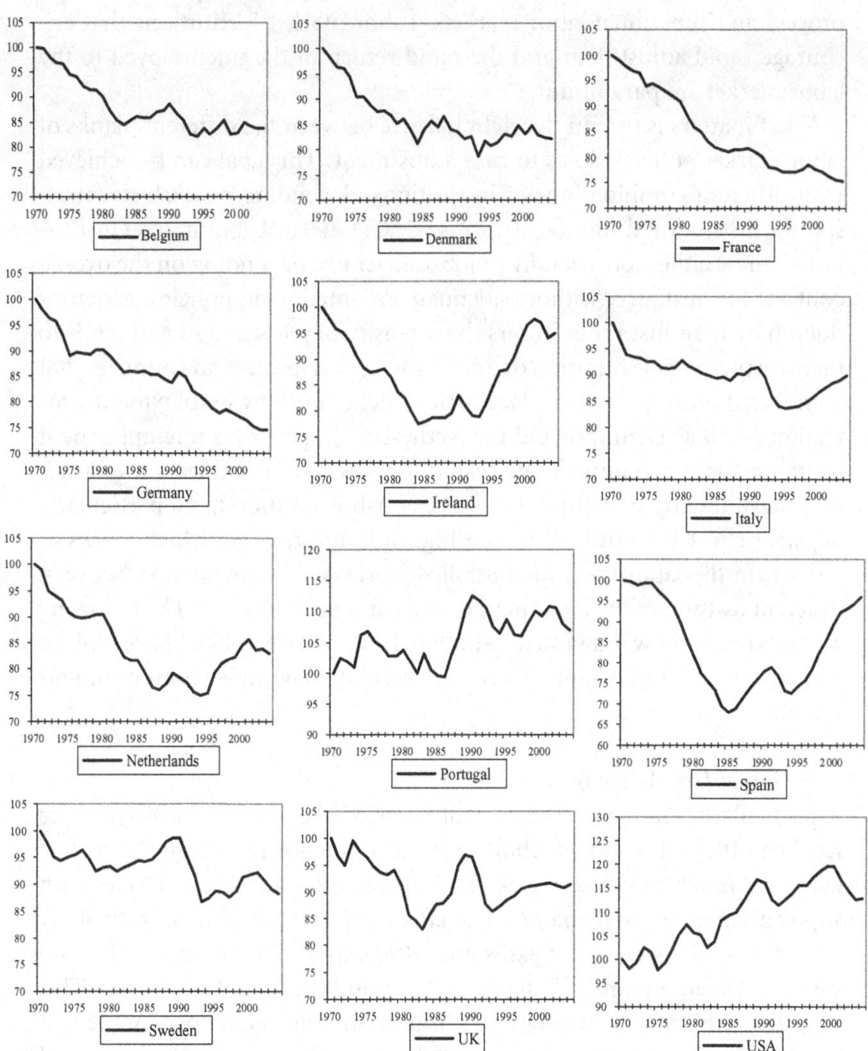

Chart 6.3. Different trends in labor use, 1970–2000 (1970 = 100). *Source*: OECD.

Italy, more than 50 percent of the job seekers are long-term unemployed (i.e., registered for one year or more), suggesting poorly functioning labor markets and over-prolonged periods of adjustment. In these countries, the cost of adjustment is likely to be high because insiders will not agree to negotiate lower wages until unemployment reaches very high levels. In other countries

(Denmark, Finland, the United Kingdom, and Sweden), the share of long-term unemployment is closer to 20 percent, suggesting a rapid adjustment process and functional labor markets. Labor market institutions that encourage rapid adjustment and the rapid return of the unemployed to the labor market are paramount.

What matters is to find the right balance between the different planks of labor market policies, so as to ease adjustment. This goal can be achieved with different combinations of institutions, depending on each country's specific institutional and social norms (OECD, 2004). Labor market institutions can be either job-friendly or job-unfriendly, depending on the overall context. For instance, without adequate accompanying policies, generous unemployment insurance lowers the intensity of job searches and tends to increase the average duration of unemployment. However, in countries that combine it with active job placement policies and low employment protection (such as Denmark and the Netherlands), generous unemployment insurance does not impede the search for new jobs and does not increase long-term unemployment. Likewise, high labor taxation has a particularly negative effect in countries with a high minimum wage, which works as a floor on the labor costs for unskilled workers. The interaction between different features of the labor market plays an important role. The following sections review how individual features of labor market policies have evolved recently, but it is important to keep in mind that their impact is multidimensional.

Taxation of Low-Wage Earners

A particularly important category of labor market reform in recent years has been the reduction in labor taxation. High taxes increase the cost of labor inasmuch as workers seek to compensate higher levels of taxes with supplementary wage demands. The effect of labor taxation is particularly large for workers with few skills and little experience because it drives a wedge between their marginal productivity and the cost of their labor. This is particularly true when a statutory minimum wage sets a floor on the cost of labor. In view of this, governments have sought to lower the burden of labor taxation on targeted categories of workers, notably through cuts in social security contributions and other labor taxes.

Chart 6.4 uses indicators of labor taxation compiled to measure the tax burden of typical workers at various levels of income and in different family situations. As shown, the taxation of low-wage earners declined between 1998 and 2004 in all EU countries, with more pronounced cuts in Ireland, France, and Belgium. Chart 6.5 examines the progressivity of the tax system

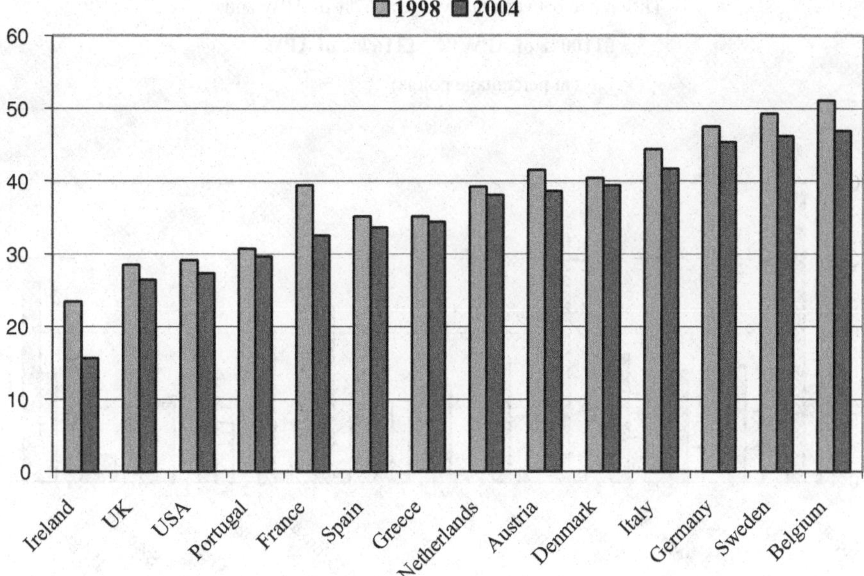

Chart 6.4. The tax wedge declined for low-wage earners from 1998 to 2004. Graph shows income tax plus social security contribution in percentage of labor costs for single people without children at 67% of average earnings. *Source*: OECD.

measured by the differences among tax rates at different levels of income. In several countries (notably, Ireland and France) the tax rates are significantly lower on low-wage earners than on average or high-wage earners. In the case of France, however, the cost of unskilled labor is nonetheless the highest in the OECD because a substantial share of the cuts in labor taxes was used to offset very strong increases in the minimum wage.

Financial Incentives to Retire Early

Another important reform in labor market policy has related to the participation of older workers. Past decades saw governments react to rising unemployment with measures meant to encourage the early withdrawal of older workers from the labor force, notably through early-retirement schemes. These schemes, together with traditional features of old-age pension schemes, have been detrimental to the labor market participation of older workers. Retiring early or at the statutory age of retirement entitles the older worker to a number of benefits, while continued work implies deferring benefits without necessarily increasing their levels. The tax and benefit consequences of working beyond the age of retirement have been

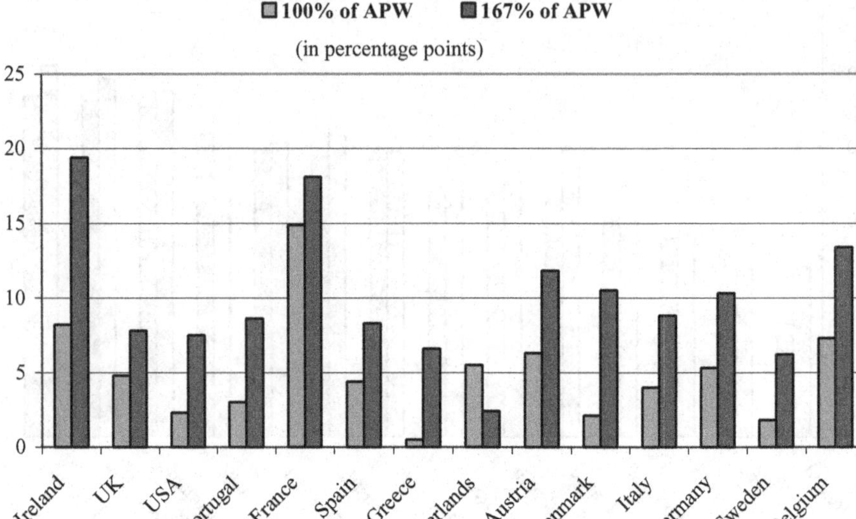

Chart 6.5. Differences in progressivity of the tax wedge across countries. "APW" = wage of an average production worker.

evaluated by a new OECD indicator, the "implicit tax on continued work" (Duval, 2003). The indicator takes into account the net present value of additional contributions paid in case of continued work as well as the potential increase in pension benefits accrued when workers decide to continue working past the retirement age. Before recent pension reforms, EU workers aged fifty-five to sixty faced implicit taxes of nearly 60 percent if they decided not to take advantage of early-retirement and regular old-age pension benefits. Such high rates of taxation severely depressed the employment rates of older workers.

Faced with the prospect of population aging, several EU governments have reformed their pension regimes to restore long-term financial sustainability. These reforms often changed the main parameters of pension benefits as well as the age of entitlement. Together with stricter eligibility for early-retirement benefits, they have lowered the implicit tax on continued work in several EU countries (e.g., Germany, France, and Belgium), and the average EU-15 implicit tax has dropped from about 60 percent to close to 45 percent of income (Chart 6.6). An example of such a measure is the 2004 French pension reform, which introduces an element of actuarial neutrality in the

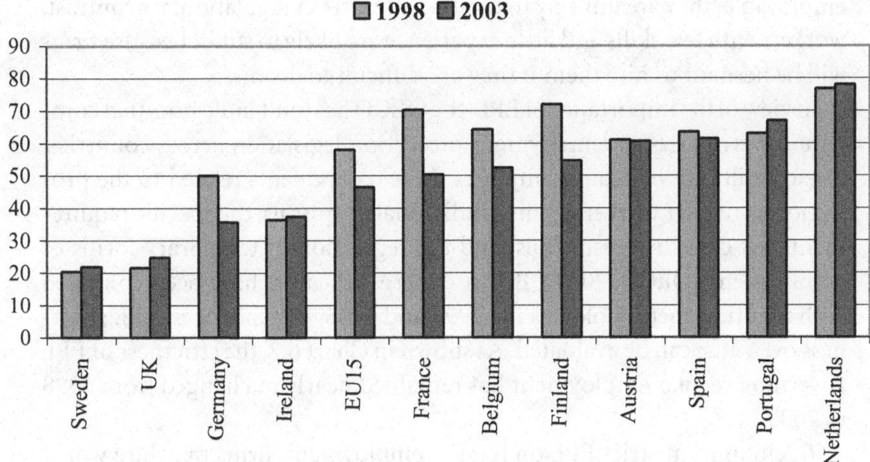

Chart 6.6. The implicit tax on continued work declined from 1998 to 2003. Graph shows average of implicit tax on continued work in early retirement route, for 55 and 60 years old, in percentage of average workers earning. *Source*: OECD, 2005.

pension system and lowers the disincentive to work longer, while increasing the freedom to retire early with a reduced pension. In several countries, sector-specific early-retirement schemes have been closed. This decline in the implicit tax has been associated with an increase in the labor participation of older workers, even though factors other than taxation have probably been at play (notably, the increase in life expectancy).

Stringency of Employment Legislation

Employment protection legislation (EPL) is a third category of labor market policy that limits the adaptability of labor markets. While such legislation is necessary to govern the relations between employers and employees, excessively strict legislation increases the cost, time, and legal complexity of dismissing workers. By making it more costly and difficult to make workers redundant, EPL limits the labor market outflows and reduces inflows. Faced with strict EPL, employers will be more reluctant to hire workers, knowing that it will be difficult to dismiss them.

Because it reduces both outflows and inflows, strict EPL has ambiguous effects on employment. What is unambiguous, however, is the asymmetry of effects on various groups of workers. Strict EPL generally protects insiders, but penalizes outsiders. While skilled and experienced workers are easily employable, they are unlikely to be affected by strict regulation. By contrast, workers with few skills and little experience are likely to suffer because firms will be hesitant to hire them if they are difficult to dismiss.

In view of the importance of EPL, the OECD has built indicators that compare the strictness of employment protection legislation across countries. The overall EPL indicator combines three components related to the protection of regular workers against individual dismissals, the specific requirements for collective dismissals, and the regulation of temporary forms of employment (OECD, 2004). Because these indicators have been compiled with identical methodologies for 1998 and 2003, the change in EPL strictness over time can be evaluated. As shown in Chart 6.7, the strictness of EPL governing regular employment has remained nearly unchanged from 1998 to 2003.

To circumvent strict EPL on regular employment, firms may hire workers under temporary contracts, which many countries regulate less strictly. Chart 6.7 shows that EPL on temporary contracts has been eased more frequently than EPL on regular contracts. As a result of this divergence, some countries have stricter EPL regimes for regular work than for temporary work. This encourages labor market dualism because firms can have recourse to regular and protected contracts for skilled workers and temporary contracts for the others (OECD, 2004). Although not an optimal solution, the easing of EPL on temporary workers has helped to foster the creation of temporary jobs. This might be one of the reasons for the rapid increase in the employment rate of female workers, which are overrepresented in the group of temporary workers, notably in the services sectors and in part-time jobs.

Unemployment Insurance

Little change has occurred in the level of unemployment benefits. These benefits, while providing a sense of income security, have the potential to lower search intensity and increase the duration of average unemployment spells. High levels of income replacement may translate into a rigid wage formation process and therefore increase the cost of adjustment in the aftermath of a negative shock. Chart 6.8 shows the rate of replacement income for unemployment in 2002 compared with its previous measure in 1999. The chart illustrates the great heterogeneity of unemployment insurance policies, with replacement rates ranging from 50 percent of previous earnings (United Kingdom) to nearly 90 percent (Sweden). Little has been done in the most generous countries to cut these entitlements.

■ 1998 ■ 2003

Protection legislation on permanent employment

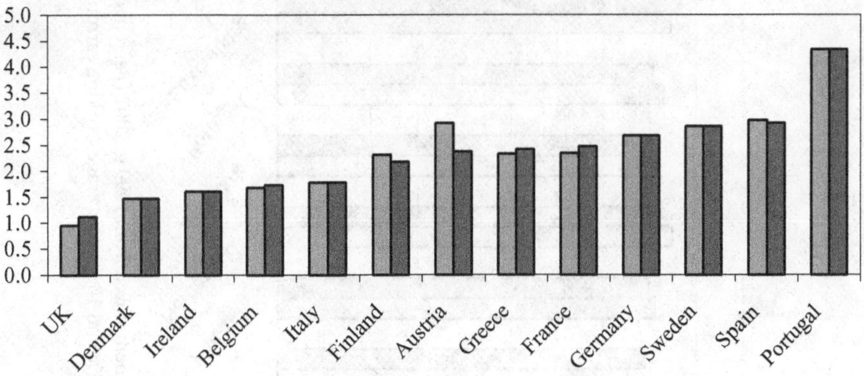

Protection legislation on temporary employment

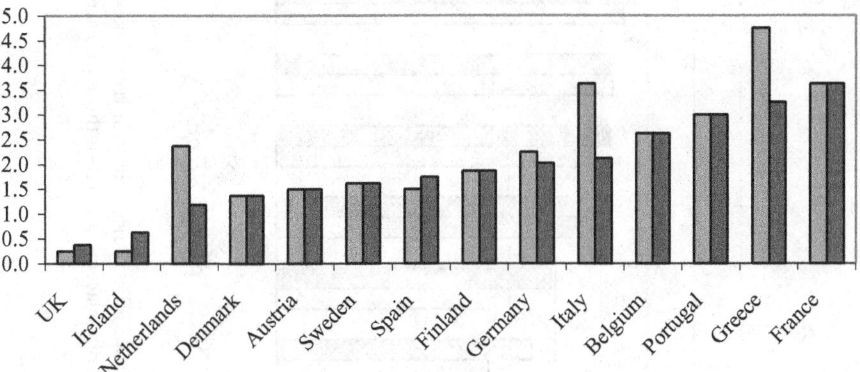

Chart 6.7. Employment protection legislation has not changed, except for temporary work between 1998 and 2003. The scale of indicators is 0–5, from least to most restrictive. *Source*: OECD, 2004.

The social cost of reform might explain governments' reluctance to change. The replacement income of job seekers would fall immediately, while structural changes in employment trends would take time to appear. Perhaps this is why countries have emphasized job placement policies, such as the recent measures under the German Agenda 2010 plan, which limit the duration of unemployment benefits and lower their level, but increase the resources available for personalized job search assistance.

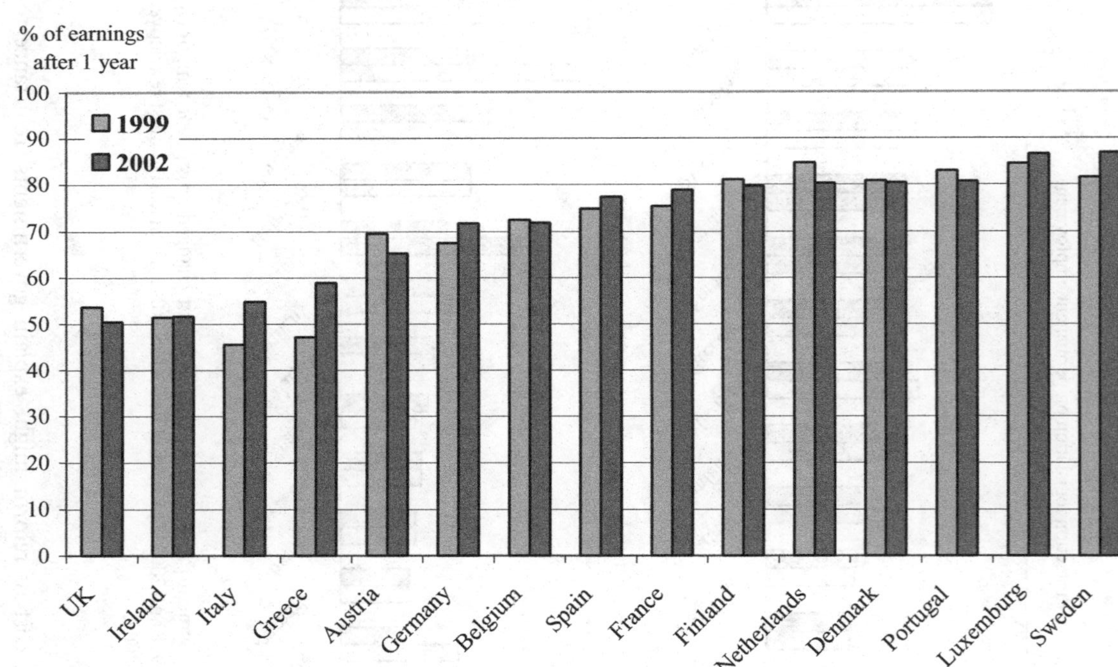

Chart 6.8. This graph shows little change in income replacement for unemployed from 1999 to 2002 (percent of earnings after one year). Average of replacement rates for those who earned 67% and 100% of average working earnings. *Source*: OECD.

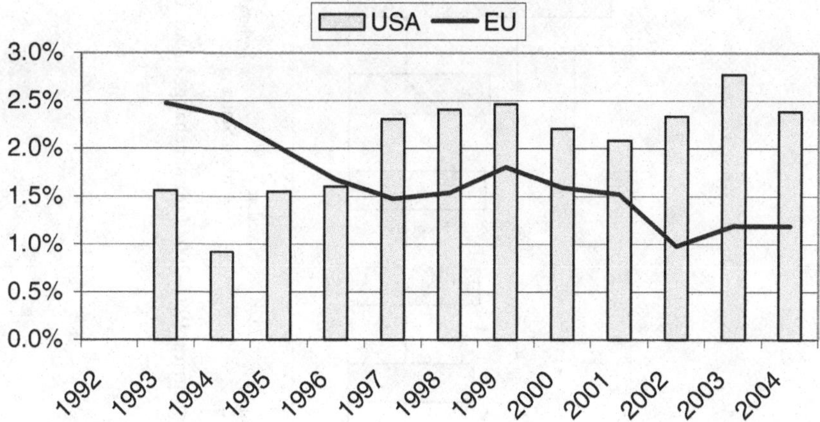

Chart 6.9. EU hourly labor productivity growth fell below the U.S. level, 1992–2004. Graph shows labor productivity per hour (real GDP divided by total hours worked; annual growth, moving average for three years). *Source*: OECD.

To summarize, European employment trends have changed, not only thanks to the cyclical rebound of the late 1990s, but due to more fundamental improvement. Yet a large degree of heterogeneity prevails across countries. Where employment has improved, this seems to have resulted from a combination of changes in policies that made the labor market function better. In high-unemployment countries, structural reforms have either been insufficiently ambitious, combined in a suboptimal way, or implemented too recently to produce significant observable effects. There is wide agreement that labor market reforms need to be implemented in a comprehensive and coherent fashion (European Commission, 2005). The way to achieve this policy coherence depends on country circumstances and institutions (OECD, 2004). Given the country-specific nature of labor market reforms, there is little room for a unique and centralized approach at the EU level. This has implications (discussed below) for the Lisbon Strategy.

Productivity and Product Market Competition

Increasing productivity growth is another important goal of the Lisbon Strategy. Despite the importance of this goal, Charts 6.9 and 6.10 show that the trend of hourly productivity has fallen in recent years, preventing

Chart 6.10. There was a wide disparity in productivity growth rates across countries, 1998–2004 (annual change in %). Graph shows annual percentage in GDP per hour. *Source:* OECD.

the EU from gathering speed. Hourly labor productivity growth has barely exceeded 1 percent annually in the EU during 2000–2004, sharply less than the pace of 2 percent to 2.5 percent recorded in the United States. Hence, the productivity gap between the two regions is widening.

In the United States, productivity accelerated in the mid-1990s, a development that is often attributed to the diffusion of new information and communication technologies and the associated surge in business fixed investment. In Europe the diffusion of the same new technologies did not increase productivity growth. The EU productivity growth even slowed down after the mid-1990s. While some sectors benefited from the use of IT (notably, telecommunication), a majority of other industries saw their productivity growth decline significantly (O'Mahony and Van Ark, 2003). The continuation of divergent U.S. and EU productivity trends over a decade suggests that this was more than a simple cyclical phenomenon. A fundamental change has occurred.

Within the EU, productivity growth differs across countries. A few economies have achieved levels of productivity growth similar to that of the United States (Ireland, Sweden, and United Kingdom), while in other countries productivity nearly came to a standstill (Spain and Italy). This suggests that policy settings have influenced productivity outcomes. Although governments do not influence productivity directly, a variety of structural policies, including those related to education, innovation, and investment, influence it indirectly. Likewise, the type of labor market reforms discussed in the first part of this chapter may exert a temporary drag on productivity insofar as low-productivity workers are reabsorbed into the labor force.

There is growing evidence that the degree of competition in product markets has an important influence on productivity (Nicoletti and Scarpetta, 2003; European Commission, 2004b). High competition influences firms' incentives to seek efficiency gains via the adoption of technological and organizational best practices. Combined with labor market reform, a greater degree of product market competition reduces the level of mark-ups and reduces the bargaining power of insiders, with beneficial impact on employment trends. In addition, relatively "liberal" regulatory policies are often associated with loose employment protection legislation.

Product market regulation indicators, compiled by the OECD for 1998 and 2003, measure the change in policies influencing competition (Conway et al., 2005). These indicators were developed to describe broad differences in product market policies across OECD countries. They evaluate regulations that have the potential to reduce competition in areas of the product market where technology and market conditions make competition viable. The structure of indicators, which are based on questionnaires sent to OECD governments, takes the form of a pyramid with sixteen detailed indicators at the base. These are aggregated successively to produce indicators in three domains (state control, barriers to entrepreneurship, and barriers to trade and investment), which are summarized in one product market regulation indicator at the top. Detailed aspects of regulatory practices (such as licensing requirements or trade tariffs) are combined with industry-specific regulations (such as rules governing retail trade) to produce an overall assessment of regulatory stance. Production of the indicator incorporates a variety of verifications, for instance, to ascertain the quality of answers to the questionnaires and to test different weights used in the aggregation. Nonetheless, the indicators remain largely confined to formal regulatory policy and do not directly account for informal regulatory practices or the strictness of implementation.

The indicators, which were initially produced for 1998, have been recently updated for 2003 with the objective of ensuring full comparability. Between these two dates, the regulatory stance of all OECD member countries has eased significantly (Chart 6.11). State controls have been lowered, price controls have been lifted, state ownership of enterprises has been reduced, barriers to entry have been removed, trade barriers have been eliminated, and countries have become more open to foreign direct investment. In Europe, the implementation of single market directives has helped to boost cross-border competitive pressures, especially in the goods market. Other European initiatives have fostered competition in various sectors, such as telecommunications and air transport, notably by allowing the entry of new firms. If the past relationship between pro-competition policies and productivity growth continues to prevail, some acceleration of productivity could occur in the second half of the decade in countries that have undertaken the greatest liberalization efforts.

Important differences continue to prevail across EU member states, despite the adoption of EU directives on the functioning of the single market and competition policy. The United Kingdom, Ireland, and Denmark have implemented pro-competition policies, while other member states adopted stricter regulatory stances. This large variance is possible because many policy areas related to competition, such as the extent of state ownership, do not belong to the prerogatives of the European Commission. Some member states do not fully implement EU directives or transpose them late. Overall, product market competition has intensified in the EU, but much remains to be done.

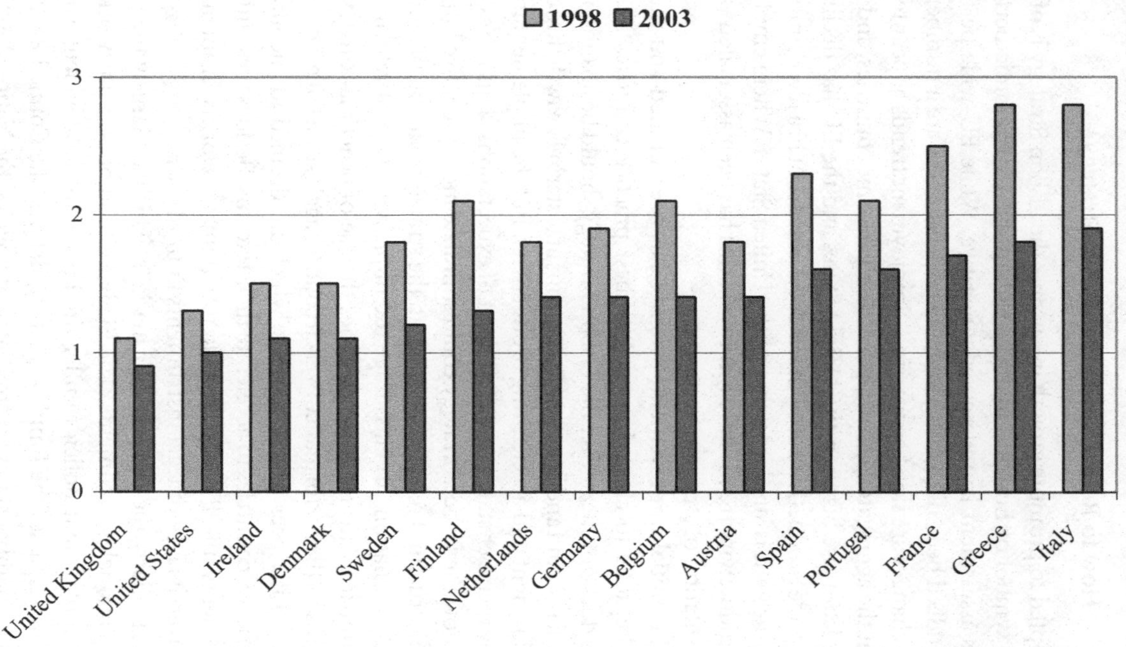

Chart 6.11. Product market regulation became less stringent from 1998 to 2003. The scale of indicators is 0–6, from least to most restrictive. *Source*: Conway et al. (2005).

How to Reinvigorate the Lisbon Strategy?

Initially adopted to promote growth in Europe, the Lisbon Strategy is often viewed as a symbol of Europe's inability to improve its economic performance. This assessment is undeservedly negative. While EU-wide performance has indeed been dispiriting in many respects, there are a number of areas where changes are slowly occurring. Employment trends appear to be improving at the aggregate EU level, particularly in some countries, and the large gap in labor use between the United States and the EU has declined slightly. EU-wide productivity growth has decelerated, but in a few countries productivity growth is similar to that of the United States. Where employment and productivity trends have improved, this has been associated with the implementation of structural reforms.

Despite this initial improvement, progress has been limited and much remains to be done to close the gap with best practice countries in the OECD. This does not mean that the Lisbon Strategy should be abandoned. Its framework is sound and it appropriately aims at fostering growth through higher employment and accelerating productivity. But the implementation of policies by member states has fallen short of expectations. This raises the question of how the Lisbon Strategy could stimulate more proactive implementation of structural reforms. At present, the strategy relies on the "open method of coordination" to encourage the implementation of reforms in member countries. This method combines the use of benchmarking exercises, which assess the performance of each country against a set of numerical targets, and regular peer review sessions, which are deemed to encourage lower-performing countries to accelerate their reforms. Besides these informal arrangements, the EU can do little to stimulate reforms in member countries, given its lack of legal instruments in most areas.

This is particularly the case in labor markets, which are largely the prerogatives of national governments. The EU has established a framework to coordinate employment policies under the European Employment Strategy, which encompasses the Employment Guidelines, the Council Recommendations to member states on employment policies, the National Action Plans on employment policies, and the Joint Employment Report. While this framework aims at coordinating the employment policies of member states, there is widespread belief that structural reforms in this area are based on national objectives rather than EU guidance (Alesina and Perotti, 2004).

There is support for maintaining decentralization in labor market reforms (Boeri, 2004). As noted, countries can improve their labor markets in different ways, and notably with different combinations of policies, depending on their circumstances and institutions. What seems to matter is coherence in the setting of the various instruments, so as to obtain maximum synergies. Given the various interactions between instruments and country-specific features, most decision making needs to remain at the national level.

Based on past experience, EU policy initiatives are successful when they produce a common good. For instance, they have been successful in removing intra-EU customs barriers, because this produced a common good with obvious benefits, notably lower prices for consumers and easier market entry for firms. Similarly, the formation of the monetary union, the launching of the euro, and the establishment of the ECB led to lower transaction costs, exchange rate stability, and low inflation in all member countries.

Against this backdrop, the Lisbon Strategy might be more successful if refocused on areas where a common good could be produced. Fostering product market competition, notably in the services sector, is a good candidate in this respect. The benefits of enhancing competition within Europe should be obvious to all, including consumers benefiting from lower prices, firms taking advantage of lower barriers to entry, and workers finding jobs in deregulated sectors. The spillover effects of enhanced competition could be particularly important in the euro area: increased competition could translate into faster productivity and increased potential growth, facilitating faster activity without rekindling inflationary pressure.

In view of the large externalities that could be obtained, it would be appropriate to refocus the Lisbon Strategy on enhancing product market competition. The EU should seize the new Lisbon Strategy for Growth and Jobs, together with its periodic National Reform Programs, as an opportunity to complete the single market, notably for the cross-border provision of private services. By putting this goal at the center of the Lisbon Strategy, the enlarged EU would improve its chances to become a very competitive and dynamic region by 2010.

References

Alesina, Alberto, and Roberto Perotti. 2004. "The European Union: A Politically Incorrect View." *Journal of Economic Perspectives* 18, no. 4: 27–49.

Blanchard, Olivier. 2004. "Explaining European Unemployment." NBER *Reporter*. Cambridge, Mass.: National Bureau of Economic Research.

Blanchard, Olivier, and Justin Wolfers. 1999. "The Role of Shocks and Institutions in the Rise of European Unemployment: The Aggregate Evidence." NBER Working Paper 7282. Cambridge, Mass.: National Bureau of Economic Research.

Boeri, Tito. 2004. "Reforming Labor and Product Market: Some Lessons from Two Decades of Experiments in Europe." Mimeo.

Conway, Paul, Véronique Janod, and Giuseppe Nicoletti. 2005. "Product Market Regulation in OECD Countries: 1998 to 2003." OECD Economics Department Working Paper 419. Paris: OECD.

Duval, Romain. 2003. "Retirement Behavior in OECD Countries: Impact of Old-Age Pension Schemes and Other Social Transfer Programs." OECD Economic Studies 37. Paris: OECD.

European Commission. 2004a. "Labor Markets in the EU: An Economic Analysis of Recent Developments and Prospects." *The EU Economy 2004 Review.* Luxemburg: European Communities.

European Commission. 2004b. "The Link between Product Market Reforms and Productivity: Direct and Indirect Impacts." *The EU Economy 2004 Review.* Luxemburg: European Communities.

European Commission. 2005. "The Economic Costs of Non-Lisbon: A Survey of the Literature on the Economic Impact of Lisbon-type Reforms." Directorate-General for Economic and Financial Affairs Occasional Paper 16. Brussels.

International Monetary Fund. 2004. "Euro Area Policies: Staff Report." Country Report 05/265. Washington, D.C.: IMF.

Kok, Wim. 2004. "Facing the Challenge: The Lisbon Strategy for Growth and Employment." Report from the High Level Group Chaired by Wim Kok. Luxemburg: European Communities.

Mourre, Gilles. 2004. "Did the Pattern of Aggregate Employment Growth Change in the Euro Area in the Late 1990s?" ECB Working Paper 358. Frankfurt: ECB.

Nickell, Stephen. 1997. "Unemployment and Labor Market Rigidities: Europe Versus North America." *Journal of Economic Perspectives* 11, no. 3: 55–74.

Nicoletti, Giuseppe, and Stefano Scarpetta. 2003. "Regulation, Productivity and Growth: OECD Evidence." *Economic Policy* 18, no. 36: 9–72.

O'Mahony, Mary, and Bart Van Ark, eds. 2003. *EU Productivity and Competitiveness: An Industry Perspective.* Luxemburg: European Communities.

OECD. 2004. *OECD Employment Outlook: 2004.* Paris: OECD.

OECD. 2005. *Economic Policy Reforms: Going for Growth.* Paris: OECD.

SEVEN

Recovery Growth as a Stage of Post-Socialist Transition

Yegor T. Gaidar

The complexity of post-socialist transition was unprecedented. Initially, no one could accurately predict its pace or foresee how soon and to what extent it would be accomplished.

For example, when Solidarity's victory in the 1989 elections opened the "window of opportunity" for Polish reformers, it was impossible to assess the extent of Poland's problems and foresee the difficulties that would arise as the society and the economy adapted to market conditions. But today the stage of transformational recession, as well as the discussion about its causes and consequences, belongs to the past. Although major difficulties still have to be overcome, the economies of post-socialist countries largely display stable GDP growth and effective market mechanisms.

Transformational recession can be explained rather simply. The dismantling of the socialist economic structure revealed a sad circumstance: a substantial part of the economic activities carried out under socialism would never be needed in a market economy or democracy. The redistribution of resources concentrated in those activities cannot occur overnight. Processes that occurred at this stage of post-socialist recession were reminiscent of what Joseph Schumpeter (1950) described as "creative destruction," but they occurred on a scale unprecedented for market economies. It is vital to understand that both post-socialist recession (the adaptive decrease in production) and the subsequent recovery are part and parcel of a single process, whose essence is the structural rebuilding of the economy.[1]

[1] Describing the specifics of transformational recession as compared with normal recessions in market economies, Janos Kornai (1994) points out the following two specific factors: the need to move from a seller's market to a buyer's market and the introduction of hard budget constraints. Olivier Blanchard (1997) defines the key processes of the post-socialist transition as the combination of two elements: reallocation of resources from the old types of economic activities to the new ones (closing of enterprises and their

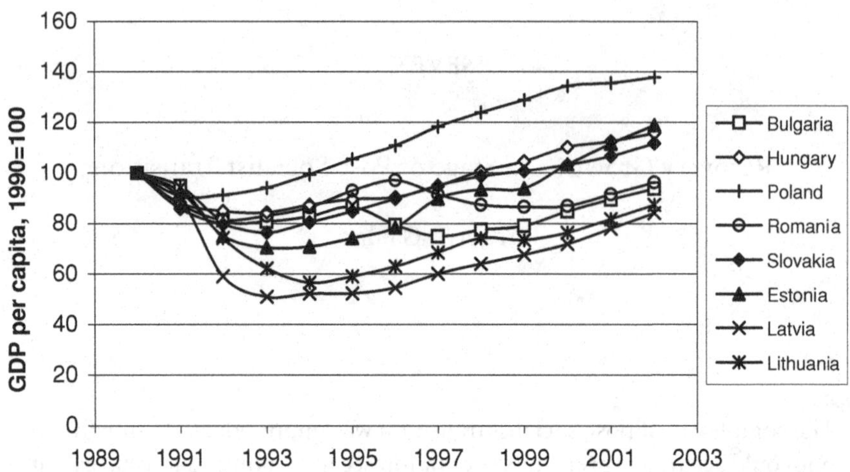

Chart 7.1. Dynamics of per capita GDP in the Central and Eastern European countries and Baltic states, 1990–2002. *Source*: IMF (2004).

This process has taken different forms in different countries. Polish reformers, the pioneers of post-socialist transformation, emphasized instant price liberalization, economic openness, the introduction of a convertible national currency, rapid disinflation through monetary and fiscal policy, wage controls, and structural reforms, first and foremost, privatization. The combination of these measures has come to be called "shock therapy." Other countries, such as Romania, preferred an evolutionary path. A third group of countries attempted some kind of middle way. Russia, for example, tried shock therapy to begin with, but under pressure from populist forces it was quickly forced to backtrack to gradual reforms, which some considered more "compassionate." Despite the varying results, which were obviously better in the first group of countries and worse in the second and third groups, the overall picture of economic development was surprisingly similar: first came a deep output fall, which was less severe in the first group and more dramatic in the second and third, and then a gradual economic recovery, which occurred earlier in the first group and later in the second and third (Charts 7.1 and 7.2).

Now, with the recession over, it is relevant to focus on the new economic growth. In Russia, where the economy has grown since 1999, two principal

bankruptcies in combination with establishment of the new ones) and the restructuring of the most important companies (innovation, change in the structure of production, and new investments). On the causes of the recession in the early stage of post-socialist transition, the need for change in the structure of production (to reflect an effective market demand), and the imposition of hard budget constraints, see Havrylyshyn et al. (1998).

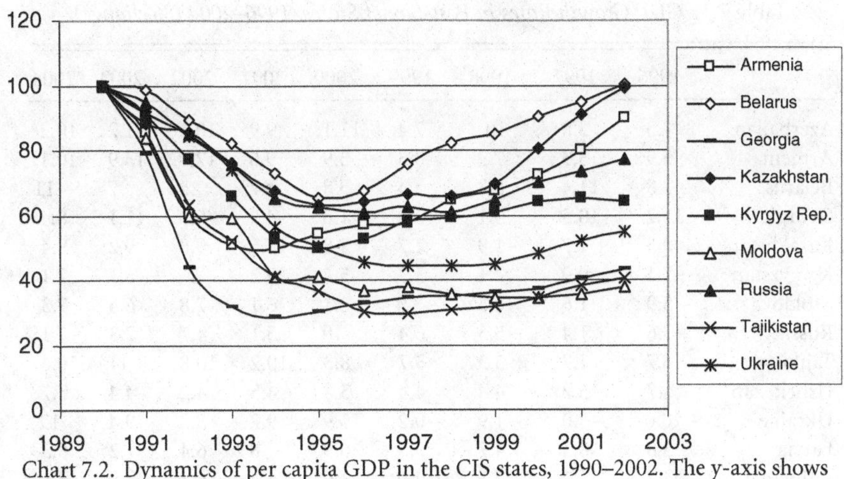

Chart 7.2. Dynamics of per capita GDP in the CIS states, 1990–2002. The y-axis shows GDP per capita (1990 = 100). *Source*: IMF (2004).

points of view prevail. The first compliments the government: when Vladimir Putin came to power, political stabilization and structural reforms followed, which caused growth.[2] The second view denies the government's merits and links the growth to high oil prices and the depreciation of the ruble.[3]

Unfortunately, almost no one expresses the third point of view: the economic growth is a direct consequence of prior reforms that improved the macroeconomic and microeconomic conditions in which both Russian and foreign companies operate. Participants in the Russian debate too often ignore the experiences of nearly thirty countries that, like Russia, were forced to adapt after the collapse of socialism.[4] At present, economic growth is happening in all post-Soviet states (Table 7.1).

All post-Soviet countries experienced output decline from 1991 to 1994. From 1995, the first indicators of economic growth became evident, primarily in those countries that had been drawn into wars or were subject to economic blockade, and especially where the preceding output fall was the

[2] For further analyses that attribute growth in Russia to the actions of the current government, see Fedorenko (2003), pp. 54–57.

[3] See Ellman (2000), Åslund (2002), Gaddy (2002), and Berglöf et al. (2003). The mere reference to the depreciation of the ruble as a factor behind economic growth suggests that market incentives have taken hold in the Russian economy.

[4] Leon Aron (2001) has noted that the processes of post-socialist transition in most countries of Eastern Europe and in the post-Soviet territories are normally studied in a comparative context against developments that take place in other post-socialist countries, while Russia (because of its vast territory) is often studied individually. The same idea is underlined by Pekka Sutela (2003).

Table 7.1. *GDP Growth Rates in Post-Soviet States, 1996–2004 (% change)*

	1996	1997	1998	1999	2000	2001	2002	2003	2004
Azerbaijan	1.3	5.8	10	7.4	11.1	9.9	10.6	11.2	10.2
Armenia	5.9	3.3	7.2	3.3	5.9	9.6	12.9	13.9	10.1
Belarus	2.8	11.4	8.3	3.4	5.8	4.7	5	7	11
Georgia	11.2	10.5	3.1	2.9	1.8	4.8	5.5	11.1	8.4
Kazakhstan	0.5	1.7	−1.9	2.7	9.8	13.5	9.8	9.2	9.4
Kyrgyzstan	7.1	9.9	2.1	3.7	5.4	5.3	0	6.7	7.1
Moldova	−5.9	1.6	−6.5	−3.4	2.1	6.1	7.8	6.6	7.3
Russia	−3.6	1.4	−5.3	6.4	10	5.1	4.7	7.3	7.1
Tajikistan	−6.7	1.7	5.3	3.7	8.3	10.2	10.8	11	10.6
Uzbekistan	1.7	5.2	4.4	4.4	3.8	4.5	4.2	4.4	7.7
Ukraine	−10.0	−3.0	−1.9	−0.2	5.9	9.2	5.2	9.4	12
Latvia	3.8	8.3	4.7	3.3	6.9	8	6.4	7.2	8.3
Lithuania	4.7	7	7.3	−1.7	3.9	6.4	6.8	9	6.6
Estonia	4.5	10.5	5.2	−0.1	7.8	6.4	7.2	5.1	6.1

Sources: The Interstate Statistical Committee of the CIS (2004); IMF (2005).

sharpest. Within the next two to three years, rickety growth spread to other parts of the post-Soviet territories.[5] Growth finally stabilized in 1999 and became omnipresent a year later.[6]

Among the post-Soviet states in the period 1995–2002, some are net exporters, while others are net importers of oil and oil products. Some countries' currencies appreciated in real terms, while others depreciated (see Table 7.2). None of these countries conducted reforms similar to those carried out in Russia in 2000–2003, but nearly all of them are regarded as countries with growing economies.

Since production decreased in nearly all post-Soviet states in the early 1990s and started to grow by the end of the decade, there is evidence for the idea put forth above: both the fall and the subsequent rise are components of a single process that is determined by common historical and economic rules. It depends only to a limited extent on the people and parties that came to power in one or another country in that period.

[5] One can associate GDP growth in the CIS in 1993–2003 with the growing prices on Russian, Kazakh, and Azerbaijani oil, which in turn promoted growth in other CIS countries exporting to oil producers. However, a sustained decrease of the share of Russia and other oil producers in the foreign trade of non-oil-producing CIS countries seriously weakens the above hypothesis (Havrylyshyn, 2006).

[6] Kyrgyzstan, where growth slowed down in 2002, was an exception. A natural disaster brought the largest gold-mining enterprise to a virtual standstill for a few months. In 2003, economic growth resumed.

Table 7.2. *Index of the Real Exchange Rates of National Currencies to the U.S. Dollar in Post-Soviet States at Year End (the year 1995 = 100%)*

	1996	1997	1998	1999	2000	2001	2002	2003
Azerbaijan	126.1	134.5	131.5	104.5	98.7	93.1	92	...
Armenia	106.6	104.2	105.8	103.9	94.5	93.2	89.1	94.3
Belarus	110.1	88.9	43.9	56	39.5	46.2	53.3	59.6
Georgia	130.1	134	98.7	107.4	105.4	103.1	105.6	...
Kazakhstan	117.9	131.3	124.9	80.3	84	85.2	86.2	96.2
Kyrgyzstan	86	99.6	64.1	55.1	59.5	62.7	65.2	68.9
Latvia	110.2	110.8	118.2	116.4	109.9	104.4	113.6	124.9
Lithuania	121.1	128.8	133.3	131.4	128.4	126.5	150.9	174
Moldova	113.2	119.7	70.4	72.2	85.8	86.6	85.1	97.2
Russia	119.8	125.3	45.5	63.2	70.8	78.1	84.5	101.3
Ukraine	165.9	187	112.8	89	106.1	118.3	116.7	120.1
Estonia	110.1	103.2	117.6	102.5	95.4	93.3	112.6	134.3

Source: IMF (2004).

In the initial stages of post-socialist transformation, the nonmarket sector releases more resources than the market can absorb. The supply of resources exceeds the effective demand. When the market sector's demand grows larger than the resources released from the nonmarket sector, the transformational recession ends and recovery growth begins.[7]

Total factor productivity in the post-socialist transition begins to grow earlier than total output.[8] In Russia, it has grown since 1995. The 1997–1998 financial crisis caused insignificant fluctuations in this index (Entov et al., 2004). Recovery growth stalls from time to time primarily due to financial crises, but the latter have become rare since the mid-1990s in Eastern Europe and the Baltic states and since the late 1990s in the Commonwealth of Independent States (CIS) countries.

The term "recovery growth" was introduced by the Russian economist V. Groman in the 1920s.[9] According to his conception, the recovery growth process utilizes the previously created production capacities and trained labor force. To unleash recovery growth, it is necessary to stop the economic disorganization and rebuild economic links. Groman (1925a) underscored

[7] The most interesting works dedicated to the analysis of post-socialist recessions and subsequent growth include De Melo et al. (1997), Berg et al. (1999), Havrylyshyn and Wolf (1999), and Åslund (2002).

[8] Total factor productivity is defined as a ratio of aggregate output to aggregate costs. Growth in total factor productivity (or output per unit of cost) is related to growth in efficiency caused by technical progress and better organization of production.

[9] The same issue was extensively studied by Bazarov (1925) and Mau (1993).

that despite the destruction of physical capital during the civil war, the main cause of the recession was the disruption of economic links. Their restoration would activate idle production capacity and start recovery growth.

Comparing the recovery growth of the 1920s with that of the present day, two factors deserve particular attention: first, the moment when the resources of extensive (recovery) growth are exhausted, and, second, the role and dynamics of finances in economic recovery. The exhaustion of resources for recovery growth does not equal the achievement of the pre-crisis production level. In the mid-1920s, researchers of "recovery regularities" made exactly this mistake. In a market economy, such as the Russian economy in 1913, there is always reserve capacity. The exploitation of this reserve capacity made it possible for the Soviet Union to maintain high growth rates for some time after the pre-crisis level was reached. This mistake cost V. Bazarov and V. Groman dearly: they were accused of anti-Soviet activities and attempting to halt "socialist restructuring."[10]

A different situation has arisen in post-communist Russia. The Soviet Union was overloaded with production capacity, designed to satisfy artificial demand created by centralized state planning. Because of the closed nature of the national economy, demand was maintained for low-quality products. Furthermore, the Soviet bloc countries imported those products utilizing effectively free and irrevocable Soviet loans. Some capacities that have survived the collapse of socialism are in fact economically useless. In this situation, the completion of recovery growth must occur long before the attainment of the 1989 GDP level. The illusion that the pre-crisis levels of production and monetization of the economy are attained simultaneously must be avoided. In practice, no logic of "recovery proportionality" can be applied to analysis of financial problems in a new economic system.

During the extremely high inflation from 1917 to 1923, monetization decreased dramatically in Soviet Russia. Groman and Bazarov presumed that with the beginning of the recovery, the demand for money would promptly grow and that this would permit a considerable increase in credit expansion without risk of inflation. Such considerations formed the basis

[10] Vyacheslav Molotov: "Bazarov admits that real life refutes his theory of 'a decaying curve.'" Joseph Stalin: "Really?!" Molotov: "Only two years ago Bazarov wrote a book with a great number of tables and diagrams in which he tried to assert quite the opposite. Now, he renounces his 'research'" (Yakovlev, 2000, vol. 5, p. 219).

for the calculation of plan targets for 1925 and 1926.[11] Their hypothesis did not turn out to be correct. The reason for this forecast error can be explained by the very nature of recovery growth. The methods that are normally used to forecast GDP are not adequate during a sudden rise in economic activity.

In the 1920s, initially high growth rates, one of the characteristic features of recovery growth, surprised both experts and the political elite. None of the State Planning Committee experts expected the growth rate to be so high in 1923–1924, after the monetary reform had been carried out and the currency stabilized (Groman, 1925b). It was suggested that by 1927, due to economic growth alone, without major capital investments, the national income of the Soviet Union would amount to approximately 50 percent of Russia's national income in the last pre-war year (Davies et al., 1994). But reality exceeded all expectations: over that period the Soviet Union caught up with pre-war Russia in terms of national income. Though data from that period are rather controversial (the index in question is estimated to be within 90 to 110 percent of the 1913 GDP level), the overall picture remains clear.[12]

Something similar can be observed today. In 1999, the Russian government presumed that in the ensuing year GDP would either increase slightly (by 0.2 percent) or even fall (by 2.2 percent). The International Monetary Fund forecast growth of 1.5 percent. In reality, GDP increased by 9 percent and industrial production by 11 percent. In Ukraine, where GDP growth was 9 percent in 2001, the IMF had forecast a mere 3.5 percent increase (IMF, 2000).

Recovery growth with its initially high rates arrives unexpectedly and is received as a gift. But then its less pleasant peculiarity emerges: by nature it is fleeting.[13] It is predicated on existing production capacities[14] and the previously trained labor force. In any country such resources are unlimited,

[11] See "Kontrolnye tsifry narodnogo khoziaystva na 1925–1926 gody," 1925.

[12] On different evaluations of correlation between the GDP of the Soviet Union and that of Russia in the 1913–1928 period, see Kafengaus (1994); *Narodnoye khozyaystvo RSFSR za 60 let* (1977); Fedorenko (2003), p. 121–122.

[13] "What is the rate of growth in the total value of the mass of commodities . . . ? In 1922–1923, it amounted to 28 percent, the next year, to 25 percent, while in the last year of the period under review, to 17 percent. Here is a definite law of slow-down in growth rates" (Groman, 1925a, p. 113).

[14] Capital investments in the 1924–1925 period (385 million rubles) somewhat exceeded depreciation deductions (277 million rubles) (Kviring and Krzhizhanovski, 1929).

so after a dramatic initial takeoff, the rate of growth tends to decline. This was true of the USSR in the 1920s and of Russia in 2001–2002.

The highest initial rates of recovery growth determine the orientation of economic policy. In the 1920s, the Soviet government tried to prevent a slowdown in growth rates. The efforts to speed up economic expansion through increased capital investments resulted in 1925–1926 in monetary expansion, price rises, and shortages. Despite these negative phenomena, economic recovery reserves persisted, and the Soviet government tried to escape the dilemma by balancing monetary policy and fighting inflation (Yurovsky, 1996).

In 1927–1928, the Soviet Union made a new effort to speed up economic growth in a new situation: the main recovery reserves were exhausted and the growth rate started declining.[15] Once again, effects of these financial disproportions came to the fore – inflation and shortages of goods. The government tried to tackle these new financial imbalances by giving up the market-driven new economic policy (NEP), instead confiscating grain from peasants and undertaking forced collectivization, rather than by restoring monetary and fiscal equilibrium.[16]

In 2002–2003, debate arose in Russia whether the government was right to opt for a modest 4 percent GDP growth and give up more ambitious plans. Those familiar with Russian economic history will remember an incident at the meeting of the Politburo of the VKP(b) in March 1928, where Alexei Ivanovich Rykov, the chairman of Sovnarkom (the Council of

[15] In 1925–1926, increases in production costs demonstrated that recovery growth reserves were exhausted. The price increase was connected to dramatic growth in wages and salaries and exhaustion of earlier created production and technical reserves (Malafeyev, 1964).

[16] Earlier classified materials of the Central Committee of the VKP(b), published in 2000, illustrate well how the preservation of high growth rates was related to the rollback of the new economic policy. A. Rykov, Chairman of Sovnarkom, said in a speech: "In this period, the rate of growth in investments in industry may slow down. No fetish is to be made of growth rates. We need to ensure such 'feeding' of industry as will permit it to occupy leading positions in the entire economy in minimum time, so that our efforts in innovation and restructuring of the economy will not be confined by a lack of engines, tractors, chemical fertilizers, experts and skilled workers who could carry out that restructuring" (Yakovlev, 2000, vol. 5, p. 38). In a speech to the November Plenum of the Central Committee of the VKP(b) in 1928, he said: "When discussing the issue of the rate of growth, we should not think that a constant increase in the rates of growth or even preservation of those rates from year to year is a law of the transition period" (Yakovlev, 2000, vol. 3, pp. 37–38). In a speech to the April Plenum of the Central Committee of the VKP(b) in 1929, J. Stalin said: "The issue of the rates of development of industry and new forms of merger of cities with villages. . . . It is one of the principal issues of our differences. . . . [T]he Plan of Comrade Bukharin is a plan for a slow-down of the rates of industrial development and subversion of a merger of cities with villages" (Yakovlev, 2000, vol. 4, pp. 477–480).

Table 7.3. *Growth Rates in Real Wages and Salaries in CIS Countries, 1996–2003 (% change)*

Year Country	1996	1997	1998	1999	2000	2001	2002	2003
Azerbaijan	19.0	53.0	20.0	20.0	18.0	16.0	18.0	...
Armenia	13.0	26.0	22.0	11.0	13.0	5.0	9.9	14.8
Belarus	5.0	14.0	18.0	7.0	12.0	30.0	7.9	3.2
Georgia	53.0	37.0	25.0	2.0	3.0	22.0	...	...
Kazakhstan	2.0	5.0	4.0	7.0	12.0	13.0	11.0	6.9
Kyrgyzstan	1.0	12.0	12.0	−8.0	−2.0	11.0	13.3	9.9
Moldova	5.0	5.0	5.0	−13.0	2.0	15.0	20.8	15.3
Russia	6.0	5.0	−13.0	−22.0	21.0	20.0	16.2	10.9
Tajikistan	−14.0	−2.0	29.0	0.3	8.0	11.0	25.9	37.1
Ukraine	−5.0	−2.0	−3.0	−6.0	1.0	21.0	20.1	37.1

Source: The Interstate Statistical Committee of the CIS (2004).

People's Commissars), tendered his resignation in protest over other party leaders' demands to further accelerate the industrial development of the country (Yakovlev, 2000). That was not an easy decision. Renowned Soviet economist S. Strumilin said: "I would rather advocate high growth rates than be imprisoned for low ones" (Mau, 2002).

In 2002, it became obvious that the resources of economic recovery would soon be exhausted. From 1998 to 2002, the number of workers employed in the Russian economy rose from 58.4 million to 67.3 million. The shortage of skilled workers resulted in a dramatic growth of real wages and salaries: they increased by 70 percent from 1999 to 2002. A similar trend occurred in other CIS countries (Table 7.3). These data starkly show another characteristic of the recovery process: real wages grow faster than labor productivity, as Groman noted in his works in the 1920s (Groman, 1925a).

Market surveys carried out by the Institute for the Economy in Transition have shown that production capacity relative to demand changed from 1998 to 2001. A lack of equipment and skilled workers increasingly hindered production growth. A drop in the growth rate, after it has peaked and the most available resources are utilized, prompts economic and political debates on the causes of the slowdown and possible remedies. Since the sources of recovery growth have been exhausted, a new issue arises: how to ensure economic development beyond the recovery period. Growth is now based on the creation of new production capacity, new investment in fixed assets, and employment of new skilled workers.[17] This can be achieved only with an efficient market and economic incentives.

This in turn requires strengthened property rights and profound structural reforms. In 2000–2001, the Russian government began to carry out a series of such reforms, and in some areas many useful reforms were carried out. While such reforms do not pay off immediately, they lay a foundation for long-term economic growth.

For example, in the last few years Russia has made positive changes in its Criminal Procedural Code. At the same time, the Russian judicial system suffers from many shortfalls, as before, and problems connected with its malfunctioning will persist for a long time.

Important measures have been taken to legalize private ownership of land. It is debatable whether the adopted Law on Transfer of Agricultural Land is good or bad, but that the private transfer of land is legalized and sanctified undoubtedly facilitates long-term economic growth in Russia. The same logic applies to other measures: the new Labor Code and the pension reform. Changes that produce positive results in the short term (for example, the reform of the income tax) are rare exceptions.

As mentioned above, high oil prices were an important factor in Russia's economic situation in the early 2000s. Under these conditions, the Russian government carried out a prudent fiscal and monetary policy for several years, which deserves respect. This was not at all the case in the previous period of anomalously high oil prices in the 1970s. In 1979–1982, real oil prices were significantly higher than today (Chart 7.3), but the Soviet authorities senselessly squandered these revenues.

Structural reforms proceed slowly and promise no miracles. While oil prices remain high, populist demands for measures that promise immediate payoffs and "breakthroughs" rise. Calls to speed up growth rates and searches for countries that need to be "caught up with and overtaken" have played a major role in Russia's twentieth-century economic history. Recall Nikita Khrushchev's efforts to catch up with the U.S. per capita production of meat or a situation from the more recent past: the economic catastrophe of the USSR in the late 1980s and the early 1990s, which started with an attempt to speed up economic growth.

Russia does not have a monopoly on such economic pursuits. For example, in Chile the economic policy of the Salvador Allende government also tried

[17] On the limited role of investments in recovery growth during post-socialist transitions, see Wolf (1999). On specifics of recovery growth, where increased investment is not an engine of growth but rather follows it, see De Melo et al. (1997), Havrylyshyn et al. (1998), and Åslund (2002).

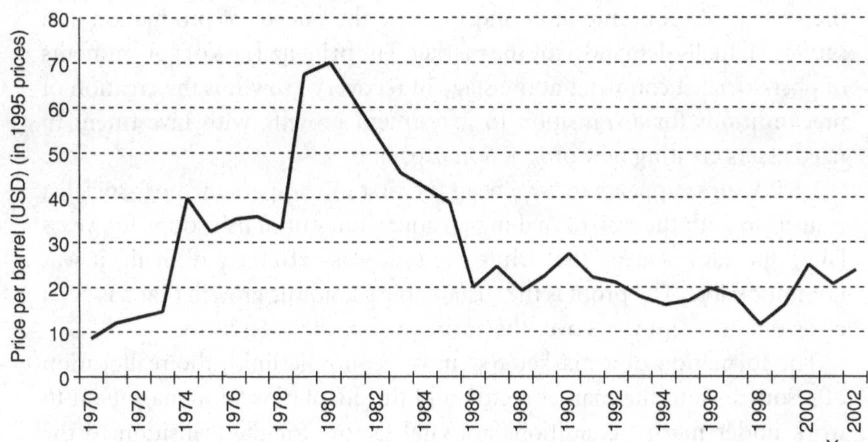

Chart 7.3. Dynamics of world oil prices (Brent; U.S. dollars per barrel). *Source*: IMF (2003).

to speed up economic growth by abandoning orthodox models, removing financial constraints and pumping money into the economy. These policies caused a deep political and economic crisis, which took Chile a decade to overcome. But in the initial stage, in 1971, they did boost the economic growth rate. It is instructive that in Chile macroeconomic manipulation was attempted not after protracted economic stagnation but after a period of economic expansion, followed by a decline in the growth rate and in the price of copper – the country's most important export commodity (Dornbusch and Edwards, 1991, p. 200).

What Russia needs today is to learn to develop stably in the changing conditions of the post-industrial world, to avoid being drawn into wars, to escape domestic upheavals, and not to panic over short-term fluctuations in growth rates. Russia needs to rid itself of the pattern, long characteristic of the country, of growth spurts followed by stagnation and crisis. Russia needs to learn to go forward, utilizing not instruments of state enforcement, but private incentives and initiative. To do this is more difficult than to boost economic growth for a short time. It requires hard and consistent efforts that do not produce immediate political dividends. But such a policy can lead to sustainable economic growth.

Let us draw some conclusions. The economic growth that began three to seven years after the collapse of socialism is recovery growth. It is based on the new market economic institutions, which make it possible to reorganize the system of economic links and increase the output of production and services actually demanded by the market. The principal task of governments of post-socialist countries at the stage of recovery growth is the creation of preconditions for a transition to investment growth, with investment in fixed assets creating new production capacity.

Lech Wałęsa appears to have been the first to compare the post-socialist transition with the task of making an aquarium out of fish soup. Ten years later, one cannot deny that while the task was extremely difficult, it was not impossible. The proof is the sustainable economic growth that has been observed in recent years over the entire post-socialist territory.

The formation of a market system of economic links, the reallocation of resources into the market sector, and the adaptation of management to work under market conditions are vital factors for the transition to the stage of post-socialist growth. This process took place in the first half of the 1990s in Eastern Europe and at the end of the 1990s in the CIS states. The specific features of the national macroeconomic situation, the dynamics of prices on exports and imports, and exchange rate policy all influence this process. These factors affect the national course of development, but within the framework of the general process of post-socialist recovery growth.

The disorganization of economic links and the collapse of former administrative channels of coordination in the absence of new ones seriously impact industries manufacturing technically complex products. However, after the stabilization of market mechanisms, precisely these industries enjoy the most dynamic growth (Entov et al., 2004).

All this proves is that today Russia, like the majority of other post-socialist countries, is a country with a market economy. This fact has received wide international recognition.[18] The historical transition from a socialist command economy, under which generations of Russians lived, to a market economy, has been concluded.

Needless to say, numerous important parameters of post-socialist states, including Russia, differ from those of market economies that did not go through the socialist experiment. First of all this concerns demography. Even so, judging from key indices, countries emerging from socialism are

[18] The European Union and the United States recognized Russia as a country with a market economy in June 2002. According to B. Marshall, Vice President of the Russian-American Council on Business Cooperation, at the hearings in the U.S. Department of Commerce on March 27, 2002, "To deny official recognition of Russia as a country with a market economy is equal to the negation of the present-day reality" (Hearing before the U.S. International Trade Association, 2002).

Table 7.4. *Individual Parameters of Development of Russia, Brazil, Mexico, and Spain, Second Half of the Twentieth Century*

Country	Russia	Brazil	Mexico	Spain
Year[a]	2001	1998	1980	1966
Share of the urban population, %	72.9	79.9	66.4	62.2
Share of the population engaged in agriculture, %	12.7	23.4	36.3	29.0 (1970)
Share of the population employed in industry, %	30.5[b]	20.1	29.1	36.0 (1970)
Share of the population engaged in the service sector, %	56.8	56.5	34.6	35.0 (1970)
Public expenditure on education, % of the GDP	3.2	5.0 (1999)	4.6	1.2 (1966)
Public expenses on health-care, % of the GDP	3.1	...	...	2.3 (1970)
Child mortality (at the age of under one year) per 1,000 live-born children	18.1	32.0 (2000)	56.0	36.0
Child mortality (at the age of under five years) per 1,000 live-born children	21.0	38.0 (2000)	74.0	45.5 (1965)
Number of fixed and mobile phones per 1,000 persons	281	165	53 (1988)	94
Number of Internet users per 1,000 persons	30	15	...	...
Number of cars per 1,000 persons	140 (2000)	129	60	33

[a] Corresponds to the level of per capita GDP in the amount of US$ 5,437 in Russia, US$ 5,459 in Brazil, US$ 5,582 in Mexico, and US$ 5,538 in Spain.

[b] Employment in industry, including construction.

Sources: Maddison (1995); Mitchell (1998); World Bank (2003); OECD (health-care expenditure of all the countries except Russia); UN Common Database; the State Statistics Board of Russia; and the Ministry of Finance of the Russian Federation.

fairly close to market economies of a corresponding level of development (Table 7.4).

For this reason, when we discuss long-term problems of economic development, we can base our analysis on the cumulative experience of the countries that were the modern economic growth leaders over the past fifty years, while taking into account the specifics of the socialist experiment.

Most important of all today is to continue reforms, which are necessary to ensure that the economic growth becomes sustainable and for the formation of the social and economic foundations of post-industrial society in our countries. This determines the essence of the current transformation and the main challenges facing virtually all the post-socialist countries in the coming decades.

References

Aron, Leon. 2001. "Structure and Context in the Study of Post-Soviet Russia: Several Empirical Generalizations in Search of a Theory." *Russian Outlook*. Washington, D.C.: American Enterprise Institute.

Åslund, Anders. 2002. *Building Capitalism: The Transformation of the Former Soviet Bloc*. New York: Cambridge University Press.

Bazarov, Vladimir A. 1925. "'O vosstanovitelnyh protzessah' voobshche i ob 'emissionnyh vozmozhnostyah' v chastnosty (On 'Recovery Processes' in General and 'Issuing Possibilities' in Particular)." *Ekonomicheskoe Obozrenie* 1. Moscow.

Berg, Andrew, Eduardo Borensztein, Ratna Sahay, and Jeromin Zettelmeyer. 1999. "The Evolution of Output in Transition Economies: Explaining the Differences." IMF Working Paper 73. Washington, D.C.: International Monetary Fund.

Berglöf, Erik, Andrei Kunov, Julia Shvets, and Ksenia Yudaeva. 2003. *The New Political Economy of Russia*. Cambridge: MIT Press.

Blanchard, Olivier. 1997. *The Economics of Transition in Eastern Europe*. Oxford: Clarendon Press.

Davies, R. W., Mark Harrison, and Stephen G. Wheatcroft, eds. 1994. *The Economic Transformation of the Soviet Union, 1913–1945*. Cambridge: Cambridge University Press.

De Melo, Martha, Cevdet Denizer, and Alan Gelb. 1997. "From Plan to Market: Patterns of Transition." In Mario I. Blejer and Marko Skreb, eds., *Macroeconomic Stabilization in Transition Economies*. Cambridge: Cambridge University Press.

Dornbusch, Rudiger, and Sebastian Edwards. 1991. *The Macroeconomics of Populism in Latin America*. Chicago: University of Chicago Press.

Ellman, Michael. 2000. "The Russian Economy Under El'tsin." *Europe-Asia Studies* 52, no. 8: 1417–1432.

Entov, Revold, Oleg Lugovoy, Yevgenya Astafeva, Vladimir Bessonov, Ilya Voskoboinikov, Marina Turuntseva, and Denis Nekipelov. 2004. "Faktory ekonomicheskogo rosta rossiyskoi ekonomiki (Factors of Economic Growth in the Russian Economy)." Institute for the Economy in Transition Working Paper 70. Moscow: Institute for the Economy in Transition.

Fedorenko, Nikolay. 2003. *Rossiya na rubezhe vekov (Russia at the Turn of the Century)*. Moscow: Ekonomika.

Gaddy, Clifford G. 2002. "Has Russia Entered a Period of Sustainable Economic Growth?" In Andrew C. Kuchins, ed., *Russia After the Fall*. Washington, D.C.: Carnegie Endowment for International Peace.

Groman, Vladimir. 1925a. "O nekotoryh zakonomernostyah, empiricheski obnaruzhivaemyh v nashem narodnom khozyaystve (On Some Regularities in National Economy Established Through Experiments)." *Planovoe Khozyaystvo*, 1–2.

Groman, Vladimir. 1925b. "Konyunkturnyj obzor narodnovo khozyaystva SSSR za pervoe polugodie 1924 i 1925 goda (Survey of the National Economy of the USSR in the First Six Months of 1924 and 1925)." *Planovoe Khozyaystvo*, 6.

Havrylyshyn, Oleh. 2006. *Divergent Paths in Post-Communist Transformation: Capitalism for All or Capitalism for the Few?* Palgrave Macmillan.

Havrylyshyn, Oleh, and Thomas Wolf. 1999. "Growth in Transition Countries 1991–1998: The Main Lessons." Paper presented at the conference "A Decade of Transition," International Monetary Fund, February 1–3, 1999, Washington, D.C.

Havrylyshyn Oleh, Ivailo Izvorski, and Ron van Rooden. 1998. "Recovery and Growth in Transition Economies 1990–1997: A Stylized Regression Analysis." IMF Working Paper 141. Washington, D.C.: International Monetary Fund.

Hearing Before the U.S. Department of Commerce's International Trade Administration. 2002. "The Status of the Russian Federation as a Non-Market Economy Country Under the Antidumping and Countervailing Duty Laws." Comments by Z. Blake Marshall. Http://www.usrbc.org/Transcripts-Summaries-testimonies/2002/Commerce%20Hearing%20march%2027.asp.

International Monetary Fund. 2000. *World Economic Outlook: Focus on Transition Economies.* Washington, D.C.: IMF, October.

International Monetary Fund. 2003. *International Financial Statistics Yearbook, 2003.* Washington, D.C.: IMF.

International Monetary Fund. 2004. *International Financial Statistics Yearbook, 2004.* Washington, D.C.: IMF.

International Monetary Fund. 2005. *International Financial Statistics Yearbook, 2005.* Washington, D.C.: IMF.

Interstate Statistical Committee of the Commonwealth of Independent States. 2004. *The Commonwealth of Independent States in 2003: Statistical Yearbook.* Moscow: The Interstate Statistical Committee of the CIS.

Kafengaus, Lev B. 1994. "Evolyutziya promyshlennovo proizvodstva v Rossii: poslednyaya tret' XIX – 30-ye gody XX v. (Evolution of Industrial Production in Russia: The Last Thirty Years of the 19th Century and the First 30 Years of the 20th Century)." Moscow.

"Kontrolnye tzifry narodnovo khozyaystva na 1925–1926 gody. Utverzhdennyj prezidiumom Gosplana SSSR doklad komissii po kontrolnym tzifram (Planned Targets of the National Economy for the 1925–1926 Period. Report of the Commission on Planned Targets approved by the Presidium of the State Planning Committee of the USSR)." 1925. *Planovoe Khozyaystvo.* Moscow.

Kornai, Janos. 1994. "Transformational Recession: The Main Causes." *Journal of Comparative Economics* 19: 39–63.

Kviring, Emanuel, and Gleb Krzhizhanovski. 1929. "Osnovnye problemy kontrolnyh tzifr narodnogo khozyaystva na 1928–1929 (Principal Issues of Planned Targets of the National Economy in 1928–1929)." *Planovoe Khozyastvo.* Moscow.

Maddison, Angus. 1995. *Monitoring the World Economy 1820–1992.* Washington, D.C.: OECD.

Malafeyev, Alexei. 1964. *Istoriya tsenoobrazovaniya v SSSR: 1917–1963 (History of Price Formation in the USSR: 1917–1963).* Moscow: Mysl.

Mau, Vladimir. 1993. *Reformy i dogmy 1914–1929 (Reforms and Dogmas: 1914–1929).* Moscow: Delo.

Mau, Vladimir. 2002. "Alternativa Strumilina (Strumilin's Alternative)." *Vedomosti* 51: 614.

Mitchell, Brian R. 1998. *International Historical Statistics: Europe 1750–1993.* London: Macmillan.

Narodnoye khozyaystvo RSFSR za 60 lyet (The National Economy of the RSFSR in the Past 60 Years). 1977. Moscow: Roskomstat.

Schumpeter, Joseph A. 1950. *Capitalism, Socialism and Democracy*. New York: Harper.

Sutela, Pekka. 2003. *The Russian Market Economy*. Helsinki: Kikimora.

Wolf, Holger C. 1999. *Transition Strategies: Choices and Outcomes.* Princeton, N.J.: International Finance Section.

World Bank. 2003. *The World Development Indicators.* Washington, D.C.: The World Bank.

Yakovlev, Andrei, ed. 2000. *Kak lomali NEP: stenogrammy plenumov TSK VKP(b) 1928–1929 gg (How the New Economic Policy (NEP) Was Liquidated: Records of Plenums of the Central Committee of the VKP(b) in 1928–1929).* Moscow: Rossia XX vek.

Yurovsky, Leonid. 1996. *Dyenyezhnaya politika sovetskoy vlasti: 1917–1927 (Monetary Policy of the Soviet Government: 1917–1927).* Moscow: Nachala-Press.

EIGHT

Comparative Oligarchy

Russia, Ukraine, and the United States

Anders Åslund

Introduction

Oligarchs have become one of the big political and economic issues after communism, and one of the biggest policy questions in both Russia and Ukraine is what to do with them. Russia has seen the lawless confiscation of its biggest oil company, Yukos, through taxation, while Ukraine has flirted with widespread re-privatization. The resolution of the problem of the oligarchs will greatly influence the future of the economic systems of these countries.

To design a suitable policy for the treatment of oligarchs, we need to examine what oligarchs actually are, the economic and legal reasons for their emergence, how they act politically, and why they provoke such popular outrage. Our endeavor is to discuss oligarchs as a social phenomenon rather than a moral matter.

Economically, oligarchs have proven highly useful. They are a natural product of large economies of scale and weak legal security, and very large enterprises can hardly develop without them. A major problem is that oligarchs spend inordinate amounts to assure their property rights. The best cure would be to guarantee private property rights to all people, including the oligarchs. If not even the property of the richest is safe, how can anybody trust his or her property rights? Such a guarantee of property rights marks the crossing of the threshold to mature capitalism. Oligarchs may become more palatable politically if they are charged additional taxes or induced to undertake large-scale charitable donations. What must be avoided is the redistribution of property and legal limbo. Ultimately, the acceptance of oligarchs is a matter of ideology. Do we accept the very rich or not? Mature capitalism does, while lesser systems do not.

In the second section, I shall consider the meaning of the concept of "oligarch." The third section discusses the economics of oligarchy; the fourth section moves on to its political aspects; and the fifth section presents the standard complaints about oligarchs. The sixth section suggests that the reaction might be of ideological nature, while the seventh section reviews the current dilemma in Russia and Ukraine. The eighth section discusses what should be done to improve the situation, whereas the ninth section looks back on how privatization should have been done in light of these new insights. The last section summarizes my conclusions.

What Is an Oligarch?

"Oligarch" is an ancient concept, and an "oligarchy " is defined as "government in the hands of a few" by the Oxford English Dictionary. In Russia and Ukraine, "oligarch" came into use as a popular label for certain businessmen around 1994, as the first truly rich people emerged. The meaning of oligarch in the two countries is similar.[1] An "oligarch" is a very wealthy and politically well-connected businessman, a dollar billionaire, or nearly one, who is the main owner of a conglomerate of enterprises and has close ties with the President. It might be more appropriate to call the oligarchs plutocrats, because they focus on making money rather than ruling the state. Joel Hellman (1998) has coined the phrase "state capture" to characterize the relationship between big businessmen and the state in a country such as Ukraine, because these big businessmen influenced the state by multiple means.

Oligarchs are by no means unique to Russia and Ukraine. Andrei Shleifer and Daniel Treisman (2004) have pointed out that oligarchs are typical of most middle-income countries and even many Western countries. Much of the discussion about economic populism in Latin America circles around the entrenched power of oligarchs (Dornbusch and Edwards, 1991). In the former Soviet Union, people talk about oligarchs in Kazakhstan, but hardly at all in small, poor countries like Georgia, Kyrgyzstan, Moldova, and Tajikistan, and not at all in lingering socialist economies, that is, Turkmenistan, Belarus, and Uzbekistan.

The most prominent oligarchs in world history were the "robber barons" in the United States. The *New York Times* referred to the new big businessmen in America as "robber barons" in the 1850s, alluding to the knights who lived

[1] See two excellent studies of the Russian oligarchs: Freeland (2000) and Hoffman (2002).

in castles along the Rhine and extorted fees for passage. This label stuck. The robber barons were the men who built great industrial and transportation empires in the late nineteenth century in the United States (Steele Gordon, 2004, pp. 211–2).

The oligarchs in Russia and Ukraine have displayed much greater similarities with the American robber barons than is usually understood, because time has beautified American history. The argument of this chapter is that we can better understand the Russian and Ukrainian oligarchs if we compare them with the American robber barons. In all three cases, big businessmen have responded rationally to a peculiar set of economic, legal, and political conditions.

The Economics of Oligarchy

Oligarchs or robber barons are few and tremendously wealthy. Bradford DeLong (2002, p. 179) has suggested that a present-day billionaire would be a good proxy for a "robber baron." John Steele Gordon (2004, p. 207) aptly quotes U.S. President Herbert Hoover: "The trouble with capitalism is capitalists. They're too damn greedy." Let us look more closely at the conditions that generated oligarchs in the United States as well as in the former Soviet Union.

One fundamental cause of this generation and concentration of wealth was the sudden achievement of great economies of scale in certain industries, especially metals, oil, and railways. Such economies of scale cannot be attained in a small country. The super-rich can emerge only in countries with large markets, which explains why they have arisen only in the three largest post-Soviet economies (Russia, Ukraine, and Kazakhstan).

A second feature common to the American industrialization and postcommunism was rapid structural change, which facilitated great accumulation of wealth among those few who knew how to take advantage of the trends of the day. In Central Europe, large enterprises remained state-owned and unprofitable for many years. Sometimes, they have finally been sold to foreign investors, but the hapless foreigners have usually turned out to be clueless facing these communist mastodons. As a result, nearly all large industrial enterprises in Central Europe have closed down. In Russia and Ukraine, by contrast, the large oil and metallurgical industry is booming as never before, thanks to able local entrepreneurs, who have naturally became immensely rich.

A third economic characteristic is the presence of rent, which is often difficult to distinguish from economies of scale. The U.S. anti-trust case against

Microsoft attempted to determine whether Microsoft's profits depended on rent or economies of scale, and failed to make this distinction to anyone's satisfaction. Most of the original U.S. robber barons made their money on railways, which easily generate monopoly rents. Other robber barons focused on the natural rents of resource industries, John D. Rockefeller on oil and Andrew Carnegie on steel.[2] Today, the Russian oligarchs are typically preoccupied with oil and metals. Out of twenty-six Russian billionaires identified by *Forbes* in 2005, twelve had made most of their money on metals, nine on oil, and two on coal (Kroll and Goldman, 2005),[3] while six of the biggest Ukrainian oligarchic groups concentrate on steel.[4]

Free distribution of state assets, notably land around the railways, and cheap credits were also important causes of enrichment in the United States (DeLong, 2002), and the cheap sale of old assets either through direct privatization or on the secondary market has characterized Russia and Ukraine.

Prevailing legal conditions also determine the nature of oligarchs. Well-functioning legal systems are a recent invention, and even within the West legal systems are subject to many flaws. Joint stock companies emerged in the nineteenth century, but many Western countries have adopted insider legislation only in the last two decades. As multiple corporate accounting scandals, from Enron to AIG, illustrate, corporate governance remains poor in the West even today. John Steele Gordon (2004, pp. 207–208) has eloquently captured the state of law in the United States in the 1860s, which saw the rise of the robber barons:

> Nowhere was . . . corruption more pervasive than in New York, and especially on Wall Street. . . . In 1868 the New York State Legislature actually passed a law the effect of which was to legalize bribery. . . . In 1868 the popular English *Fraser's Magazine* wrote that "in New York there is a custom among litigants as peculiar to that city, it is to be hoped, as it is supreme within it, of retaining a judge as well as a lawyer."

Thus, the current legal practices in Russia and Ukraine appear just about normal for this stage of legal development. Poor judicial systems breed poor corporate governance, impeding the evolution of financial markets. Without strong corporate legislation and a potent judicial system, partners find it difficult to agree or to resolve conflicts. Nor can principals (owners) control their agents (executives), so they are compelled to manage their companies

[2] J. P. Morgan was an odd man out in finance, and so was Jacob Astor in real estate (DeLong, 2002).

[3] In oil: Yukos, Lukoil, Surgut, TNK, Sibneft; in metals, Rusal, SUAL, Norilsk Nickel, Severstal, Evrazholding, NLMK, MMK, Mechel, and UMMK.

[4] System Capital Management, Interpipe, Privat Group, Industrial Union of Donbass, Zaporozhstal, and Zavod imeni Ilicha in Mariopol.

themselves. As a consequence, businessmen with concentrated ownership tend to be more successful than those who have to deal with many minority shareholders. Conversely, businessmen rationally opt for vertical integration to avoid the hazards of arbitrary court judgments about contracts; that is, they prefer corporate hierarchies to markets (Williamson, 1975).

In post-communist Russia many oligarchic groups are run by tight groups of friends, typically school friends, while the American robber barons tended to be more lonely. This suggests that the current degree of trust in Russia is much greater than in the United States a century ago, contrary to common assumptions. A consequence of the surprisingly great trust among Russian partners is that several of the big enterprise groups generated multiple billionaires: Yukos seven, Alfa three, Interros two, Mechel two, and so on (Kroll and Goldman, 2005). The uncommonly large number of billionaires in Russia is partially explained by the country's strong partnerships. Ukraine is more like the United States under the robber barons, displaying less trust, but even there two of the big oligarchic groups (Privat Group and Industrial Union of Donbas) have three billionaire owners each.[5]

The combination of large economies of scale, vast economies, fast structural change, the prevalence of rents, and poor legal systems naturally led to the concentration of fortunes in oil, metals, and railways in the United States in the nineteenth century as well as in Russia and Ukraine today. It is difficult to see how a market economy could be introduced under these conditions without generating super-rich businessmen. The emergence of oligarchs is a natural consequence of the prevailing conditions. The actual alternative to the oligarchs would be devastation of much of the truly large-scale sectors of the economy, as has occurred in Central Europe.

The Politics of Oligarchy

The key legal problem in emerging capitalism is property rights. Hernando de Soto (2000) has pointed out how the absence of property rights harms the poor in middle income countries and the developing world today. Under emerging capitalism the rich also face the same hazard.

Under early post-communism the business world was Hobbesian. "In the state of nature, property exists only as long as it can be protected by the claimant," as Vadim Volkov (2002, p. xi) has formulated it. Before the oligarchs, organized crime prevailed: "[s]ince the actions of the state bureaucracy and of law enforcement remain arbitrary and the services provided

[5] Interviews with owners of both groups in March 2003 and December 2004, respectively.

tend to have higher costs, private enforcers (read: the Mafia) outcompete the state and firmly establish themselves in its stead" (Volkov, 2002, p. 19).

The oligarchs represented a breakthrough in this world of organized crime. To begin with, they established their own security services, which were cheaper and more reliable than criminal gangs. Over time, however, they increasingly purchased state services, or politics, to re-insure their shaky property rights. Admittedly, oligarchs also use politics to extract more state resources and to undermine the property rights of others, but their fundamental demand is the defense of their feeble rights to newly acquired property.

Politics offer a number of attractive goods. Starting from the top, businessmen can buy presidential decisions, usually not from the President but from his family or closest aides. The difference between the administration of Ulysses Grant (1869–1877) and that of Boris Yeltsin or Leonid Kuchma is less than people want to recognize. Although the U.S. robber barons arose in the 1850s (Commodore Cornelius Vanderbilt), it was not until the early 1900s that President Theodore Roosevelt effectively stood up against them.

The second kind of political good on sale is legislation from the national parliament. The United States has not prohibited the purchasing of legislation, or lobbying, but rather legalized this process and made it transparent. President Putin has complained that Yukos could block minor tax legislation directed against oil companies in Russia, but the United States cannot tax energy because of its strong energy lobby. The corporate lobbies in the Parliaments of the United States, Russia, and Ukraine are strengthened because parliamentary elections are dominated by one-man constituencies.[6] Individual candidates need to mobilize their own campaign financing, which is much easier to do if the candidates themselves are rich or if each contribution is relatively large. The U.S. Senate was even called a Club of Millionaires in the gilded age of the 1880s. The same is true of the Ukrainian Parliament today, and U.S. congressmen remain greatly dependent on their donors. The situation in the U.S. Congress is quite similar to that in the Russian Duma, where individual oligarchs finance a few parliamentarians in return for their attention to corporate interests. Since the March 2002 elections, Ukraine has had the most oligarchic Parliament. It is commonly said that 300 out of the 450 deputies in the Supreme Rada are dollar millionaires, and until the Orange Revolution, half the Supreme Rada was dominated by nine

[6] Admittedly, only half the deputies in Russia and Ukraine are elected in that way, but many slots on party lists are bought by wealthy businessmen.

oligarchic factions, each representing the interests of one major business group.

A third group of political goods is government decisions. This is straightforward corruption. Several of the ministers of President Ulysses Grant's administration were direct beneficiaries of corrupt payments from railway companies (Steele Gordon, 2004, p. 219), and corruption of cabinet ministers has been a patent problem in the United States. With the American revolving doors between government and the private sector, conflicts of interests slightly detached in time have become almost impossible to prosecute.

By contrast, in the 1990s it was amazing how little attention the Ukrainian and Russian oligarchs devoted to government posts. Ministers tended to be civil servants, some of whom were corrupt. In Russia, the half-year appointments of Vladimir Potanin and Boris Berezovsky to senior government posts were exceptions. Russian businessmen prefer to buy services from officials or purchase public jobs for their helpers. At present, Russian ministerial posts and governorships are reportedly traded for multiples of $10 million. The prices depend on the post and to whom the payment is being made, while deputy ministerial posts are being traded in a closer range of $8–$10 million. Today, the Russian administration has become more pervasively corrupt than ever before.[7]

Again, Ukraine has been far more oligarchic than Russia. Two prime ministers in the 1990s, Yukhum Zviahilsky (1993–1994) and Pavlo Lazarenko (1996–1997), were major businessmen themselves (Åslund, 2000). Even so, the Ukrainian government remained dominated by civil servants until November 2002, when the country's first coalition government was formed under Prime Minister Viktor Yanukovych, and big businessmen moved from Parliament to top government jobs. Viktor Yushchenko promised to draw a sharp line between business and government, but his first administration contained three substantial businessmen (Yevhen Chervonenko, Petro Poroshenko, and David Zhvania).

A fourth political good of great value is court decisions. The quote above about New York courts in the 1860s says it all about American courts at that time. In Russia and Ukraine, the use of courts has risen steadily as law has evolved (Hendley et al., 1997). Alas, as courts have become more important, they have also become more corrupt, and the prices of court decisions have likewise risen (Kaufmann and Siegelbaum, 1996).

[7] Interviews with insightful Russian businessmen, March 2005.

Media is a fifth kind of political good, although it is mostly private and only influences the government. In the United States, media owners have enjoyed a free hand for a long time. Publicity has long been traded freely in Russia and Ukraine, which is completely legal. In Russia under President Yeltsin, the oligarchs Boris Berezovsky and Vladimir Gusinsky dominated the media. President Vladimir Putin has gradually expanded government control and ownership over media, but the trade in publicity for commercial purposes is continuing as before, and public relations agencies in Moscow provide price lists, specifying how much it costs to buy news reporting by various prominent TV personalities.[8] In Ukraine, oligarchs (primarily Viktor Medvedchuk and Viktor Pinchuk) purchased a lot of media, especially television stations, before the presidential elections in October 1999, inspired by the Russian presidential elections of June 1996. "Oligarch" even acquired the additional meaning of "media owner."[9] The main media have so far stayed in the hands of a few oligarchs.

Thus, considering the economic, legal, and political conditions of oligarchy, the Russian and Ukrainian oligarchs are by no means atypical. They are responding rationally to the prevailing conditions in order to maximize profit and security.

Complaints About Oligarchs

Oligarchs are a controversial phenomenon, and so were the American robber barons (Veblen, 1994 [1899]). Let us scrutinize the most common complaints about the current oligarchs.

The primary political complaint about oligarchs is their excessive wealth. The number of billionaires is large in Russia. By its number of billionaires, Russia ranks as the third country in the world after the United States and Germany (Kroll and Goldman, 2005).

A related argument derives from the purportedly extraordinary inequality in Russia and Ukraine. The Gini coefficients for Russia and Ukraine, however, are similar to those of the United States, and far below the average of Latin America (World Bank, 2004). Inequality is substantial but hardly inordinate. Nor is it increasing. It seems more or less constant, which means that poverty falls with rising growth.

Criticism of the oligarchs has focused on purportedly flawed privatization, which is perceived as the key to their wealth. This is the dominant popular

[8] A Russian peculiarity is that enterprises can also pay to avoid negative publicity (interview with Boris Fedorov in the spring of 2001).

[9] I owe this observation to Olena Prytula.

view in Russia and Ukraine, and it is much cherished by Western critics, such as Joseph Stiglitz (2002) and Marshall Goldman (2004). Alas, that a view is widespread does not mean that it is well founded. Ukraine illustrates the problems with this perception. Until 2000, all oligarchs focused on gas trade and little else. One of the leading oligarchs, Ihor Bakai, stated famously in an interview in 1998 that "[a]ll really rich people in Ukraine have made their money on gas" (Timoshenko, 1998). No privatization was required for that, and the big controversial privatization in Ukraine took place in 2002–2004, after the oligarchy was fully established.

Volumes have been written about the loans-for-shares privatizations in Russia, which occurred in late 1995, widely seen as the year that marked the rise of the Russian oligarchs.[10] In reality, the relationship between privatization and oligarchs is not at all that clear. To begin with, the oligarchs in question were all known as oligarchs before, and they did not become oligarchs through the loans-for-shares privatizations. Even more strikingly, most oligarchs did not participate in the loans-for-shares privatizations.[11] Unlike in many other privatizations, substantial money was actually paid in the loans-for-shares deals. Even if the amounts were paltry in comparison with the potential values of the enterprises, they were larger than in virtually all other privatizations. Most of the enterprises involved in loans-for-shares, notably Yukos and Sibneft, did extremely well. Yukos and Sibneft led the revival of the Russian oil industry. Soon, they paid as much in taxes in one year as anybody could possibly have asked in return for these enterprises in 1995 (Shleifer, 2005).

Economically, the Russian loans-for-shares privatizations were an unmitigated success. The state would have lost greatly if it had kept them and privatized them later, regardless of the eventual sale price. The contrast with Central Europe's now moribund steel industry and coal mines, which were privatized much later, if at all, is overwhelming. The old management mismanaged these state properties and stole most of the proceeds. People tend to detest privatizations more than straightforward theft of money, because privatized factories can be seen with the naked eye. Another political problem with privatization is that it is too transparent, making the wealth of the few apparent to ordinary people (Shleifer and Treisman, 2000; Åslund, 2002).

In Ukraine, privatization was later and messier than in Russia (Yekhanurov, 2000), which only seems to have bolstered the power of the oligarchs.

[10] The best are Freeland (2000) and Hoffman (2002). See also Blasi et al. (1997).
[11] Only the Yukos group, the Interros duo, Boris Berezovsky, and Roman Abramovich did.

The rent-seeking excesses of the oligarchs delayed economic recovery much more in Ukraine than in Russia. Finally in 2000, substantial economic policy changes occurred against the will of the Ukrainian oligarchs, which contributed to high economic growth (Åslund, 2001). Although the oligarchs increased their wealth more than ever, competition from emerging big businessmen challenged the very system of oligarchy. After the Orange Revolution, popular anger targeted the two leading oligarchs, Viktor Pinchuk and Rinat Akhmetov, who had made the transition from commodity trading to production. The shadier oligarchs escaped the brunt of the critique. Pinchuk and Akhmetov possess large steel corporations, whose corporate structures appear both transparent and efficient. Admittedly, they were the beneficiaries of the most disputed privatization in Ukraine, which was somewhat reminiscent of the loans-for-shares privatizations in Russia. In summer 2004 they acquired the huge Kryvorizhstal steelworks. The privatization generated substantial revenue ($800 million), and it was comparatively transparent, though not competitive. Pinchuk plausibly alleges that this privatization alone netted the state more than all other privatizations of steelworks in Ukraine. Nonetheless, the Yushchenko government reversed the privatization and sold Kryvorizhstal to Mittal Steel for $4.8 billion.

A standard complaint about oligarchs is that they bribe, steal, and commit all kinds of crime. The profound problem with post-communist society, however, was that it was lawless in the exact meaning of the word. Multiple ordinary human rules were not codified in law. Worse, many obvious human rules were criminalized. Trade was long labeled "speculation," considered criminal according to the lingering Soviet laws. Law was at best contradictory. The judicial system was even worse, and legal collection was all but non-existent. Under such circumstances, it was difficult to establish the requirement for legal behavior. Even if some individuals refrained from certain acts out of moral compunction, others would exploit the huge legal loopholes. Some of the latter were bound to make fortunes.

Another common view is that oligarchs are disliked because they are parasites, not producing anything, but this popular mood does not reflect economic reality. The less rent-seeking and the more productive oligarchs become, the more unpopular they become. This is particularly evident in Ukraine, where the oligarchs focused and made most of their money on commodity trade until 2000. Other early sources of wealth were subsidized state credits, steel exports, oil trade, coal subsidies, and agricultural and chemical exports – in short, anything but production (Åslund, 2000). At the time of the Orange Revolution in 2004, Ukraine's GDP was growing at a staggering pace of 12 percent a year; much of its steel was produced in the oligarchs' mills; and many other branches of industry were taking off in the oligarchs' hands. The real issue appears to be transparency, which people find hard to tolerate. People do not react when billions of dollars are spirited out of the state treasury, since they do not see them. The oligarchs are subject to much greater public criticism when they no longer steal but instead produce, because the factories are seen by the people, who draw their own conclusions about personal wealth.

Similarly, the popular reaction against the Russian oligarchs caught on around 2000 after several of the major oligarchs had decided to become fully legal and legitimate, pay taxes, declare their ownership, and spend substantial amounts on charitable donations. In hindsight, it can be argued that this voluntary transparency was the greatest mistake the Russian oligarchs ever made. The increase in popular dislike of them was palpable.

It is commonly argued that American robber barons were better than the oligarchs in one way or the other. Marshall Goldman (2004) insists that the former differed by investing and building new enterprises, but that distinction hardly holds up. The U.S. robber barons mainly made their fortunes on railways, which involved free distribution of vast areas of government land and subsidized state financing, both of which were critical for the success of railways (DeLong, 2002). Naturally, the first railways enjoyed monopoly rents. Resources and rents are characteristic of oligarchs throughout the world. Since the Russian and Ukrainian oligarchs seized their enterprises, they have invested heavily by any standard (Shleifer, 2005). Moreover, why should big old enterprises be wasted? Empirically, only oligarchs have been able to save them.

There appears to be a negative correlation between economic utility and popular acclaim. Insider privatization, which dominated in the early transition, has been found economically less effective, but it is politically more easily accepted. If the first beneficiary wasted his funds, he is easily forgiven, or at least forgotten. Also, if somebody buys a mismanaged privatized enterprise on the secondary market for a penny, nobody seems to complain. Nor do people seem to react if somebody takes over a well-managed company at a low price after ordering law enforcement agencies to engage in lawless persecution.

The *sense morale* is not pretty. The shadier the machinations on which oligarchs make their money, the safer they are from public condemnation. The more productive they become, the more disliked they are. The more transparent they are, the more condemned they are. The more taxes they pay, the more exposed they become. Just look at Yukos! Admittedly, time heals all wounds, and so does failure. Today, few are concerned about the retired organized criminals who emigrated (even if they are serial killers) or state enterprise managers who lost their fortunes after having run their ill-gotten enterprises aground.

A Matter of Ideology

So what is the problem with oligarchs? There is a lot of noise in this discussion, but the comparison with the United States helps to clarify the debate. People dislike successful capitalists for purely ideological reasons. Some of the anti-oligarchic literature makes this plain (Stiglitz, 2002; Goldman, 2004). The United States government did not react against the robber barons in the 1860s and 1870s, when their excesses were worst. It did so only in the early 1900s, when populism grew strong under the influence of Thorstein Veblen's *The Theory of the Leisure Class* (1899) and Theodore Roosevelt (it was in this era that Andrew Carnegie gave away his wealth at an unprecedented pace).

In the end, the acceptance of large fortunes and certain inequality is a matter of ideology. If people are to accept that some are very rich, they must believe that great riches are permissible. The outstanding example of the acceptance of the great wealth of others under democratic conditions is the United States, and the United Kingdom comes in second, with both largely embracing classical liberalism. In his book *The Constitution of Freedom,* Friedrich Hayek (1960) has formulated this ideology, accepting both the formation of wealth and its inheritance.

Edward Luttwak (1999, pp. 17–21) has taken the argument quite a bit further, arguing that capitalism could succeed in the United States because of the country's intrinsic Calvinism. Religion compels Americans to work hard and save. They see the desire to become rich as praiseworthy and success in doing so as a moral achievement. Wealth is an indication of virtuous life. Yet the American outlook is also puritanical. Winners are not supposed to indulge in hedonism but to keep working hard to become even richer. Therefore, American wealth does not become all that ostentatious. Conversely, people who do not make money are not virtuous, and should be ashamed of themselves. Those who do not know better, but instead steal, find themselves in prison; the United States has one of the proportionately largest prison populations in the world.

Hilary Appel (2004) has compared privatization in the Czech Republic and Russia, and she has come to the conclusion that in the Czech Republic, Vaclav Klaus wisely used classical liberal ideology to facilitate privatization.

Although the Russian privatizers were equally radical liberals, they decided that they were better off justifying privatization in terms of concrete material benefits, advocating relevant shares for various groups of stakeholders (Boycko et al., 1995; Chubais, 1999). The Russian public felt cheated when their expected material benefits did not appear, while the Czechs happily reelected Klaus, because he had not promised concrete benefits but an ideology, although the Czech Republic persistently underperformed in economic growth (EBRD, 2004).

The riches of the Russian and Ukrainian oligarchs can hardly be accepted by the public if people in these countries do not embrace capitalist ideology. This is not a legal matter. Nothing could be done by law in a situation when laws were in disarray, the courts unreformed, and the law enforcement was ineffective at best but more likely corrupt (Gaidar, 2003). Therefore, both the state and the market had to fail in the transition, and the best that could be done was to guide society pragmatically toward a normal situation (Shleifer and Vishny, 1998; Shleifer and Treisman, 2000).

The main enemy of liberalism is no longer socialism, even if many of its sentiments linger. Its place has been taken by populism. Much of the discussion about economic policy in Latin America in the 1970s and 1980s concerned populism. At that time, populism was primarily directed against the laws of macroeconomics (Dornbusch and Edwards, 1991). Now, the importance of macroeconomic stability is widely understood throughout the world, as the Washington Consensus has effectively won.

Instead, the new economic populism pokes into a less well understood area of economics, namely, property rights, agitating for redistribution. As usual, populism is driven by a combination of forces. Some suffer from the lack of justice, while others want to make fortunes by undermining the construction of a sound capitalist order. But no sound capitalism can develop without respect for property rights. The origins of Western property rights are not pretty – indeed, they made Pierre Joseph Proudhon exclaim, "Property is theft" in 1840 (Kolakowski, 1981, p. 204) – but capitalism succeeds in the West because property rights are accepted even so.

Current Trends in Russia and Ukraine

The oligarchs were not an economic problem. Indeed, they led the economic recovery in Russia and Ukraine. The real source of criticism is evident from the identities of the critics. The two main forces criticizing the oligarchs are emerging big businessmen, aspiring to seize their property, and populist politicians, agitating people against the rich. There is also a liberal concern, however, namely, that the oligarchs are benefiting from privileges and that the playing field is not level.

Russia under President Vladimir Putin has singled out one big company, Yukos, for confiscation through arbitrary taxation, and jailed its main owner, to great popular applause. This has jeopardized both the excellent tax reform and the judicial reform. The credibility of property rights has been undermined. Less noticed is what has happened to the rest of the big business world. The oligarchs have been forced to "re-insure" their property rights repeatedly with large and arbitrary amounts extorted by the Kremlin for various purportedly charitable funds.

Paradoxically, these practices probably enrich the oligarchs further, because smaller up-and-coming businessmen who encounter this extortion tend to sell their enterprises to the established oligarchs, who thus acquire dynamic enterprises for very reasonable prices. Meanwhile the oligarchs also benefit from less competition. The logical expectation is that Russia's high economic growth will taper off, partly because of less competition, partly because of less investment by cautious oligarchs. The drawback is social, because this is probably a significant cause of Russia's economic growth being less than the average for the CIS for the last four years (EBRD, 2004).

The Yushchenko government in Ukraine contemplated a second option, re-privatization of enterprises that had been improperly privatized. The dominant motive was revenge against the oligarchs who supported the old regime. Second, big businessmen close to the new regime wanted to seize the assets of the old oligarchs. A third goal was to level the playing field, and a fourth objective was to collect more state revenues. Clearly, the first two objectives contradicted the third one, which was the legitimate goal. One idea was that the privatization should be annulled, with compensation paid to the prior owner for his initial payment, and then the enterprises should be sold anew by the state at a competitive auction. This was the course eventually adopted with Kryvorizhstal. Another idea was that some of the old owners should be compelled to make additional payments, but be allowed to keep their loot.

The redistribution of property is often considered a characteristic of a revolution (Mau and Starodubrovskaya, 2001), and the complications of a large-scale re-privatization would be immense. Only very recent privatizations could be effectively reversed, because many enterprises have changed hands. How would partial sales and investments be considered? Obviously, the oligarchs would resist their expropriation, and their willingness to spend money on politics and courts in a corrupt state makes it likely that most of them would win. New case-by-case privatization would probably not be very successful either, because it rarely exists in weak post-communist states (Havrylyshyn and McGettigan, 2000). In a revolutionary situation, many businessmen, especially respectable foreigners, are prone to stay out of competitive privatizations. In Ukraine, however, the prior local oligarchs might be replaced by Russian oligarchs, who are not tainted by cooperation with the old regime. The old owners would undoubtedly sue the state, and court cases would be long-lasting. Yushchenko and his second Prime Minister, Yuri Yekhanurov, did well to abandon the idea of wholesale re-privatization.

East Germany showed how harmful the unlimited pursuit of property rights through the courts can be, leaving millions of properties unused for years, although the East German courts were the least corrupt in the post-communist region. Property strife reduces the propensity to invest, which is vital for economic growth. The center of Warsaw is another example of an area that has been dilapidated by property strife, because Poland has so far failed to promulgate a restitution law. Given Ukraine's limited ability to legislate, it is doubtful that the country will ever manage to enact a re-privatization law. The Ukrainian rage for re-privatization was more economically destabilizing than the Yukos affair in Russia. The initial reaction among Ukrainian businessmen was to stop investing, though this trend reversed with the sacking of Prime Minister Yulia Tymoshenko.

Neither in Russia nor in Ukraine were the recent approaches to re-privatization likely to lead to a reinforcement of property rights or a more level playing field. The state might temporarily have been able to extract more revenues, but the legal system was being undermined. Increased uncertainty is almost always likely to lead to less investment and thus less economic growth.

What Should Be Done?

The question remains, what can and should be done to cure the problem with oligarchs? The criticism of the recent Russian and Ukrainian schemes does not imply that nothing should be done, because property rights remain insecure. If we want to change the oligarchs' status, we can impose reasonable demands on them, change their incentives, or alter the economic, legal, and political environment. If the problem is that the oligarchs have paid too little to the state, that issue should be settled once and for all, while their property rights should be reinforced.

My proposal consists of three elements. The first and most important element is a strong government commitment to the principles of economic freedom, including property rights – even for billionaires. Hayek (1960) has formulated the principles, and Hilary Appel (2004, p. 172) has laid out the economic rationale for such an ideology: "the implementation of a program of transformation is least costly and most effective when the ideas underlying those programs are easily compatible with the existing ideological context."

The second element should be an invitation to the oligarchs to pay up, that is, to make a substantial once-and-for-all contribution to the Treasury. The oligarchs could be invited one after another to meet with a group of top officials, and a price would be conclusively agreed on. As a result, the State Treasury would be filled up, and a stable settlement could be accomplished. Judging from recent public statements from the Ukrainian oligarchs under attack (Viktor Pinchuk and Rinat Akhmetov), this was their preferred solution. They stated that they wanted to sit down with the responsible state officials and arrive at a final and definite deal, and they alleged that they were happy to pay what the government demanded. This solution has several advantages. The oligarchs could be co-opted, as this would amount to a real compromise. The state would get substantial revenues, which would give it a strong case to the public. Taxation is preferable to redistribution of property rights, as it is far less disruptive to the economy.

As the result of such a lump-sum payment, it would be politically possible for the government to provide the third element of a solution, namely, to give the oligarchs amnesty for prior violations and guarantee their property rights. A legal way of facilitating this would be to legislate a three-year statute of limitations for privatization complaints, as President Putin suggested in his meetings with the Russian oligarchs in March 2005. Property rights are fundamental rights that should be guaranteed by the Constitution. If the state can effectively guarantee the property rights of the oligarchs, their need to re-insure their property rights through huge political expenditures diminishes. State capture would ease and corruption could more easily be brought under control. Arguably, the privatization of more enterprises remains so attractive that an amnesty can become effective only after almost all the major privatizations have been completed.

After the Rose Revolution the new Georgian regime did something similar. It arrested dozens of businessmen that it considered criminals and let them out for a fee, arbitrarily set at an amount from $300,000 to $1 million. In tiny Georgia, the positive effect on the Treasury was palpable. The public complained that friends of the new regime were not asked to pay up, regardless of how they had earned their money. The amounts were perceived as arbitrary extortion, while the guarantees of property rights have not been proven.[12] In comparatively wealthy countries, such as Russia and Ukraine, the amounts to be paid would be in much greater dispute and a more formal and open arbitration mechanism would have to be established.

An alternative policy option would be to guarantee the oligarchs full property rights without asking them for compensation. This is, of course, the preferred choice of the oligarchs, but it is hardly realistic in the current political climate. With sizable charitable donations primarily to the social sector, the Russian oligarchs are trying to develop this option, and after the Yukos debacle President Putin appears to be approaching such a fallback position. Given the public outrage that became evident in the Ukrainian Orange Revolution, however, amnesty for oligarchs without direct compensation to the state appears implausible in Ukraine. Yet huge charitable donations of the kind Andrew Carnegie and the Rockefeller family provided may lead to a solution.

Oligarchs can also be combatted through a social democratic approach, with high progressive taxation. The advantage of this method is that the problem of assessing any once-and-for-all tax disappears. Bradford DeLong (2002) points out that the United States generated hardly any billionaires from 1930 to 1980, because even in the United States social democracy was victorious for half a century. The outstanding feature of this period was high progressive taxation, which exceeded 90 percent for the truly rich after World War II (Steele Gordon, 2004, p. 359). But that is exactly the problem. Even under the generally liberal conditions of the United States, high progressive taxes on the very rich can stem the development of newly rich people. High progressive taxes almost define social democracy as distinct from a liberal market economy. They change the economic system permanently and are likely to harm both entrepreneurship and economic growth for the foreseeable future, as the current Eurosclerosis illustrates so well. Would Microsoft, Intel, Wal-Mart, and so on have developed if the United States had maintained a marginal income tax of over 90 percent? To introduce high marginal taxes would be to throw the baby out with the bathwater. Fortunately, such taxes are against the mood of our time, which cherishes flat taxes. Moreover, the oligarchs are likely to avoid such taxes, either by buying themselves sufficient legislative clout or through emigration. The wealthy aristocracy persists in many European countries in spite of high

[12] Personal information from Theresa Freese, a journalist living in Georgia, interviewed on May 12, 2005.

progressive taxes, while new entrepreneurs have perished. But countries with few entrepreneurs need to cherish them. Numerous political reforms can also be undertaken to reduce both corruption and the power of the oligarchs, but that is a topic for another paper.

How Should Privatization Have Been Done?

The current discussion about oligarchs sheds new light on the efficacy of various forms of privatization. The two critical factors are the establishment of private ownership and respect for private property rights, which lead to good economic performance in the long term.

Direct sales to new outside strategic investors have widely been considered the economically most rational approach. This method was widely applied to big enterprises in Central Europe, but it failed extraordinarily, because few such enterprises remain. Many dwindled under state ownership, waiting for the perfect privatization. Others were sold to big foreign companies of good repute, which either closed them or kept just some workshop. Either foreign owners failed because they did not know how to run such a company or they reduced production as a part of their overall rationalization.

By contrast, direct sales to Russian and Ukrainian businessmen, such as the loans-for-shares deals, have been economically successful. These owners knew what to do, and they did it well (Shleifer and Treisman, 2004). They knew how to manage both authorities and workers. They eliminated the most criminalized parts of an enterprise, reduced the work force, expanded production, and improved quality by astute small investment in bottlenecks, drawing on old equipment and engineering skills. Profits surged. Alas, the public does not appreciate their achievements but harps on how cheaply they bought the enterprises from the state. At present, these political problems appear almost insurmountable in Russia and Ukraine.

On balance, the most successful privatizations were insider privatizations by the old management and workers, such as the voucher privatizations in Russia and Ukraine. For years, incompetent old state managers vegetated and stripped assets, but after several years they tended to sell their run-down enterprises to aspiring young businessmen, who could buy them very cheaply, notably after the Russian financial crash of 1998. Even if prices are lower than if the state had sold the enterprises directly to outsiders, ownership arising from secondary sales tends to be respected. The oligarchs can utilize this insight and resell all properties that they have bought directly from the state among themselves.

These observations cast doubt on the relevance of a large literature measuring the effects of privatization. First, its time perspective is too short. Mass privatization looks much better in a longer perspective than in the medium term. Second, the key to good long-term economic performance is the sanctity of property rights, on which medium-term economic performance offers little or no guidance. Third, this literature ignores the peculiar problems of very big enterprises. The whole discussion about the purported importance of the economic quality of privatization is irrelevant.

Conclusions: Make a Deal with the Oligarchs and Preach Capitalism

Ironically, the key problem of our time is to safeguard the generators of the unprecedented boom in Russia and Ukraine. In the mid-1990s, young local men took on the challenge of transforming seemingly moribund Soviet smokestacks. They succeeded beyond any expectation, revitalizing old factories and spawning economic recovery. Soon, some new owners became conspicuously rich, as economies of scale were great, rents ample, and only enterprises with concentrated ownership could make it because of the weakness of the legal system. Since their property rights were weak, the new entrepreneurs, commonly called oligarchs, re-insured their property rights by buying politicians, judges, and other officials, which is called corruption or state capture.

Currently, both Russian and Ukrainian politics are driven by a popular urge to defeat corruption, identified with oligarchs. The United States faced the same dilemma: how to quell the excesses of the new big businessmen in the late nineteenth-century Gilded Age, when Andrew Carnegie made a fortune on steel and John Rockefeller on oil. Russia under Putin has instigated confiscatory taxation of the biggest oligarch and extorted the rest with periodic payments. Ukraine considered a large re-privatization scheme, which destabilized both politics and economics, not to mention law.

The problem with these schemes is that they are driven by the wrong ideology: a populist dislike of the rich plus a desire by rising businessmen to grab the assets of the old oligarchs. Neither should be encouraged. The emergence of oligarchs must be understood as a natural consequence of the prevailing economic, legal, and political conditions and be accepted by the public. This requires that the public understand and embrace the fundamental principles of capitalism.

Yet there is a liberal argument for the leveling of the playing field, doing away with old privileges and possibly making the oligarchs pay for some past benefits. In return for substantial additional payments to the Treasury, their property rights should be guaranteed. The new government in Georgia has done approximately that. It has forced its big businessmen to pay a certain amount to the state, but then guaranteed their property rights. This deal should be made once and for all.

Naturally, law must be imposed, which means that the oligarchs must be disciplined. They are much more easily accepted if they discipline themselves. They have already developed large-scale charity, as in the United States, but they could go much further. If the state is able to guarantee property rights to big businessmen, their need to capture the state with large political payments will plummet. Then a normal legal system, which can discipline the oligarchs, can evolve.

The worst alternative is the repetitive redistribution of property, which would periodically disrupt economic activity. The other alternative is the introduction of high marginal income taxes, which would not only impede the evolution of new businesses of many kinds, but probably also preserve the old ones and brake economic growth.

In the end, no political solution is likely to hold if it is not supported by a strong and broad ideological commitment. If people are not convinced that they need capitalism for their own good, they are not likely to accept the perseverance of the super-rich.

References

Appel, Hilary. 2004. *A New Capitalist Order: Privatization and Ideology in Russia and Eastern Europe*. Pittsburgh, Pa.: University of Pittsburgh Press.

Åslund, Anders. 2000. "Why Has Ukraine Failed to Achieve Economic Growth?" In Anders Åslund and Georges de Ménil, eds., *Economic Reform in Ukraine: The Unfinished Agenda*. Armonk, N.Y.: M. E. Sharpe, pp. 255–277.

Åslund, Anders. 2001. "Ukraine's Return to Economic Growth." *Post-Soviet Geography and Economics* 42, no. 5: 313–328.

Åslund, Anders. 2002. *Building Capitalism: The Transformation of the Former Soviet Bloc*. New York: Cambridge University Press.

Blasi, Joseph R., Maya Kroumova, and Douglas Kruse. 1997. *Kremlin Capitalism: Privatizing the Russian Economy*. Ithaca, N.Y.: Cornell University Press.

Boycko, Maxim, Andrei Shleifer, and Robert W. Vishny. 1995. *Privatizing Russia*. Cambridge: MIT Press.

Chubais, Anatoly B., ed. 1999. *Privatizatsiya po-rossiiski (Privatization the Russian Way)*. Moscow: Vagrius.

DeLong, Bradford. 2002. "Robber Barons." In Anders Åslund and Tatyana Maleva, eds., *Ocherki o mirovoi ekonomiki: Vydayushchiesya ekonomisty mira v Moskovskom Tsentre Karnegie (Series of Lectures on Economics: Leading World Experts at the Carnegie Moscow Center)*. Moscow: Carnegie Endowment for International Peace, pp. 179–208.

de Soto, Hernando. 2000. *The Mystery of Capital: Why Capitalism Triumphs in the West and Fails Everywhere Else*. New York: Basic Books.

Dornbusch, Rudiger, and Sebastian Edwards, eds. 1991. *The Macroeconomics of Populism in Latin America*. Chicago: University of Chicago Press.

European Bank for Reconstruction and Development (EBRD). 2004. *Transition Report 2004*. London: EBRD.

Freeland, Chrystia. 2000. *Sale of the Century: Russia's Wild Ride from Communism to Capitalism*. New York: Crown Business.

Gaidar, Yegor T. 2003. *State and Evolution: Russia's Search for a Free Market*. Seattle: University of Washington Press.

Goldman, Marshall. 2004. *The Piratization of the Russian Economy*. New York: Routledge.

Havrylyshyn, Oleh, and Donal McGettigan. 2000. "Privatization in Transition Countries." *Post-Soviet Affairs* 16, no. 3: 257–286.

Hayek, Friedrich A. 1960. *The Constitution of Freedom*. London: Routledge & Kegan Paul.

Hellman, Joel S. 1998. "Winners Take All: The Politics of Partial Reform in Postcommunist Transitions." *World Politics* 50: 203–234.

Hendley, Kathryn, Barry W. Ickes, Peter Murrell, and Randi Ryterman. 1997. "Observations on the Use of Law by Russian Enterprises." *Post-Soviet Affairs* 13, no. 1: 19–41.

Hoffman, David. 2002. *The Oligarchs*. New York: Public Affairs.

Kaufmann, Daniel, and Paul Siegelbaum. 1996. "Privatization and Corruption in Transition Economies." *Journal of International Affairs* 50, no. 2: 419–458.

Kolakowski, Leszek. 1981. *Main Currents of Marxism*, vol. 1: *The Founders*. Oxford: Oxford University Press.

Kroll, Luisa, and Lea Goldman, eds. 2005. "The World Billionaires." *Forbes*, March 10. Http://www.forbes.com/lists/2005/03/09/bill05land.html, accessed on June 2, 2005.

Luttwak, Edward. 1999. *Turbo-Capitalism: Winners and Losers in the Global Economy*. New York: HarperCollins.

Mau, Vladimir, and Irina Starodubrovskaya. 2001. *The Challenge of Revolution: Contemporary Russia in Historical Perspective*. Oxford: Oxford University Press.

Shleifer, Andrei. 2005. *A Normal Country: Russia after Communism*. Cambridge, Mass.: Harvard University Press.

Shleifer, Andrei, and Daniel Treisman. 2000. *Without a Map: Political Tactics and Economic Reform in Russia*. Cambridge: MIT Press.

Shleifer, Andrei, and Daniel Treisman. 2004. "A Normal Country." *Foreign Affairs* 83, no. 2: 20–38.

Shleifer, Andrei, and Robert W. Vishny. 1998. *The Grabbing Hand: Government Pathologies and Their Cures*. Cambridge, Mass.: Harvard University Press.

Steele Gordon, John. 2004. *An Empire of Wealth: The Epic History of American Economic Power*. New York: HarperCollins.

Stiglitz, Joseph E. 2002. *Globalization and Its Discontents*. New York: Norton.

Timoshenko, Viktor. 1998. "Vse bogatye lyudi Ukrainy zarabotali svoi kapitaly na rossiiskom gaze (All Rich People in Ukraine Made Their Money on Russian Gas)." *Nezavisimaya gazeta*, October 16.

Veblen, Thorstein. 1994 [1899]. *The Theory of the Leisure Class*. New York: Penguin.

Volkov, Vadim. 2002. *Violent Entrepreneurs: The Use of Force in the Making of Russian Capitalism.* Ithaca, N.Y.: Cornell University Press.
Williamson, Oliver E. 1975. *Markets and Hierarchies.* New York: Free Press.
World Bank. 2004. *World Development Indicators.* CD-ROM.
Yekhanurov, Yuri I. 2000. "The Progress of Privatization." In Anders Åslund and Georges de Ménil, eds., *Ukrainian Economic Reform: The Unfinished Agenda.* Armonk, N.Y.: M. E. Sharpe.

NINE

The Economic Rationale of the "European Neighbourhood Policy"

Susanne Milcher, Ben Slay, and Mark Collins

Introduction

The accession of ten new member states to the European Union on May 1, 2004, brought deep changes to Europe's political economy, both toward the new member states and the EU's "new neighbors" to the east and south. To formulate a policy toward these "new neighbors," the European Commission (EC) presented the European Neighbourhood Policy (ENP) strategy paper, setting out a new framework for relations and financial support for the neighborhood countries in May 2004 (EC, 2004a). The neighbors in question were Ukraine, Belarus, Moldova, Algeria, Egypt, Israel, Jordan, Lebanon, Libya, Morocco, Syria, Tunisia, and the Palestinian Authority, with the recommendation to also include Armenia, Azerbaijan, and Georgia. Russia was included as a privileged partner. Then European Commission President Romano Prodi described the goal of the ENP as seeking to create a "ring of friends" around the EU, by offering close cooperation on issues ranging from political dialogue to economic integration. This initiative was supposed to allow these neighbors to participate in major EU policies and programs, and ultimately in the EU's single market. ENP participants were expected to form a relationship with the EU similar to that of the European Economic Area (EEA) members, such as Norway, Iceland, and Liechtenstein.

This chapter describes the general framework of the EU's emerging relationship with its new neighbors and explores the potential economic impact of the ENP, both for the EU itself and for its neighbors in the Commonwealth of Independent States (CIS): Armenia, Azerbaijan, Belarus, Georgia, Moldova, Russia, and Ukraine. In particular, it seeks to develop an answer to the question of whether the ENP is sufficiently attractive so as to induce CIS governments to adopt (or accelerate the adoption of) the types of economic and governance reforms that were implemented in the new member states during their accession processes. These include trade liberalization, privatization, convergence to EU legislation, and the development of state capacity needed to execute the *acquis communautaire*, as required in accession agreements. This task is complicated by the fact that many of the ENP's specifics are still unresolved, while the initiative and its associated financial assistance are not scheduled to go into effect until 2007.

While "a significant degree of integration" for non-EU members is a goal, the ENP was originally conceived of as an alternative to accession (EC, 2004a; Verheugen, 2004). This point was reiterated in early 2006 by EC External Relations Director Landaburu, who emphasized that "the neighborhood policy was launched as an explicit alternative to enlargement" rather than a precursor to accession (EU Observer, 2006). By excluding the possibility of accession, the ENP would seem to run afoul of the Amsterdam Treaty, which declared that EU membership is open to all European countries that fulfill the Copenhagen criteria of the Union's market democracy.[1] Moreover, if accession is definitively precluded, the ENP may fall prey to an imbalance between obligations and commitments of the two sides, which impairs its credibility (Emerson, 2004a).

This leads to the question of whether the ENP offers sufficient incentives for the rapid reforms and harmonization with EU legislation witnessed among Central European and Baltic candidate countries prior to their accession in May 2004, for which the promise of accession was a strong pull factor in rapid and market-oriented reforms.[2] Thus it becomes reasonable to ask whether, in order to be effective, the ENP must serve as a precursor for accession negotiations, at least for some countries, such as Ukraine. What benefits will accrue to ENP countries, beyond being in a "neighborhood"? Does the ENP offer the "market access and support for market reforms" promise so intrinsic to the accession negotiations of the new member states?

This chapter explores the possible impact of the ENP on economic and political development in the western CIS countries, with an eye toward developing answers to these questions. The second section describes the main objectives and current status of the ENP. The third section presents an overview of each country's current economic situation and makes regional

[1] See http://europa.eu.int/scadplus/leg/en/s50000.htm.

[2] Slovakia is an illustrative case, which after the 1998 elections moved from being Central Europe's outcast to its most ambitious reform country within two to three years.

comparisons. The fourth section discusses the possible economic and political impacts of the ENP. The final section presents conclusions.

The European Neighbourhood Policy

In March 2003, the European Commission released a paper, "Wider Europe Neighbourhood: A New Framework for Relations with Our Eastern and Southern Neighbours," outlining the basic principles of a new European Neighbourhood Policy. In October 2003 the European Council endorsed this initiative and encouraged the Commission to take it forward. This led to the development of the strategy paper outlining the ENP's main principles that was released in May 2004. Initially, this paper was addressed to Russia, Ukraine, Belarus, Moldova, Algeria, Egypt, Israel, Jordan, Lebanon, Libya, Morocco, Syria, Tunisia, and the Palestinian Authority.

The ENP can be understood as having three main purposes. First and most generally, the ENP seeks to surround the enlarged EU with a "ring of friends" who share the EU's values and pursue security and other foreign policies that are broadly consistent with the EU's. Second, in order to do this, the ENP will offer these countries significant improvements in access to the single market and expanded technical assistance. In this way, the ENP seeks to offer its neighbors the kind of "market access for reform" grand bargain that was instrumental in the dramatic improvements in governance institutions that the new member states experienced during their accession processes of the 1990s. Third, as originally conceived, the ENP was a statement that the EU's further expansion, in terms of the potential accession of CIS and Mediterranean countries, is not anticipated. In contrast to the Stabilization and Association Protocols (SAPs) whose design and implementation is now ongoing in Southeast Europe and that are seen as preparing these countries for eventual EU membership, the ENP was conceived of as an *alternative* to EU membership.

Such an option may seem unpalatable to the countries of the western CIS (particularly Ukraine) and the Caucasus that ultimately aspire to full EU membership. The final demarcation of the EU's borders could therefore produce results that are opposite those intended. Excluding genuinely European countries such as Ukraine from EU membership by placing it into the same "neighborhood" as non-European countries, such as Morocco, may generate a perception of rejection on the part of the CIS countries. This perception may weaken political support for reform and European values within the CIS countries themselves, which could ultimately render the ENP ineffective (Emerson and Noutcheva, 2005). This underscores the importance of ensuring that the benefits of ENP membership (and the process of attaining them) are sufficiently attractive – irrespective of the question of whether, for certain countries under certain circumstances, the ENP might serve as a precursor for accession.

The 2004 ENP strategy paper led to different reactions from the addressed neighbors. While the Caucasian countries Armenia, Azerbaijan, and Georgia expressed interest in being part of the ENP, the Russian Federation refused to be called a neighbor. Ukraine and Moldova disliked the implied exclusion from EU membership and were ambivalent. After these different reactions and various consultations through the Partnership and Cooperation Agreements (PCAs) that were already in force, Ukraine, Moldova, and the countries of the Southern Caucasus joined the ENP, while the Russian Federation remains separate.[3] In Belarus the ENP is not yet "activated," since no PCA exists on which the ENP can be built.

Since then, most of the countries included in the ENP have prepared strategy papers and started negotiations on action plans, the agreements that "jointly define an agenda of political and economic reforms by means of short and medium-term (3–5 year) priorities" (EC, 2006). In February 2005, Ukraine and Moldova formally adopted their action plans, which laid out the strategic objectives for cooperation between the EU and the country for the next three years. National action plans drawn up by the Commission and neighborhood countries are to be the ENP's main operational framework. They are built on existing cooperative frameworks, such as the relatively circumspect PCAs with Ukraine and Moldova that were signed in 1994 and went into force in 1998. ENP action plan implementation will help to fulfill the provisions in these PCAs as a basis for cooperation and further integration into European economic and social structures.

The Ukraine action plan contains a comprehensive set of priorities in areas well beyond the scope of the PCA, with a particular emphasis on creating an EU-Ukraine Free Trade Area. It also seeks to strengthen institutions to guarantee democracy and crisis prevention. Further, gradual approximation

[3] The relationship between the Russian Federation and the EU is defined according to the PCA between the two, which covers cooperation with respect to political, trade, energy, environmental, transport, cultural, and crime prevention issues (EC, 1997). The EU and Russia at the St. Petersburg Summit in May 2003 decided to develop four common spaces: (1) a common economic space, (2) a common space for freedom, security, and justice, (3) a space of cooperation for external security, and (4) a space for joint research and education. Energy is a key element of the overall relationship. In the Russian case, the ENP is to serve as the legal framework for deepening and structuring these bilateral agreements and programs.

to EU standards and norms, visa facilitation, and exchanges in education and sciences are clearly targeted activities (EC, 2005e).

Although the priorities set by the Moldovan action plan are largely in line with those in the PCA, the creation of an action plan provided extra impetus and ensured that such priorities became central to the government's reform strategy (EC, 2005f). Finding a solution to the Transnistria conflict, strengthening institutions to guarantee democracy and the rule of law, and efficient state border management receive particular emphasis. Moldova also intends to work toward the EU granting Autonomous Trade Preferences and toward efficient management of migratory flows (EC, 2005d).

The action plans are designed so as to reward progress with greater incentives and benefits. This is most apparent in the processes by which the new neighbors are to attain preferential access to the single market. The action plans are intended to ultimately bring most of the EU's trade with the new neighbors under the EU's common external tariff regime. They also seek to ensure that trade flows during the transition to this regime are governed by WTO principles. For example, by facilitating convergence with EU food safety regulations, the implementation of the national action plans should promote the new neighbors' agricultural exports into the single market. Given the importance of foodstuffs in the commodity composition of their exports, this combination of liberalized market access and technical assistance could yield extensive benefits for the neighborhood economies.[4]

The anticipated creation of the European Neighborhood and Partnership Instrument (ENPI), which is to be put in place by 2007 (in time for the start of the EU's new 2007–2013 financial perspective), will be the ENP's technical assistance instrument. It will also be a key incentive for inducing neighboring country participation in the ENP. This new financial instrument, which will support cross-border and regional cooperation projects, is expected to replace some existing technical assistance instruments (e.g., TACIS programming) while better complementing others (e.g., INTERREG). In principle, the ENPI will facilitate programming under a single administrative framework for cross-border activities that would both span, and be contained by, the EU's new frontiers.

For the 2007–2013 period, the Commission intends to increase substantially the annual amounts to be allocated to the ENPI – some 15 billion euros, compared with the 266 million euros in comparable technical assistance programs available for the 2004–2006 period (EC, 2004a). However, if this is to be the only incentive in place, the ENP will most likely remain a

[4] See Åslund and Warner (2004) for more on this point.

very modest mechanism, relative to the development challenges of the new neighbors. This underscores the importance of the ENP's prospects for fostering the "market access for reform" grand bargain that the new neighbors would need to attract transformative amounts of foreign direct investment (FDI) – similar to what the new EU member states have experienced.

Economic Situation of the "New Neighbors"

Welfare levels, in terms of gross national income (GNI) per capita among the new neighbors, are all far lower than that of the EU-15 and less than half that of the EU-8 Central and Eastern European new EU members (Chart 9.1).[5] These differences complicate the process of trade integration between the EU and its neighbors, and may be an influential factor in the EC's decision to treat the ENP as an alternative (rather than a precursor) to EU accession.

However, since the end of the 1998 Russian financial crisis and its aftermath, these countries (particularly Armenia and Azerbaijan) have experienced extremely rapid GDP growth, well above the average for the EU-25 (Chart 9.2). They compare favorably with the new (and many older) EU member states in other areas as well, such as certain aspects of fiscal policy.

The Maastricht criteria for accession to the EU's Economic and Monetary Union state that countries that wish to adopt the euro should maintain consolidated government budget deficits that are no greater than 3 percent of gross domestic product (GDP). With the exception of Ukraine, during 2004–2005 all the ENP countries were well below this level. By contrast, the Central European countries – particularly Hungary and the Czech Republic, but also Poland and, to a lesser extent, Slovakia – are well above this target.

The western CIS countries also have gross government debt to GDP ratios far below the 60 percent required by the EU Maastricht criteria and – with the exception of Moldova and Georgia – below that of the EU-8 (Chart 9.3).

On the other hand, the new neighbors' apparently strong fiscal positions can also be seen as reflections of underdeveloped financial systems and unfriendly investment climates, precluding the extensive use of noninflationary forms of deficit finance. And while the relatively low (compared with EU countries) shares of GDP collected as tax and other state revenues in the ENP countries may promote the growth of private savings, consumption, and investment, they do not *ceteris paribus* facilitate the growth of

[5] These are the Czech Republic, Estonia, Hungary, Latvia, Lithuania, Poland, Slovakia, and Slovenia.

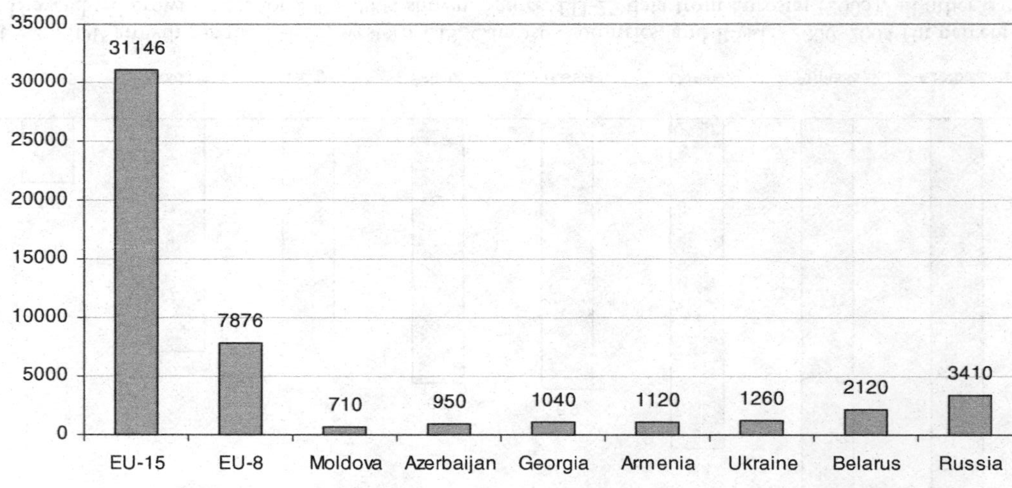

Chart 9.1. Comparison of GNI per capita for EU-15, EU-8, the Russian Federation, countries in the western CIS, and Caucasus (in international dollars). *Source*: World Bank (2005b).

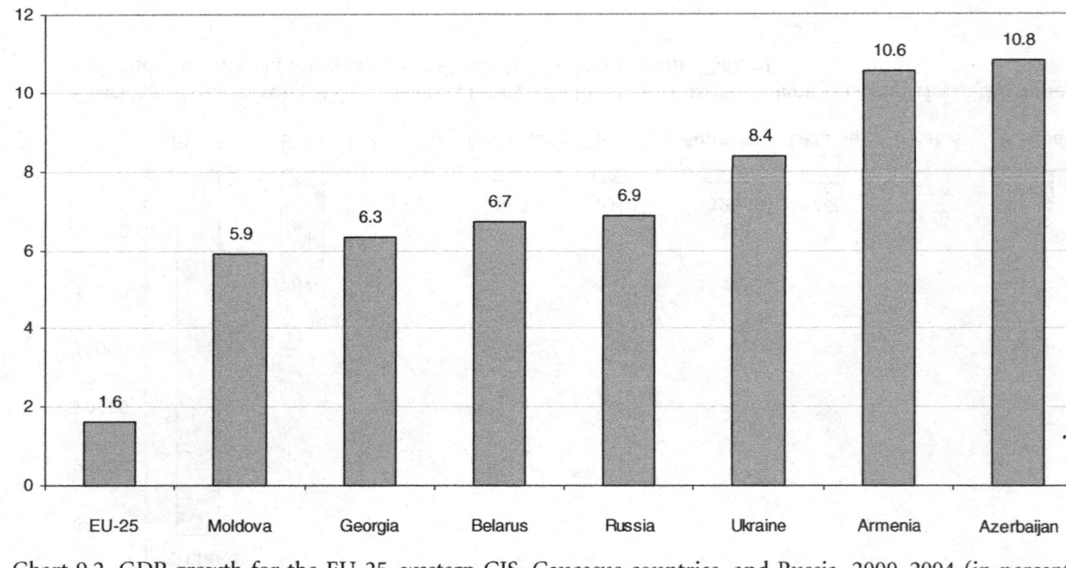

Chart 9.2. GDP growth for the EU-25, western CIS, Caucasus countries, and Russia, 2000–2004 (in percent). *Note*: Unweighted growth rates for 2000–2004 shown. *Source*: EU-25 data from Eurostat (2005), all other data from World Bank (2005b).

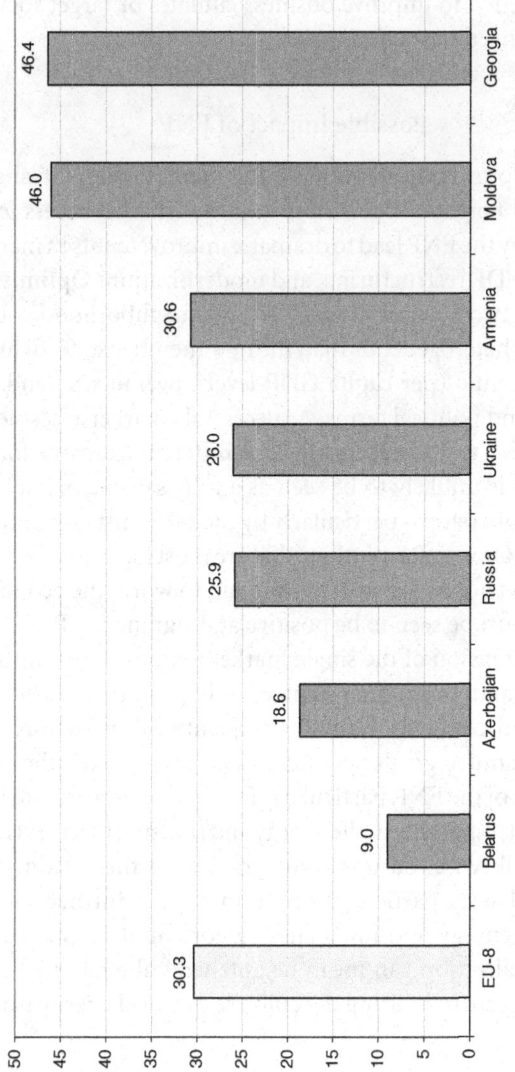

Chart 9.3. Estimated government debt for the EU-8, Russian Federation, the Caucasus, and western CIS countries in 2004 (as percentage of GDP). *Source:* EBRD (2005a).

state capacity needed to improve business climates or target social benefits to those most in need of them.

Possible Impact of ENP

Can the ENP help to replicate the new EU member states' transition successes in the new neighbor countries? Will the "market access for reform" bargain implied by the ENP lead to dramatic improvements in market access, export-oriented FDI, restructuring, and modernization? Optimists on these points must face two key questions. First, the neighborhood countries are poorer and more heterogeneous than the new member states. This is apparent both in economic (per capita GDP levels, overall size, and structural characteristics) and political terms. A successful "market access for reform" bargain for Ukraine would necessarily look different from one for Armenia. Second, the ENP is unlikely to be seen as a fully satisfactory substitute for eventual EU membership – particularly by the reformist governments (e.g., Ukraine after the Orange Revolution) that are most likely to desire accession.

For the "market access for reform" bargain to work, the economic benefits of the ENP must be seen to be positive and significant. Previous experiences with the extension of the single market to non-EU countries, such as Norway, Switzerland, or Liechtenstein, offer hope in this respect. However, the neighborhood countries have lower quality infrastructure, lower per capita GDPs, and much greater political risk. This increases the importance of other elements of the ENP, particularly financial assistance and infrastructure development, especially in the energy and transport sectors (Dodini and Fantini, 2004). Likewise, European integration for these economies could have some drawbacks, particularly in terms of the further specialization in the export of energy and raw materials for countries such as Azerbaijan. Such a specialization can mean heightened vulnerability to terms-of-trade shocks, as occurred during the collapse of world energy prices during 1998–1999.

Trade and Investment

The ENP could bring substantial efficiency and welfare gains to neighboring countries, via liberalized access to the EU's single market. Legal changes in the areas of customs and financial services should promote trade facilitation and business creation. Convergence toward EU regulatory standards may not matter much if the ENP does not significantly improve the new neighbors' access to the single market. Existing trade regimes are not particularly promising in this respect: the PCAs that govern the new neighbors' trade with the EU "are little but codification of WTO principles for non-WTO members" (Åslund and Warner, 2004).[6]

The share of exports to the EU is significantly lower among the western CIS than among the EU accession and candidate countries of Southeast Europe (Chart 9.4). This cannot be understood simply in terms of geography: Belarus shares a border with the EU-25 and is closer geographically to the center of Europe than any of the accession or candidate countries (apart from Croatia) but has far lower exports to the EU than any of them.[7]

Åslund and Warner argue persuasively that these low shares can be attributed to these countries' lack of preferential access to the EU's single market (Åslund and Warner, 2004). The EU's effective protection is especially high for agricultural goods, textiles, chemicals, and steel – goods that play a particularly large role in the commodity composition of CIS exports. In this sense, EU trade policies create obstacles for export and GDP growth for CIS countries. By the same token, significant improvements in access to the single market could have a major positive impact on the new neighbors' prospects for exports and export-related FDI. The action plans for both Ukraine and Moldova call for the removal of trade barriers, with an EU-Ukraine Free Trade Area and Autonomous Trade Preferences for Moldova the intended result (EC, 2005d; EC, 2005e).

The only western CIS countries with high proportions of exports to the EU are Azerbaijan and Russia, owing to the large role of oil and gas (which are not subject to extensive protection) in the commodity composition of their exports. The deployment of the Baku-Tbilisi-Ceyhan oil pipeline will further increase Azerbaijan's importance as an energy supplier to the EU. Russia is the EU's fifth largest trading partner (after the United States, Switzerland, China, and Japan). The enlarged EU is Russia's largest trading partner, accounting for more than 50 percent of its total trade; some 40 percent of Europe's gas supplies come from Russia (EC, 2004b). Likewise, oil exports make Azerbaijan the EU's largest trading partner in the Caucasus, although some studies suggest that even in Azerbaijan, foodstuffs, cotton, and textiles could play a large role in the country's export basket (Center for Economic Reforms, 2004).

The accession of Poland and other Central European countries to the EU in May 2004, and the resultant loss of preferential access to these markets, has resulted in at least some trade diversion: losses for Ukrainian producers were

[6] Among the neighbors, only Armenia, Georgia, and Moldova have acceded to the WTO (in 2003, 2000, and 2001, respectively).

[7] Minsk is just 1,605 km from Brussels, while Sofia, Skopje, Bucharest, and Ankara are 1,698, 1,632, 1,770, and 2,513 km from Brussels, respectively (Byers, 2000).

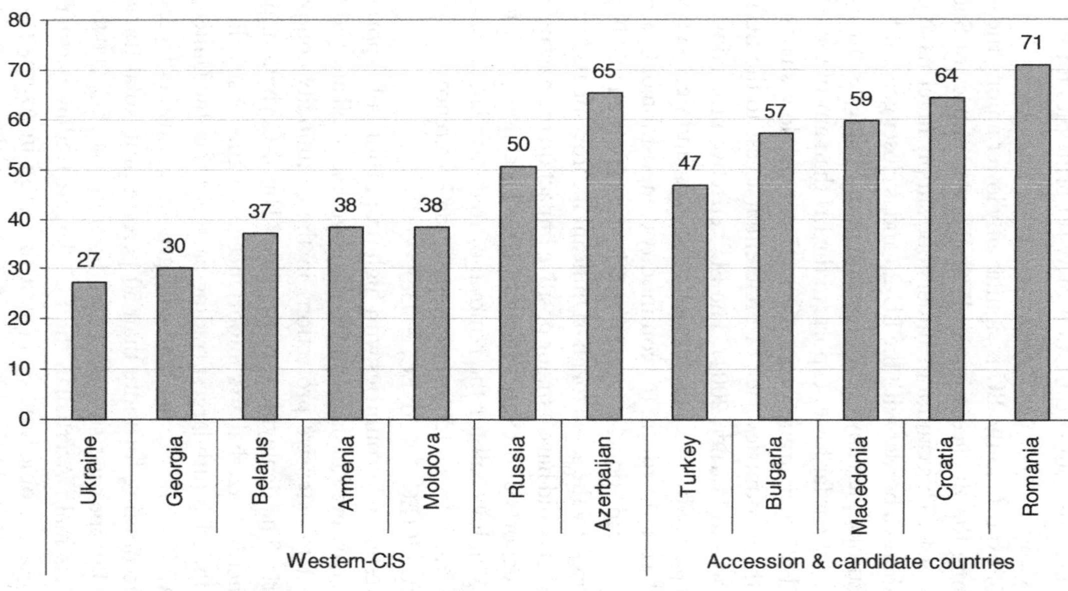

Chart 9.4. Percentage of exports to the EU-25 for EU accession, candidate, and the western CIS countries, Caucasus, and the Russian Federation in 2004. *Source*: UNCTAD (2005).

estimated at about 1 percent of exports in 2004–2005. Whether improved market access and greater support for market reforms that could come with the ENP will be sufficient to eliminate such diversion, given the EU's penchant to employ tariff and nontariff import barriers to prevent "market disruptions," remains to be seen.

The experience of the new member states suggests that the largest benefits of economic integration with the EU can come in the form of foreign direct investment (FDI) that can be attracted by geographic proximity and preferential access to the single market. As the new member states' experiences show, this FDI can have unparalleled advantages in terms of restructuring and modernizing the manufacturing, energy, and financial sectors. The bilateral EU association agreements concluded with the Central European countries in 1991, which provided asymmetric access to the single market for Central European exporters, may be instructive in this respect. In addition to encouraging rapid growth in trade overall and toward the EU in particular, the association agreements (combined with ambitious privatization programs) promoted significant FDI inflows, attracted by "export platform" possibilities (Martin and Turrion, 2001). This pattern seems to be taking hold in Southeast European countries now negotiating for EU membership, which have attracted significant FDI inflows predominately from EU-focused companies. However, such FDI inflows have been far lower in the western CIS (Chart 9.5).

Many factors – market size, geography, transport and telecommunications infrastructure, the absence of preferential access to EU markets – can explain the new neighbors' relatively low levels of cumulative per capita FDI. In contrast to the new member states, however, the new neighbors still face major challenges in developing the state capacity needed to maintain level commercial playing fields and business-friendly investment climates. This is particularly the case in terms of reforms of central administrative bodies, subnational governments, and judiciaries. Major obstacles are associated with taxation systems and high corruption levels, which generate large informal sectors.

Privatization in CIS countries has generally been focused on sales to domestic investors, and Russian capital or "round tripping" domestic capital typically plays a large role in the relatively small FDI that has come in. Perhaps for this reason, significant changes in the commodity composition of exports are yet to be registered. In Moldova, for example, food products and textiles account for almost 50 percent of total exports, while mineral products and machinery and equipment take up almost 40 percent of total imports (Economic Intelligence Unit, 2004). In the new EU member

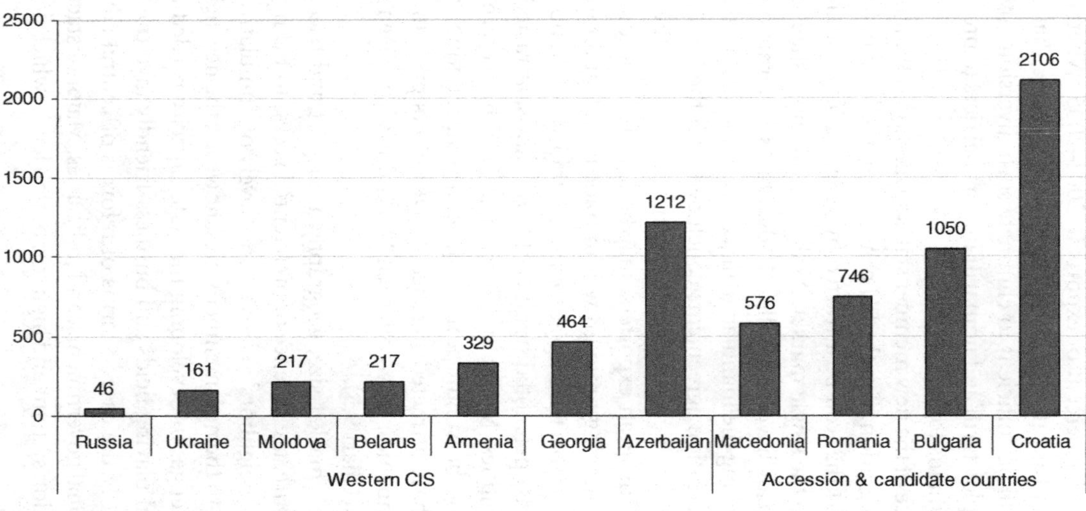

Chart 9.5. Cumulative FDI inflows per capita, 1989–2004 (in U.S. dollars). *Source*: ERDB (2005b).

states, by contrast, FDI-led modernization of manufacturing sectors has produced significant increases in the shares of exports and imports associated with electrical engineering, transport equipment, and other manufacturing products (or their components), signifying integration into European and global supply chains.

Energy

Energy security is an important component of the ENP, since neighboring countries supply or transport most of the EU's gas imports and growing shares of its oil imports. Seen in this light, the ENP is intended to reduce the technical, economic, and political uncertainties that can threaten these imports – uncertainties that were underscored by Russian-Ukrainian brinkmanship over Europe's gas supplies during the harsh winter of 2005–2006. The ENP therefore focuses on modernizing energy systems in neighboring countries, in order to facilitate their integration into EU energy markets and increase the security of energy supply and infrastructure. The ENP also calls for closer regional energy cooperation, for the benefit of the small energy-importing countries such as Armenia, Georgia, and Moldova.

In the longer term, the ENP is meant to encourage structural reforms to prepare neighboring countries for fuller participation in an expanded internal EU electricity and gas market. These reforms would be supported by EU technical and financial assistance, in order to allow energy producers in ENP countries to meet EU standards for environmental protection and infrastructure safety. Increased energy efficiency, the use of renewable energy, and cooperation in energy technologies are also promoted by the ENP. The ENP national action plans seek to address these issues by building on such existing bilateral or regional energy and transport initiatives as the EU-Russia Energy Dialogue, the Inogate Program for the Caspian basin, and the TRASECA transport project. The Commission believes that these initiatives constitute a road map for institutionalized partnership, with concrete measures to harmonize the legal and regulatory framework for energy sectors.

Energy efficiency is a major issue in ENP countries, virtually all of which consume two to three times as much energy per unit of GDP as the EU-15 countries. These inefficiencies reflect in part the incompletely reconstructed industrial bases inherited from the Soviet period. But they also reflect the continued use of extensive indirect subsidies for domestic energy users, which often take the form of nonpayments for energy supplies. According to various estimates, quasi-fiscal deficits run by utility companies in ENP countries range from 0.6 percent of GDP in Armenia to almost 12 percent of

GDP in Azerbaijan.[8] In addition to weakening fiscal discipline and delaying enterprise restructuring, these subsidies reduce incentives for energy conservation and increase energy importing countries' vulnerability to external price shocks (Saavalainen and ten Berge, 2006).

The ENP action plans for Ukraine and Moldova acknowledge the need for restructuring their domestic gas sectors, including setting tariffs at cost-recovery levels (EC, 2005d; EC, 2005e). In Azerbaijan, a 2002 presidential decree calls for stronger financial discipline in the energy sector and accelerated privatization of distribution companies. A tariff board was established as well, to ensure that energy sector regulation makes the best use of existing analytical tools and information (EC, 2005b). Since the introduction of these and similar measures has been promised before, however, it is not clear that the ENP will succeed where numerous IMF and World Bank measures have not. Still, the prospective acquisition of better access to the EU's internal energy market could provide incentives for reform that had previously been absent. The strong growth in household incomes recorded in the ENP countries since 1999 could help to take some of the sting out of the higher prices that would come with reductions in quasi-fiscal subsidies.

Whether these measures will prove sufficient to attract the investments needed in the ENP countries' energy infrastructures remains to be seen. To date, most of the FDI that has gone into these countries' energy sectors (with the exception of Azerbaijan's) has been provided by partially state-owned Russian companies such as Gazprom and UES – often in the form of debt-for-equity swaps made possible by nonpayments for Russian energy imports. More generally, the politicized nature of intra-CIS energy trade, Russia's dominance among CIS suppliers of gas and oil, and the fact that (in contrast to Russia and Azerbaijan) most ENP countries are net energy importers, seem likely to constrain the longer-term impact of the ENP's energy dimension. Instead, the dominant challenge in the ENP countries' energy policies during the coming years could be coping with the significant increases in Russian energy prices that now seem likely (Slay, 2006).

The ENP's energy dimension arguably suffers from a lack of clarity concerning the EU's strategy vis-à-vis energy security and Russia. Is the EU's medium-term energy security more consistent with developing energy supply and transport mechanisms that bypass Russia? Or, in light of potential instability in other energy supply and transport countries (in the Middle

[8] These quasi-fiscal deficits of state-owned public utilities are defined here as the difference between the actual revenue charged and collected at regulated prices and the revenue required to cover fully the operating costs of production and capital depreciation (Saavalainen and ten Berge, 2006).

East and North Africa, as well as in other CIS countries), should the EU treat the Russian Federation as a preferred energy partner – even to the point of supporting measures that would strengthen Russia's position as an energy producer and supplier vis-à-vis ENP countries? This question tends to split new EU member states, such as Poland (which favor reduced reliance on Russian energy supplies and support for the energy independence aspirations of countries such as Ukraine and Georgia), from EU-15 countries such as Germany – which is now financing the construction of a gas pipeline from Russia's Baltic coast to Germany directly. By circumventing the current pipeline infrastructure (which relies heavily on transit through Belarus, Ukraine, Poland, and Slovakia), this Baltic pipeline could significantly reduce the bargaining power of Russia's western neighbors on both sides of the Schengen border, and increase the EU's reliance on Russian energy.

Migration

Migration, which can be a key engine of European growth, is now receiving growing attention in the European Union. Migrant remittances can play an important role in economic growth and poverty reduction in ENP countries, by increasing household consumption, investment, and human capital – particularly when they are used locally to start up small enterprises that would not otherwise have access to finance (Ellerman, 2004). Remittances also make major contributions to the balance of payments in the Caucasus, Moldova, and west Balkan countries, often rivaling or exceeding levels of official development assistance and FDI.[9] For EU countries, migrant workers fill gaps in heavily regulated labor markets and help reduce the need for official assistance for the ENP countries that benefit from the remittances associated with migration.

Closer cooperation on migration between the ENP countries and the EU therefore seems highly desirable. Moldova's ENP action plan concentrates on monitoring and efficient management of migration flows, as well as adapting legislation to EU norms and standards (EC, 2005d). Ukraine's action plan deals with migration within its Justice and Home Affairs section (EC, 2005e), while in Azerbaijan a national migration plan (State Migration Management Program) has been developed.

On the other hand, key obstacles to the better utilization of migration remain on both sides of the Schengen border. In the ENP countries, state

[9] In Moldova, remittances were estimated to account for a quarter of GDP in 2002 (World Bank, 2005a), compared with 7% for FDI (World Bank, 2005b).

capacity to manage migration flows remains weak, due to limited financial and human resources and high levels of corruption. While EU countries' visa regimes vis-à-vis migrants from ENP countries are more liberal than is the case for migrants from many other countries, they are still sufficiently draconian to ensure that the bulk of labor migration continues to have an informal (if not illegal) character. This criminalization of transnational labor supply from ENP countries is a major contributor to growing problems of human trafficking from CIS to EU countries.

The liberalization of labor markets in EU countries, should it occur, should ideally be crafted so as to address these issues. More broadly, the ENP can support improvements in this regard by enhancing cooperation, financial assistance, and legal convergence through the ENP action plans. Although the action plans mention migration, concrete measures to promote increased labor migration between the new neighbors and the enlarged EU are missing. Increased technical and financial support for the ENP countries to fulfill their anti-trafficking obligations, as recent signatories to the Palermo Protocol, might also be desirable.

The ENP's incentives in terms of political and economic reform might be its strongest component, but also its most sensitive one. If "neighborhood" status is to be a substitute for rather than a prelude to EU membership, this explicit exclusion can produce results that are the opposite of the intended. The prospect of full EU membership served as a critical engine for policy reforms and institutional development in the new member states. In Southeast Europe and Turkey, this promise is already a powerful incentive for reforms in sensitive areas. In addition, the prospect of EU membership played a key role in promoting political reform in the new member states, supporting a reform consensus at key moments. It also helped to moderate more extreme political voices. Sensitive issues about which cross-border cooperation and an EU incentive-driven approach might be particularly helpful for the ENP countries include democratization, conflict resolution, environmental governance, and HIV/AIDS.

Democratization and Conflict Resolution

The remarkable success of democratization in many European countries since the 1990s is undoubtedly linked to the process of European integration. Emerson and Noutcheva (2004) argue that this linkage between democratization and the EU can be captured by a "gravity model of democratization." According to this view, the depth and pace of democratization in European countries can be explained by their proximity to the EU, and the intensity of their integration with the EU. In countries located farther from Europe's epicenter, and for which integration falls short of accession, democratization may take much longer and be subject to reversals and uncertainties.

If correct, this argument has strong implications for the ENP's prospects. First, it underscores the importance of ensuring that ENP membership per se truly is an attractive prospect, and not merely a consolation prize for countries whose membership aspirations are precluded ex ante. Second, this argument points to the importance of the EU's continued expansion. European democratization is likely to be a much more realistic proposition in the Caucasus, for example, if Turkey's progress toward accession is significant and its prospects for membership seem viable. Thus, even if the ENP is to be an alternative to EU expansion, its impact is likely to be greater if the widening process continues. On the other hand, the EU's support for the "colored revolutions" that took place in Georgia, Ukraine, and Kyrgyzstan during 2003–2005 – support that was extended under the slogan of "democracy" – exacerbated tensions with Russia. As such, the ENP's emphasis on democratization may be difficult to reconcile with the EU's desire to maintain a privileged partnership with the Russian Federation.

The ENP could help to strengthen political dialogue in the areas of security, conflict prevention, and crisis management. The ENP offers a possible framework for greater international involvement in Moldova's Transnistria. Likewise, the inclusion of Armenia, Azerbaijan, and Georgia in the ENP could increase the EU's role in the potential resolution of the "frozen conflicts" in Nagorno-Karabakh, Abkhazia, and South Ossetia in the Caucasus. On issues such as energy disputes, the ENP could provide the opportunity for the EU to have a dispute resolution role in the western CIS. On the other hand, the EU's ability to use the ENP in this way may not be fully aligned with the EU's desire for a privileged partnership with the Russian Federation, with which Brussels often finds itself at odds on methods for resolving these "frozen conflicts."

Environment and Health

The ENP also seeks to promote good environmental governance in neighboring countries. This is particularly important in the case of river and other ecosystems that overlap the EU's new eastern frontier, and in light of the new neighbors' inexperience in effective transborder environmental governance. For example, the Tisza river basin, which links parts of Hungary, Romania, Slovakia, Ukraine, and the Union of Serbia and Montenegro, has extensive biodiversity resources and ecotourism potential. It also suffers from numerous pollution hot spots, declining heavy industry, lagging economic development, high unemployment levels, regular flooding, and other tensions linked to the legacies of communism and problems of transition. The ENP could facilitate better transnational management of the Tisza river basin, as well as cross-border economic development and better relations among bordering communities.

The HIV/AIDS epidemic emerging in the western CIS countries, particularly in Ukraine and Russia, as well as in Estonia, is another serious cross-border challenge, one that is only weakly addressed in the ENP. UNAIDS estimated that some 1 million people were living with HIV in Russia at the end of 2003, and the virus continues to spread rapidly in Ukraine, Belarus, and Moldova. In addition to the high prevalence rates already recorded in Estonia, there is evidence that HIV incidence is also growing rapidly in Latvia and Lithuania (UNDP, 2004). The cross-border nature of HIV/AIDS trends, and the fact that the epidemic has already reached serious levels in new EU member state Estonia, suggests that the enlarged EU will sooner or later need to develop a concerted response to HIV/AIDS. Such a response could be based on the same values and reforms that helped the new member states to respond effectively to the epidemic. These include democratization, the modernization of state structures, and the empowerment of individuals and NGOs, which have promoted good governance and grass-roots social and behavioral changes needed to reduce the risk of contracting the virus. Its cross-border nature could render the ENP extremely useful in this respect.

Conclusions

The ENP's impact will ultimately depend on its influence on the new neighbors' economic and institutional development. So far, it is easier to find reasons for skepticism than optimism. Although the ENP seeks to promote trade through legal harmonization and convergence with EU standards, prospects for significant improvements in access to the EU's single market, and for transformative increases in FDI, seem rather distant. The lack of measures to promote increased labor migration between the new neighbors and the enlarged EU may likewise be something of a missed opportunity, one that generates significant side effects in the form of human trafficking. On the plus side, access to the single market could improve significantly under the ENP. Likewise, the new European Neighbourhood and Partnership Instrument can add more coherence to the EC's technical assistance, and better support the creation of capacities for trade infrastructures and institutional and private sector development.

Whether these benefits will be sufficient to push recalcitrant reformers to adopt robustly European policy agendas and whether such reforms would attract transformative quantities of FDI remains to be seen. Governments' interest in reforms seems largely to depend on eventual prospects of EU membership. The ENP does little to remove fears in this respect. Indeed, its genesis as a substitute for (rather than a precursor to) EU membership could make the ENP ineffective, if not counterproductive. It is not clear how strongly the countries of the western CIS and the Caucasus will be motivated by prospects of an eventual stake in the single market, or of some easing of visa restrictions. Likewise, the tensions between the EU's desire to use the ENP to extend its influence into the CIS and thereby compete with the Russian Federation as the dominant country there and the EU's desire to maintain a privileged partnership with Russia add further confusion and send mixed messages to the ENP.

The ENP's most burning problem is its confusion with the accession agenda. For countries such as Ukraine or Moldova, the argument that the ENP must necessarily be an alternative to accession is not completely credible. If the reforms promised during the Orange Revolution are eventually delivered, Ukraine will be no less qualified to begin accession negotiations than Romania was in 1999. The failure to start accession negotiations with Ukraine in such circumstances could be hard to justify, especially since the Amsterdam Treaty offers the possibility of membership to all European countries that fulfill the Copenhagen criteria.

One solution could be to make neighborhood status an explicit precursor to candidate status, irrespective of an ENP country's accession prospects. Under this scenario, successful implementation of a national ENP action plan could be a necessary – but not sufficient – condition for starting accession negotiations. Relations with neighboring countries in the Middle East and North Africa, for whom EU membership has never been viewed by the Commission as a serious prospect, could remain within the framework of the ENP. For European countries covered by the Amsterdam Treaty, this arrangement would turn the "neighborhood versus accession" dilemma into a "neighborhood and then accession" scenario. Such an arrangement could provide these countries with the benefits of the "reform for market access" grand bargain, without confusing the issue with prospective EU accession.

The ENP's prospects also depend on the national action plans. A stronger consultation process would seem desirable in many respects. Success criteria in the national action plans should be articulated more clearly and quantified where applicable. Benchmarks could help focus during implementation. A stronger emphasis on training or institution building for the ENP countries might also be desirable, in terms of making the national action plans more logical and helpful.

The ENP has yet to show what it can be. At the one extreme, it could be a modest mechanism for mitigating the unfavorable effects of EU enlargement for border regions. While such an outcome would not be trivial, it would also be a huge missed opportunity. At the other extreme, the ENP could be the driver of the next wave of "Europeanization," in the sense of political, economic, and societal transformation in neighboring states. Capturing this promise requires the clear resolution of some difficult but important decisions concerning the relationship between neighborhood and accession. As one observer noted: "the optimist can say that this is a case of a glass half full, rather than half empty. At least the glass has been constructed, it is reasonably transparent, and more can be poured into the container in due course" (Emerson, 2004b).

References

Åslund, Anders, and Andrew Warner. 2004. "The EU Enlargement: Consequences for the CIS Countries." In Marek Dąbrowski, Ben Slay, and Jaroslav Neneman, eds., *Beyond Transition: Development Perspectives and Dilemmas*. Aldershot; Burlington, Vt.: Ashgate.

Byers, John. 2000. *Great Circle: Distances between Capital Cities*. Http://www.wcrl.ars.usda.gov/cec/java/capitals.htm.

Center for Economic Reforms. 2004. *Study of Azerbaijan's Current and Potential Comparative Advantage*. Baku: Center of Economic Reforms and UNDP Azerbaijan.

Dodini, Michaela, and Marco Fantini. 2004. *The European Neighbourhood Policy: Implications for Economic Growth and Stability*. Mimeo. Brussels: CEPS.

Economic Intelligence Unit. 2004. *Country Report Moldova*. The Economist Intelligence Unit Limited.

Ellerman, David. 2004. "Migration, Transition, and Aid: Three Development Themes Relevant for South-East Europe." In Stojanov Dragoljub, ed., *The Southeast European Journal of Economics and Development*. Sarajevo: Economics Faculty of the University of Sarajevo and UNDP.

Emerson, Michael. 2004a. "European Neighbourhood Policy: Strategy or Placebo?" CEPS Working Document 215. Brussels.

Emerson, Michael. 2004b. "Two Cheers for the European Neighbourhood Policy." Brussels: CEPS.

Emerson, Michael, and Gergana Noutcheva. 2004. "Europeanisation as a Gravity Model of Democratisation." CEPS Working Document 214. Brussels.

Emerson, Michael, and Gergana Noutcheva. 2005. "From Barcelona Process to Neighbourhood Policy. Assessments and Open Issues." CEPS Working Document 220. Brussels.

European Bank for Reconstruction and Development. 2005a. *Transition Report 2005.* London: EBRD.

European Bank for Reconstruction and Development. 2005b. *Transition Report Update May 2005.* London: EBRD.

European Commission. 1997. *Agreement on Partnership and Cooperation.* Http://europa.eu.int/comm/external_relations/ceeca/pca/pca_russia.pdf.

European Commission. 2003. *Communication from the Commission to the Council and the European Parliament on the Development of Energy Policy for the Enlarged European Union, Its Neighbours and Partner Countries.* Brussels: Commission of the European Communities.

European Commission. 2004a. *European Neighbourhood Policy. Strategy Paper*. Brussels: Commission of the European Communities.

European Commission. 2004b. *External Relations.* Http://www.europa.eu.int/comm/external_relations.

European Commission. 2005a. *European Neighbourhood Policy. Country Report. Armenia.* Commission Staff Working Paper. Brussels: Commission of the European Communities.

European Commission. 2005b. *European Neighbourhood Policy. Country Report. Azerbaijan.* Commission Staff Working Paper. Brussels: Commission of the European Communities.

European Commission. 2005c. *European Neighbourhood Policy. Country Report. Georgia.* Commission Staff Working Paper. Brussels: Commission of the European Communities.

European Commission. 2005d. *EU/Moldova Action Plan.* Brussels: Commission of the European Communities.

European Commission. 2005e. *EU/Ukraine Action Plan.* Brussels: Commission of the European Communities.

European Commission. 2005f. *Implementing and Promoting the European Neighbourhood Policy*. Brussels: Commission of the European Communities.

European Commission. 2006. *The Policy: How Does the European Neighbourhood Policy Work?* Http://europa.eu.int/comm/world/enp/howitworks_en.htm.

Eurostat. 2005. *Sustainable Development Indicators.* Http://epp.eurostat.cec.eu.int/portal/page?_pageid=1996,45323734&_dad=portal&_schema=PORTAL&screen=welcomeref&open=/&product=sdi_ed&depth=2.

EU Observer. 2006. "Time for Pause in Enlargement, Top Commission Official Says." Http://euobserver.com.

International Monetary Fund. 2005. *Balance of Payments Statistics.* Washington, D.C.: IMF.

Martin, Carmela, and Jaime Turrion. 2001. "The Trade Impact of the Integration of the Central and Eastern European Countries on the European Union." European Economy Group Working Paper 11. Madrid: European Economy Group.

Saavalainen, Tapio, and Joy ten Berge. 2006. "Quasi-Fiscal Deficits and Energy Conditionality in Selected CIS Countries." IMF Working Paper 06/43. Washington, D.C.: IMF.

Slay, Ben. 2006. "Regional Growth Prospects through 2015." *Development and Transition,* March, pp. 2–5. Http://www.lse.ac.uk/collections/developmentAndTransition.

UNCTAD. 2005. *Handbook of Statistics 2005.* Http://www.unctad.org/Templates/Page.asp?intItemID=1890&lang=1.

UNDP. 2004. *Reversing the Epidemic: Facts and Policy Options, HIV/AIDS in Eastern Europe and the Commonwealth of Independent States.* Regional Human Development Report. Bratislava: UNDP.

Verheugen, Günter. 2004. "The European Neighbourhood Policy." Speech delivered at Prime Ministerial Conference "Towards a Wider Europe: The New Agenda," Bratislava.

World Bank. 2005a. *Growth, Poverty and Inequality: Eastern Europe and the Former Soviet Union.* Washington, D.C.: World Bank.

World Bank. 2005b. *World Development Indicators Online Database.*

TEN

Economic Integration of Eurasia

Opportunities and Challenges of Global Significance

Johannes F. Linn and David Tiomkin

The collapse of the Soviet Empire in 1991 opened a new frontier in globalization: the economic integration of the Eurasian "super-continent." This chapter explores the process and prospects of integration on the huge land mass that stretches from the Atlantic to the Pacific and from the Arctic Sea to the Indian Ocean, principally focusing on the economic dimensions of the integration process in Eurasia.[1] It compiles evidence on integration in the areas of energy and non-energy trade and transport, illicit drug trade, investment and capital flows, migration, and communication and knowledge. It concludes with a consideration of the institutional and political dimensions that affect regional cooperation in Eurasia and offers some broad policy recommendations.

The Eurasian continental space was integrated for centuries, if not millennia, of pre-modern history. Anthropologists speculate that much of modern humanity originated in and spread from the Mongolian steppes millions of years ago. Waves of conquerors, among them Attila the Hun and Genghis

[1] The geographic concept of "Eurasia" is here defined to include all of the traditional geographic areas of Europe and Asia, excluding the Arab peninsula, but including Turkey, Iran, and Afghanistan, with the latter two referred to as "Asia Minor" in considering regional subgroupings. This geographic boundary is of course arbitrary, but for economic, cultural, and political reasons it is for the purposes of this chapter preferable to consider the Arab peninsula as part of the geographic and economic region of the Middle East and North Africa.

The authors gratefully acknowledge the comments of participants in a seminar at the World Bank and at the CASE International Conference in Warsaw in April 2005. They also received valuable comments from Anders Åslund, Peter Thomson, and Jakob von Weiszaecker.

Khan, followed these early migrations.[2] The Great Silk Road (represented in a stylized manner in Chart 10.1) serves as the epitome of Eurasian economic and cultural connectedness. It ran east to west from the Yellow Sea through Central Asia, the Mediterranean, and on to Western Europe. The route also connected the Indian subcontinent and what are now the northern reaches of Russia (Hopkirk, 1980). Commerce, culture, and religion spread along this route, as did conflict and disease, including the Black Death of the mid-fourteenth century.[3]

Many factors contributed to the eventual disintegration of the Eurasian economic space and in particular the decline in overland communication – the decline of the great empires in and around Central Asia, a rise in instability in key regions along transit routes (especially the Caucasus and Central Asia), and the emergence of a weak and fractious China. In addition, the rise of the Tsarist Russian Empire and the expansion of Western European colonial powers in East and Southeast Asia created borders across the Eurasian continental space. Meanwhile the steamship and the Suez Canal made sea routes more attractive and economical. Finally, the rise of communism and the erection of the Iron and Bamboo Curtains sealed off much of the central and eastern parts of Eurasia.

After World War II, it was common to characterize the world as divided into three parts: the Western industrial countries; the Eastern bloc, consisting of the Soviet Union, its satellite states, and China; and the South, or Third World countries, which emerged as part of the post-war decolonization process. Beginning in the 1950s, the Western economies rapidly integrated along market principles. The West also pulled the South along gradually, if imperfectly, into this integration process. By contrast, the East did not participate in this economic globalization, although much of the region was highly integrated internally within the Soviet Empire. Moreover, from

[2] The empire of Genghis Khan "stretched from the snowy tundra of Siberia to the hot plains of India, from the rice paddies of Vietnam to the wheat fields of Hungary, and from Korea to the Balkans. [Khan] opened roads of commerce in a free-trade zone that stretched across the continents.... He took the disjoined and languorous trading towns along the Silk Route and organized them into history's largest free-trade zone" (Weatherford, 2004, pp. xviii–xix). Of course, conquerors also moved across Eurasia from the West, including Alexander the Great and later various Islamic leaders from the Arab peninsula.

[3] A recent history of the Great Plague puts it as follows: "the plague bacillus, Yersinia pestis, swallowed Eurasia the way a snake swallows a rabbit – whole, virtually in a single sitting. From China in the East to Greenland in the West, from Siberia in the North to India in the south, the plague blighted lives everywhere" (Kelly, 2005, quoted in the *Wall Street Journal Europe*, February 25–27, p. P4).

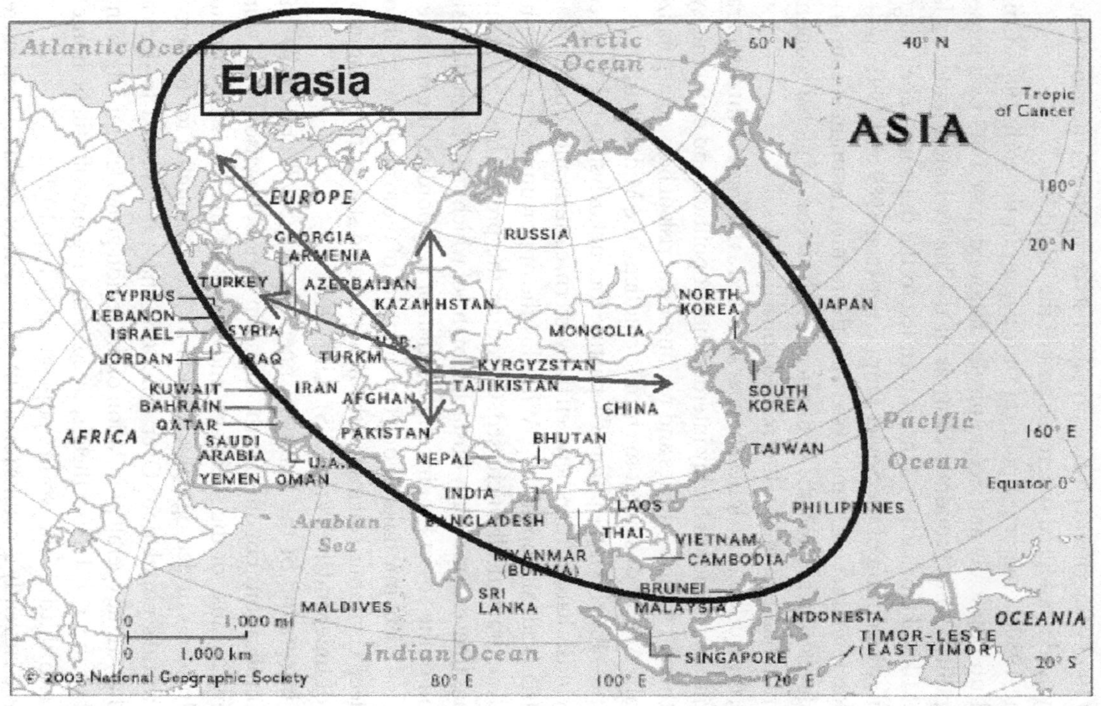

Chart 10.1. The ancient Silk Road. Reprinted with the permission of the National Geographic Society.

1950 to 1990 Western and Eastern protagonists competed in the geopolitical, military, and ideological spheres as part of the "Cold War."

In the 1980s a major geopolitical shift began. In the early 1980s China opened up politically and economically, followed after 1985 by a loosening of political and economic controls in the Soviet Union under its last leader, Mikhail Gorbachev. This in turn led to the dramatic, albeit largely peaceful, dissolution of the Soviet Empire between 1989 and 1991 and the transition to market economic systems in the former communist countries. These developments and the continued rapid process of global economic integration had two major interrelated consequences.

First, the world can no longer be characterized as falling into three separate blocs; rather, it is now a highly interdependent political and economic system, although some countries and regions are at risk of being marginalized (especially Africa) or subject to chronic conflicts (the Middle East).

Second – and this is the point of departure for our analysis in this chapter – the previously hard borders between the western, eastern, and southern parts of Eurasia gradually opened up. With this the opportunities for economic integration dramatically increased. Of course, this process has only started. It still has to overcome many obstacles, many of which stem from the disintegration of the Soviet Empire: the creation of new borders, the fracture of traditional economic links among the countries of the former Soviet Union, and a deep economic collapse in the newly created states of the Commonwealth of Independent States (CIS) (Linn, 2004).

The integration of the Eurasian super-continent will potentially have major implications not only for the Eurasian region, but also for the world economy, because of the sheer size and weight of the Eurasian economic space. In terms of demography, Eurasia in 2004 accounted for 69 percent of the world's population. Over time, this share is expected to decrease somewhat, as the overall population of the region grows less rapidly than in the rest of the world. Nonetheless, in 2050 the region will still be home to almost two-thirds of the world's population (Chart 10.2).

Eurasia currently accounts for about 53 percent of world GDP in current U.S. dollars.[4] For the future, much will depend on whether the developing and transition countries of Eurasia – East Asia, South Asia, Eastern Europe, and Central Asia – will maintain their exceptionally high growth rates of recent years. But Eurasian economic performance will also depend on whether the industrialized countries of the region – Japan and Western Europe – can recover from the economic stagnation that has gripped

[4] Based on the World Bank's *World Development Indicators, 2004.*

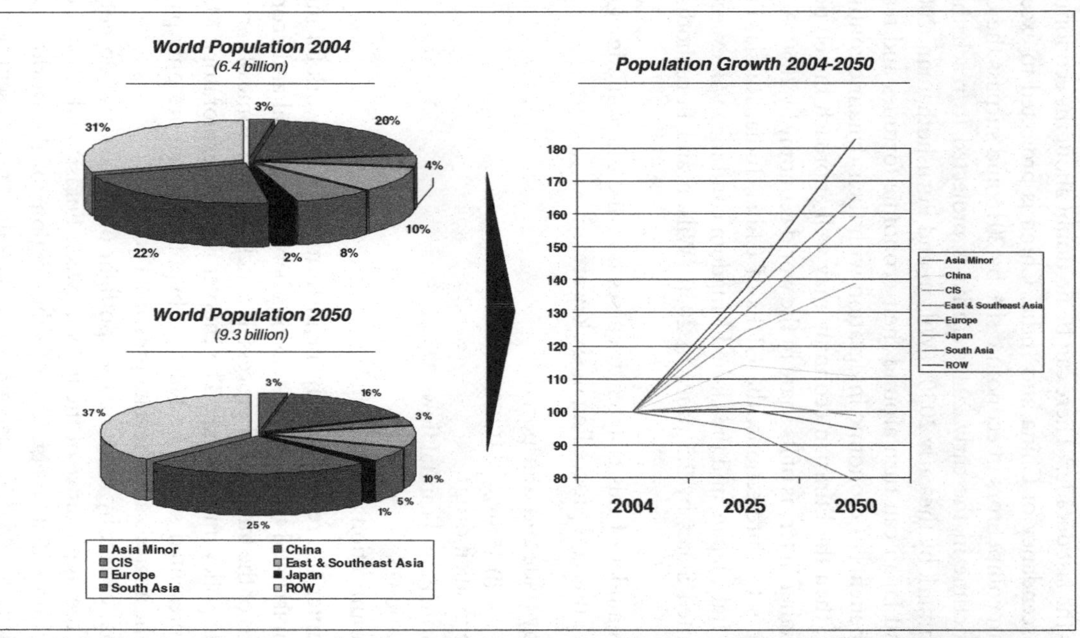

Chart 10.2. Global population growth and composition, 2004–2050. *Source*: PRB 2004 World Population Data Sheet.

them over the last decade.[5] There can be no doubt about the economic and political ascendancy of China and India. China is projected to exceed all its Eurasian competitors in economic size by 2016 and surpass the United States sometime in the early 2040s. India is projected to reach the former benchmark by the early 2030s (Wilson and Purushothaman, 2003). If Europe and Japan can turn around their economic fortunes and reap the potential benefits of economic integration with their dynamic continental neighbors, then the Eurasian economy may well approach the 60 percent mark or higher in terms of its share in the world economy by 2050. According to one set of projections, the GDPs of China, India, Russia, France, Germany, Italy, Japan, and the United Kingdom combined will exceed that of the United States by 2.5 times in 2050 (Wilson and Purushothaman, 2003).

The remainder of this chapter discusses how the economic integration process in Eurasia is proceeding in six key areas:[6]

- energy trade and transport
- non-energy trade and transport
- trade in illicit drugs
- investment and capital flows
- migration
- communication and knowledge

The chapter also reviews briefly the institutional framework for integration in Eurasia and the possible tensions between political and economic dimensions of the integration process. It concludes with some observations on possible policy implications. The chapter remains exploratory. Many of the ideas presented should be taken as hypotheses that are only partially tested by the analysis and the data presented here.

One final caveat: by focusing the spotlight on Eurasia, we do not want to belittle the importance of the links between Eurasia and the rest of the world, or imply that integration of other regions of the world – Africa, the Americas, the Middle East, and Oceania – does not present important challenges. Our core point is that integration in Eurasia, after a long delay,

[5] The developing countries of East Asia and the Pacific grew at a rate of 7.7 percent in 2003, those of South Asia 7.4 percent, and those of Europe and Central Asia 6.0 percent. Japan grew at 2.1 percent and Western Europe at about 1 percent. The United States grew at 2.9 percent, and the world economy at 2.5 percent (World Bank, *World Development Indicators 2004*).

[6] There are other areas that could be considered in terms of their relevance as region-wide integrating factors or concerns, including tourism development, environmental and natural resource (especially water) management, crime, and terrorism.

is catching up with the world-wide process of integration. This will create significant opportunities and challenges for the region and the world.

Energy Trade and Transport

The single most important force of economic integration today in Eurasia is the linkage of major oil and natural gas reserves in Russia and around the Caspian Sea with markets in Western Europe and increasingly in East and South Asia. The rapid growth of energy exports has been one of the main drivers of the recent CIS economic recovery (Hill, 2004a). Further substantial increases in oil production and exports are projected for Russia, Azerbaijan, and Kazakhstan by 2010.[7] In addition to production and exports from the CIS, there are other important energy links in Eurasia, including those from Indonesia to East Asia and potentially from Burma to India.

According to British Petroleum (BP) (2004), Eurasia accounted for around 36 percent of global oil production and just over 50 percent of global natural gas production in 2003. During the same year the region consumed around 55 percent and 57 percent of the world's oil and natural gas, respectively. For electricity there is only a small cross-border market within Europe (Chart 10.3). Most Eurasian trading blocs are net importers of energy, in particular Japan and South Asia, which export virtually no energy products. Charts 10.4 and 10.5 depict the flows of oil and gas trade, showing that Russia and Central Asia supply the lion's share of European oil imports, while the Middle East supplies the majority of Asia's oil (BP, 2004). For natural gas, flows are primarily from the CIS and Northern Europe to the rest of Europe and from Southeast Asia and the Middle East to much of the rest of Asia. Transatlantic and transpacific energy flows are relatively minor.

Data on energy trade within Eurasia show there has been rapid integration among Eurasian subregions in recent years. Energy trade within Eurasian subregions grew at an average annual rate of 8.5 percent from 1995 to 2003. During this period, energy trade between the different blocs grew annually

[7] Peter Thomson (2005) predicts that between 2003 and 2010 oil exports for Russia could increase by 2.6 million bbl per day and from Azerbaijan and Kazakhstan by a total of 1.8 million bbl per day. Of course, a lot depends on the implementation of energy development projects throughout the CIS, often financed and managed by European interests. For example, the Karachaganak oil fields in Kazakhstan – which in early 2004 produced 210,000 bbl per day – are being developed by a consortium led by British Gas and ENI (Italy). By 2010 the Karachaganak oil fields should yield 500,000 bbl per day (EIA, 2004d).

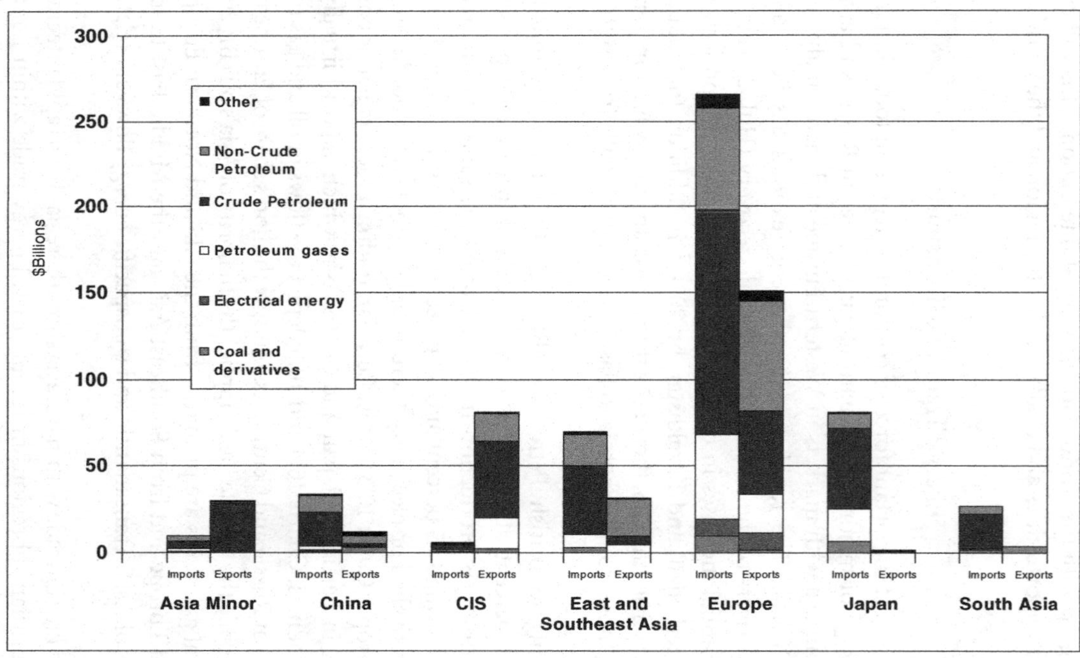

Chart 10.3. Energy imports and exports to and from Eurasian countries in 2003. *Source*: UN COMTRADE database.

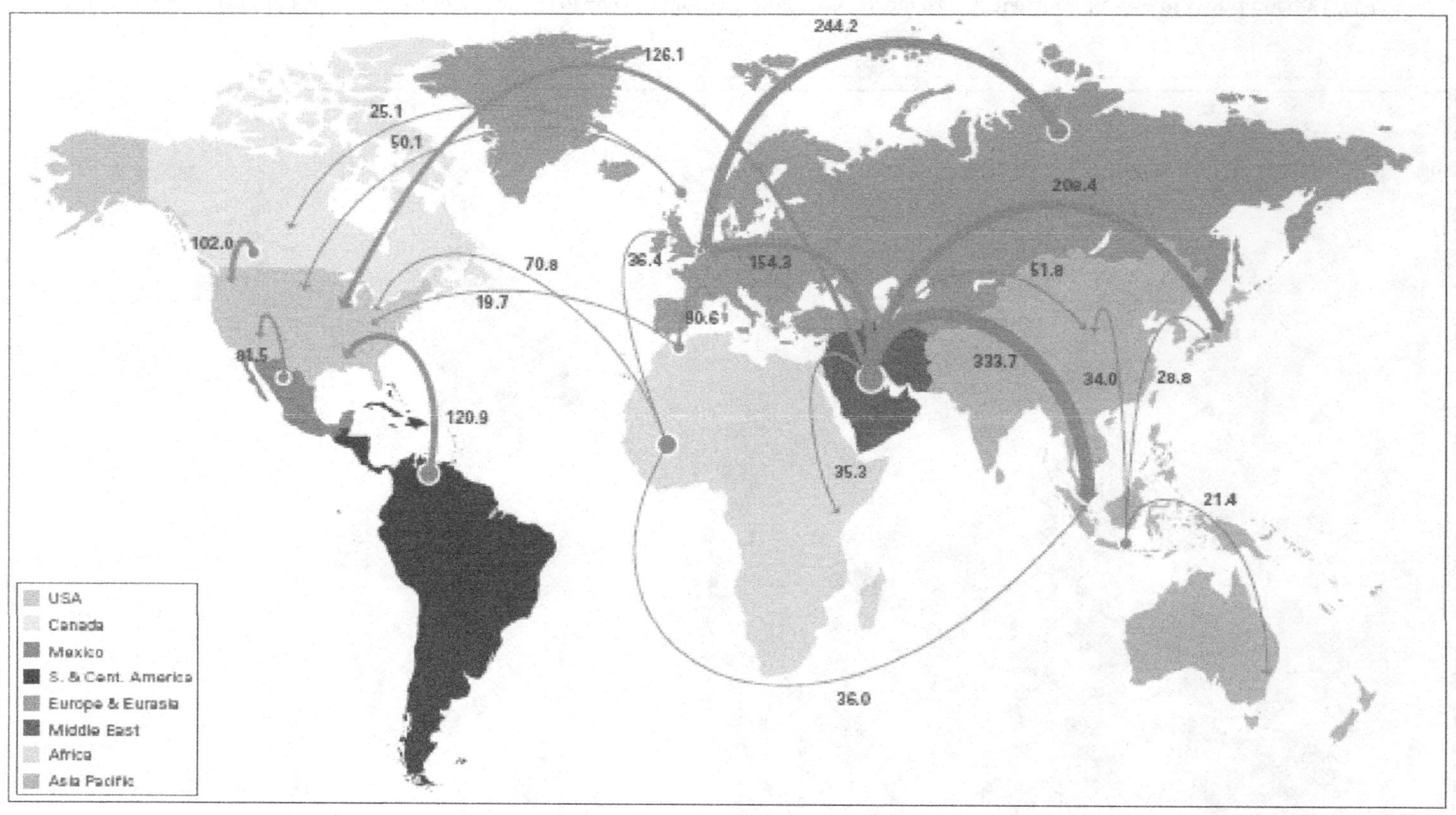

Chart 10.4. Major global oil trade movements as of 2004 (millions of tons). *Source*: BP Statistical Review of World Energy (2004).

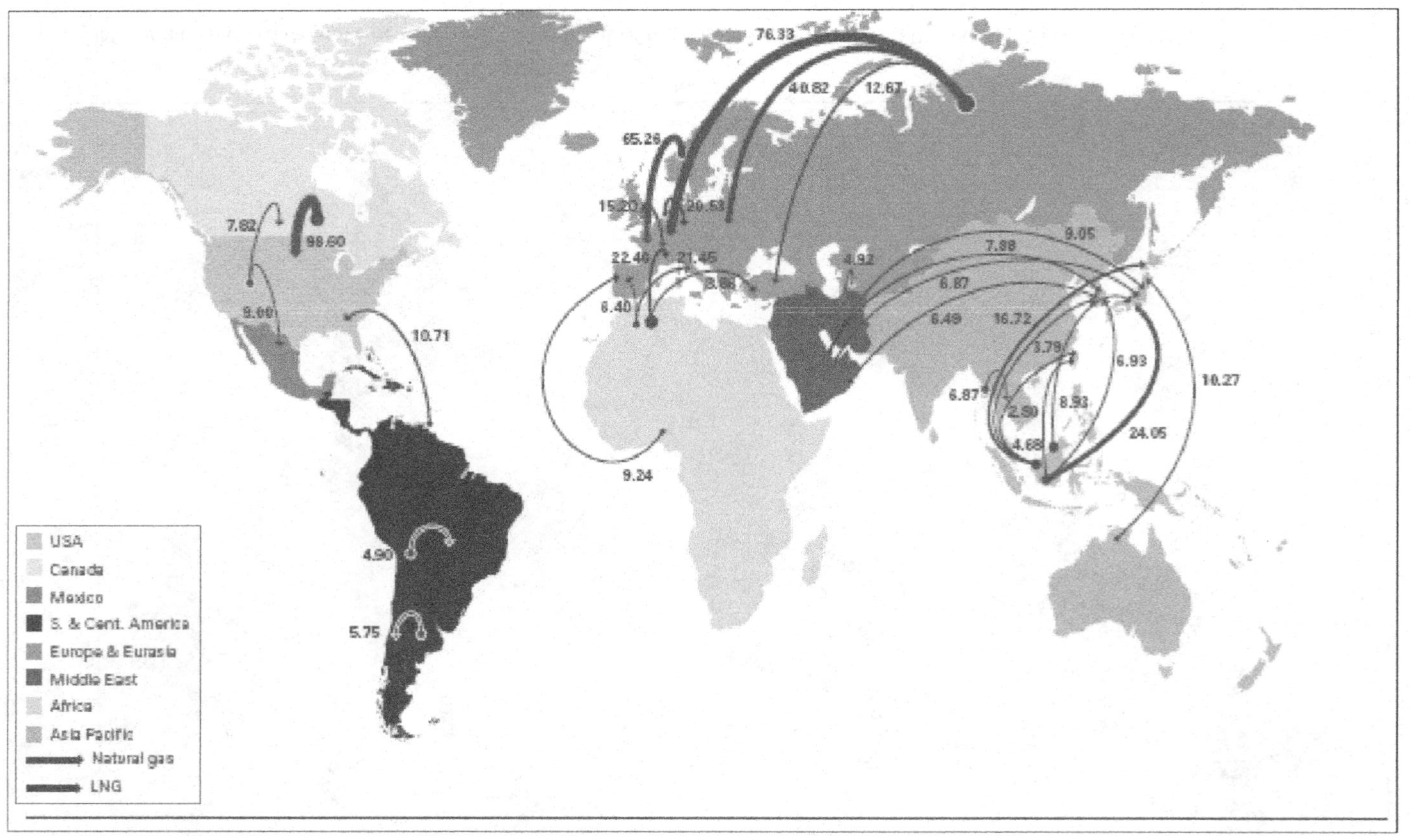

Chart 10.5. Major global gas trade movements as of 2004 (billions of cubic meters). *Source*: BP Statistical Review of World Energy (2004).

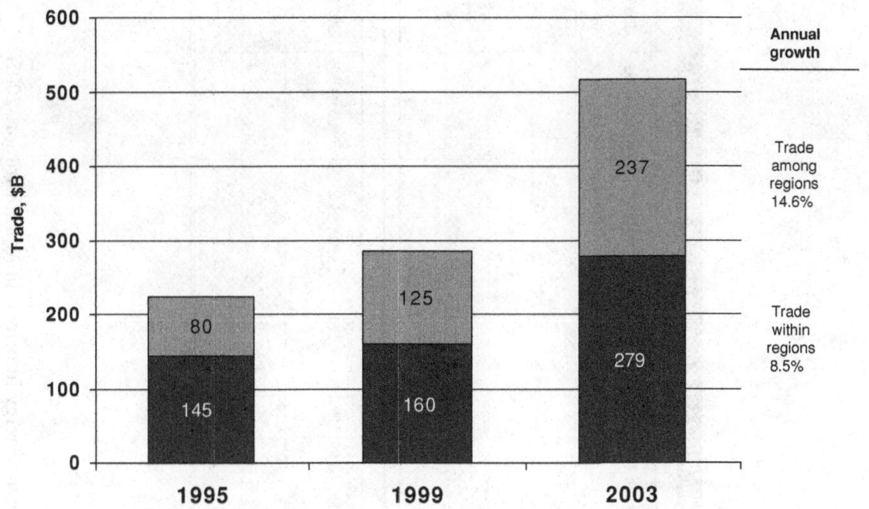

Chart 10.6. Energy trade within and among Eurasian regions, 1995–2003. *Source*: UN COMTRADE database.

by 14.6 percent (Chart 10.6). The blocs that are the most outward-focused – measured by the relative weight of imports from outside the bloc – are China, Japan, and South Asia. The former two satisfy their energy needs by importing from Eurasian countries, while most of South Asia's energy imports come from outside Eurasia.

Bilateral energy trade remains largest within Europe, but is growing fastest between the CIS and Europe and between Asia Minor and Japan and most slowly within East and Southeast Asia. In sum, the data on regional energy trade in Eurasia show growing spatial integration.

To meet the burgeoning demand for energy in the region, resource-rich areas – especially the CIS and parts of Asia Minor – have been expanding energy transport capabilities. New oil pipelines either will improve existing infrastructure and export capacity from Russia or will bring new sources of energy from the Caspian Sea region via Turkey. Natural gas pipeline networks, already considerably more dense than oil networks, will expand in much the same way: from Russia or the Caspian.

The reorientation of Eurasia's energy trade, from a Soviet north-south (Russia-Central Asia) pipeline system to an east-west network extending into Europe and East Asia, is under way. There are a number of large pipeline construction projects, many of which involve Russian production and exports (Chart 10.7), but there are currently also three large pipeline projects

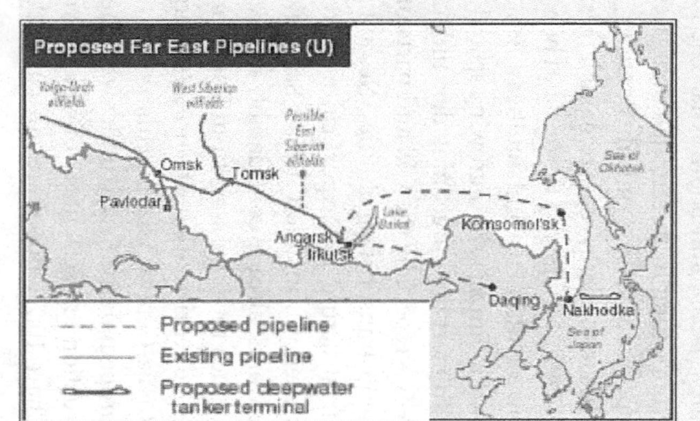

Table 1: Major Russian Oil and Natural Gas Pipeline Projects

OIL

Name	Length (miles)	Current Capacity (million bbl/d)	Expected Capacity (million bbl/d)	Location	Completion Date	Notes
Adria Reversal Project	470	0.1	0.3	Central Europe (Hungary, Slovakia) to Croatian Adriatic Port of Omisalj	Unknown - but once approval given--> immediate	Environmental hold-up in Croatia
Druzhba Expansion	2,500	1.2-1.4	same	Russia to Europe via Belarus, Ukraine, Slovakia, Czech Republic	none	Expansion proposed into Germany
Baltic Pipeline System (BPS)	1,600	1	1.24	Exports via Baltic Sea port of Primorsk	2005	
Murmansk	various	n/a	3	Baltic Sea (NE of Primorsk)	none	Project for pipeline and terminal
Taishet-Nakhodka	2,480	n/a	1	Linking from existing pipeline near Lake Baikal to Russian Pacific Coast	2008	Transneft planning spur to China

NATURAL GAS

Name	Length (miles)	Current Capacity (Billion cubic feet/yr)	Expected Capacity (Billion cubic feet/yr)	Location	Completion Date	Notes
Yamal-Europe II	n/a	1,060	n/a	Second branch from Russia via Belarus and Poland via Europe	n/a	Route undetermined
Blue Stream	750	565	same	Izabilnoye to Dzhugba (RU), under Black Sea, Samsun to Ankara (Turkey)	finished	ENI-Gazprom proposing expansions
North Trans-Gas Pipeline	1300 (737 offshore)	0	700-1000	Russia to Finland, UK via Baltic Sea, with connections to Sweden and Germany	2010	Also called N European Gas Pipeline

Chart 10.7. Major Russian oil and gas pipelines and projects. *Source*: U.S. Government Energy Information Administration, 2005.

connecting the Caspian to markets in Europe. First is the Caspian Pipeline Consortium Project, which will connect Kazakhstan's oil fields to the Russian Black Sea port of Novorossiysk. The Baku-Tbilisi-Ceyhan (BTC) pipeline, a 1,040-mile, $2.9 billion project, connects oil fields in Azerbaijan to the Turkish port of Ceyhan. It became operational in 2005 (EIA, 2004b). Azerbaijan currently lacks any infrastructure to export its natural gas. The $1 billion construction of the 550-mile Baku-Tbilisi-Erzurum or South Caucasus Pipeline will allow Azerbaijan to export 1.5 billion cubic feet of natural gas per day (EIA, 2004a).[8]

While pipeline construction feeding the European market has received the most attention, important projects have also been considered or are being undertaken connecting Russia and Central Asia to East and South Asia.[9] For example, China and Kazakhstan signed a $700 million contract in 2004 to construct a pipeline from Atasau to Xinjiang in western China. Another pipeline into China, this one from Angarsk in Russia, is being discussed. If built, it would carry as much as 1 million barrels of oil per day (EIA, 2004c). And in December 2004, Russia was reported to have "committed to building the Taishet-Nakhodka pipeline, a gargantuan 4,300 kilometer project that will cost $12 billion and is designed to provide 80 million tons of oil per year to the Asia Pacific market, including 30 million tons to China" (Cohen, 2005, p. 2). In addition, India and Pakistan, which have strong interest in Central Asian and Iranian gas, are exploring options for pipelines from Iran and Turkmenistan (Blank, 2005). However, there are considerable political uncertainties that could impede such pipeline projects, especially the continuing insecurity in Afghanistan (Siddiqi, 2004).

In addition to a growing continental interdependence in oil and gas, it is likely that there will be increasing integration of electricity grids. This will be driven in part by the efficiency benefits from integrated electricity grids and markets, and partly by the large long-term hydropower export potential of Central Asia. The Kyrgyz Republic and Tajikistan have particularly large hydro resources, which can in principle be exploited for electricity exports to the large neighboring countries and, through "wheeling" across

[8] Europe and the United States have considerable interest in diversifying access to Caspian energy resources as a way to avoid dependence on Russian exports and transit routes, especially for gas. See Cohen (2005) and Thomson (2005). In addition, the financial benefits to the transit countries can be substantial. Ukraine's revenues from gas transit amount to about $1.5 billion a year. Georgia now receives $10 million a year, which is expected to increase to $50 million when the BTC pipeline is completed. Georgia's transit revenues will be further increased when the SCP gas pipeline is completed (Thomson, 2005).

[9] With its completion in 1997, the Korpezhe-Kurt Kui pipeline, linking Turkmenistan and Iran, was the first Central Asian pipeline to bypass Russia (EIA, 2004b).

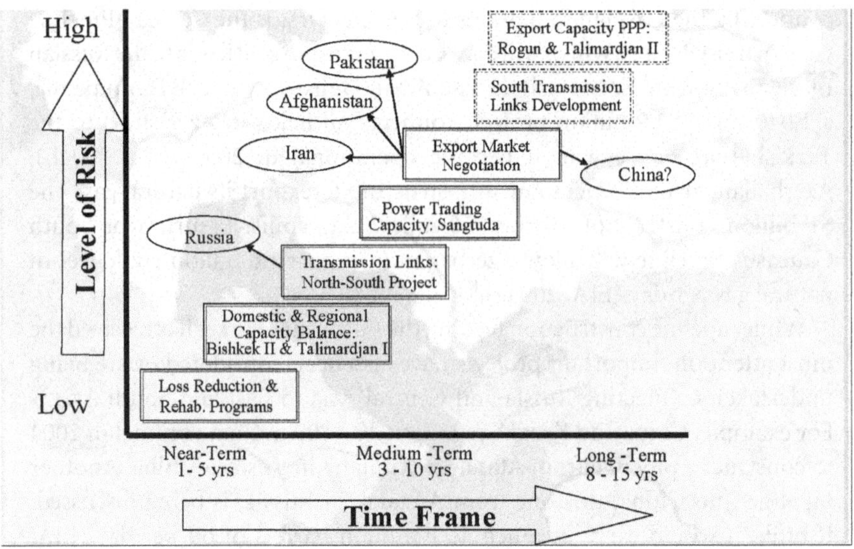

Chart 10.8. Central Asian republics' power development and trade strategy. *Source*: World Bank (2004a).

interconnected electricity grids, even to Europe, China, and India (World Bank, 2004a; Thomson 2005). However, as the World Bank (2004a) report on Central Asia's electricity export market potential makes clear (see also Chart 10.8), these are long-term development options, which will require large public and private investments. Such investments and their financing in turn will depend on several factors: firm take-off agreements and agreements on integrated electricity market management, mitigation of political and security risks along transmission routes, and improvements in the domestic market regulation, operation, and maintenance to ensure technically secure and commercially viable electricity market links (World Bank 2004a; Thomson 2005).[10]

In sum, continued development and integration of the energy sector in Eurasia is a big opportunity and a big challenge. Eurasia's continued economic growth will depend on effective energy development. At the same time, with continued rapid increases in energy demand in major consumption centers, Eurasia needs large investments in energy production and transport/transmission. Such investments will happen only if there is a

[10] Through targeted engagements (equity participation, direct investments, supply and take-off agreements) Russia's state-owned electricity company, RAO-UES, is positioning itself to play a major role in developing, managing, and supplying the regional energy markets in and around the CIS (Crane 2005; Thomson 2005).

reasonably secure political, regulatory, and investment climate in the region. The mutual dependence of key players in the energy sector will increase further over time, as will the potential for competition and even conflict among competing energy producers (Russia, Central Asia, Iran) and consumers (the EU, China, India, Japan). Eurasia accounts for a large and growing share of world energy supply and demand. Global energy prices and global economic growth will increasingly depend on how Eurasia manages energy.

Non-Energy Trade and Transport

Traditionally, economic integration has been analyzed and measured mostly with regard to trade and transport linkages. Turning from the most obvious linkages in energy to other areas, the first point to be made is that the collapse of the former Soviet Union (FSU) had a devastating impact on trade within the former Soviet regional trading bloc known as COMECON. Of course, the trade that did take place prior to 1991 in the FSU was not the result of market forces but part of a highly specialized, regionally dispersed, and highly integrated system of production and exchange under the communist command economy. The collapse of much of this trade, along with other elements of a far-reaching economic disintegration, caused a severe economic recession in the new republics of the FSU (Linn, 2004).

However, the collapse of the Soviet Union and its highly integrated internal economic structure also opened the door for a far-reaching process of integration throughout the Eurasian region, permitting the free flow of goods and services across Eurasia for the first time in centuries. Not only did trade within the FSU recover, especially after the Russian financial crisis of 1998, but the trade of the new FSU republics with the rest of the world, especially their neighbors in the Eurasian economic space, also expanded rapidly. Nonetheless, major obstacles to the free and efficient flow of trade still exist in the region: trade policies, transport infrastructure, and transit conditions remain very problematic in many parts of Eurasia. They raise the costs of trade and severely reduce competitiveness, especially for the land-locked areas of the region. This section reviews the trends in Eurasian regional trade and considers some of the opportunities and obstacles for further trade integration.

Three principal trading blocs make up the region: a European bloc, a CIS bloc, and an Asian bloc. The trade data show that much of Eurasian trade takes place within these blocs, while the trade between the combined Europe-CIS bloc and Asia exceeds that between each of these two blocs and the United States (World Bank, 2005). In other words, Eurasia is more connected internally through trade than it is with the rest of the world.

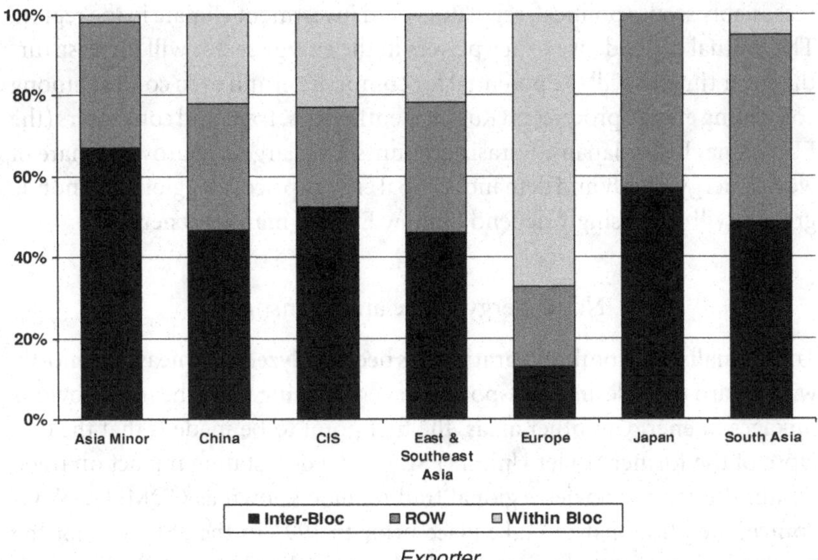

Chart 10.9. Eurasian export split by trading bloc in 2003. *Source*: WDI, BoP Data.

This picture can be refined by looking at the level, growth, and composition of trade by subregional trading blocs within Eurasia (Charts 10.9 to 10.11). The following stylized facts emerge:

- For all subregional blocs, except Europe, trade with partners outside the subregion is more important than trade within the region. For example, in 2003, CIS countries exported around $23 billion worth of merchandise to other CIS countries, but exported $83 billion to other Eurasian countries.[11] Similarly, South and Southeast Asian countries traded $136 billion worth of merchandise among each other, but $304 billion with others.
- Second, for all subregional trading blocs, intra-Eurasian trade is more important, and in most cases much more important, than trade with the rest of the world. Even in the two most outwardly focused blocs, Japan and South Asia, exports to non-Eurasian countries make up only 43 percent and 46 percent of total exports, respectively. Europe, the largest Eurasian trading bloc, sells only 20 percent of its total exports outside of Eurasia.

[11] Despite their recent recovery with regard to GDP and trade, CIS countries still underperform in terms of export levels when compared with other countries of similar per capita GDP (Freinkman et al., 2004).

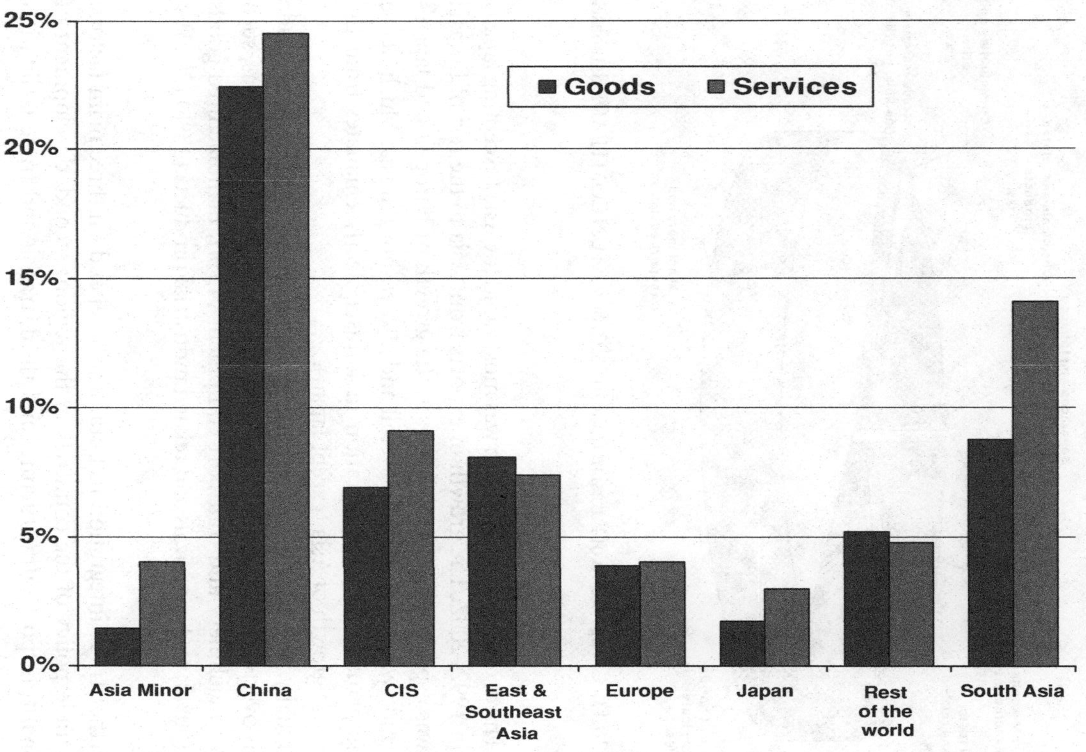

Chart 10.10. Growth in exports of goods and services by region, 1992–2002.

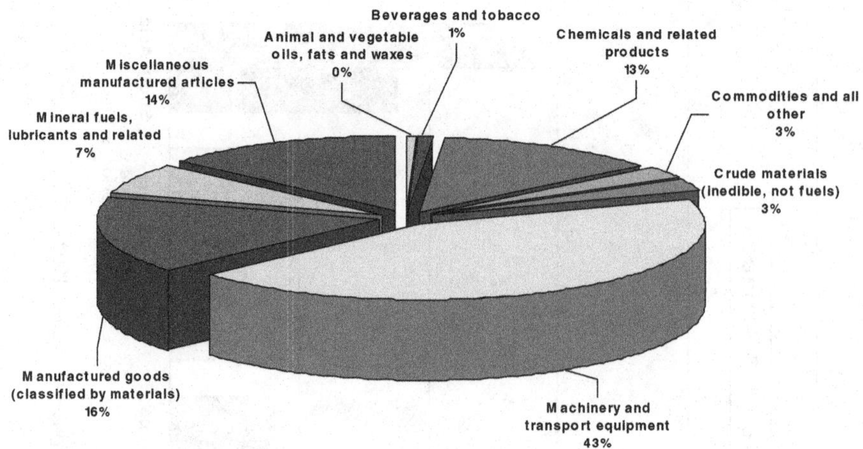

Chart 10.11. Composition of Eurasian trade in 2003. *Source*: UN COMTRADE database.

- Third, overall export growth was most rapid for Asia (excepting Japan) in 1992–2002. The growth of exports from Asia to the rest of Eurasia was especially rapid. By contrast, the growth of Europe's and Japan's trade was relatively slow overall and also within Eurasia. Much of the impetus for trade integration in Eurasia clearly emanates from the rapid growth of Asia (except Japan).
- Finally, despite the importance of energy flows in the region, trade is overwhelmingly concentrated in traditional non-energy areas, such as machinery and transport equipment (43%), manufactured goods (30%), and chemicals and related industrial products (13%) (2003).

Further trade integration in Eurasia will depend on three main factors: first, trade policy of the countries in the region; second, development of regional transport infrastructure; and third, transit and trade facilitation across and behind borders.

For trade policy, World Trade Organization (WTO) membership is a key element of global and regional integration. China's membership in December 2001 was a major step forward in this regard, but since most CIS countries are not WTO members yet, their integration into the world economy and Eurasia still lacks an important impetus. The largest of the CIS countries, Kazakhstan, Russia, and Ukraine, are expected to become WTO members in 2006 or soon after. This will significantly stimulate regional trade integration.

Countries can also pursue trade integration on a purely regional or bilateral basis. Here Eurasia shows some of the most intense activity on the globe, with regional trade agreements most significant in Europe and the CIS (Chart 10.12; World Trade Organization, 2000).

Because of their central location, the CIS countries are particularly important for permitting and facilitating Eurasian trade integration. Various reviews of regional trade policy and agreements in the CIS (Akiner, 2001; Muzafarov, 2001; Freinkman et al., 2004; World Bank, 2005) have shown that the high frequency of bilateral, regional, and global trade agreements in the CIS, while welcome in principle as recognition of the importance of regional trade integration, has not yet led in practice to effective trade cooperation. One reason for this is the complexity of the overlapping trade agreements, which leads to what is referred to as a "spaghetti bowl" effect, confusing and often unimplementable trade relations. The second, related reason is that most of the agreements have not been implemented or enforced in practice, either due to a lack of political readiness for integration or because of weak administrative capacity and corruption.

Aside from trade policy, transport infrastructure and transit facilitation are key elements that determine the costs of trading and access to world markets. These are particularly significant for the vast land-locked regions of Eurasia, most notably the countries of Central Asia. Chart 10.13 summarizes the distances to the nearest ports and some estimated costs of shipping (both in terms of money and time) for these countries.

The key question that confronts governments and private firms alike in Eurasia is whether and how the costs of shipping over land routes can be significantly reduced in the foreseeable future. One element of a solution is improvement in the transport infrastructure (rail, roads, and air). From the west, the Trans-European Network and the Transport Corridor Europe Caucasus Asia programs of the European Union have made efforts to strengthen transcontinental transport routes. From the east, the Asian Development Bank has supported regional transport infrastructure improvements in Central Asia and western China (in cooperation with other international financial institutions and the countries of the subregion under the umbrella of the Central Asia Regional Economic Cooperation (CAREC) initiative. Kazakhstan has announced that it "will start building a railway link in 2005 connecting East Asia with Europe" (Embassy of the Republic of Kazakhstan, 2004). Since 2002, with the rehabilitation of the Afghan road network and reconstruction of key bridges between Afghanistan and its Central Asian neighbors, the north-south transport corridor in Central Asia has been reopened. Plans are also being made for improved regional transport

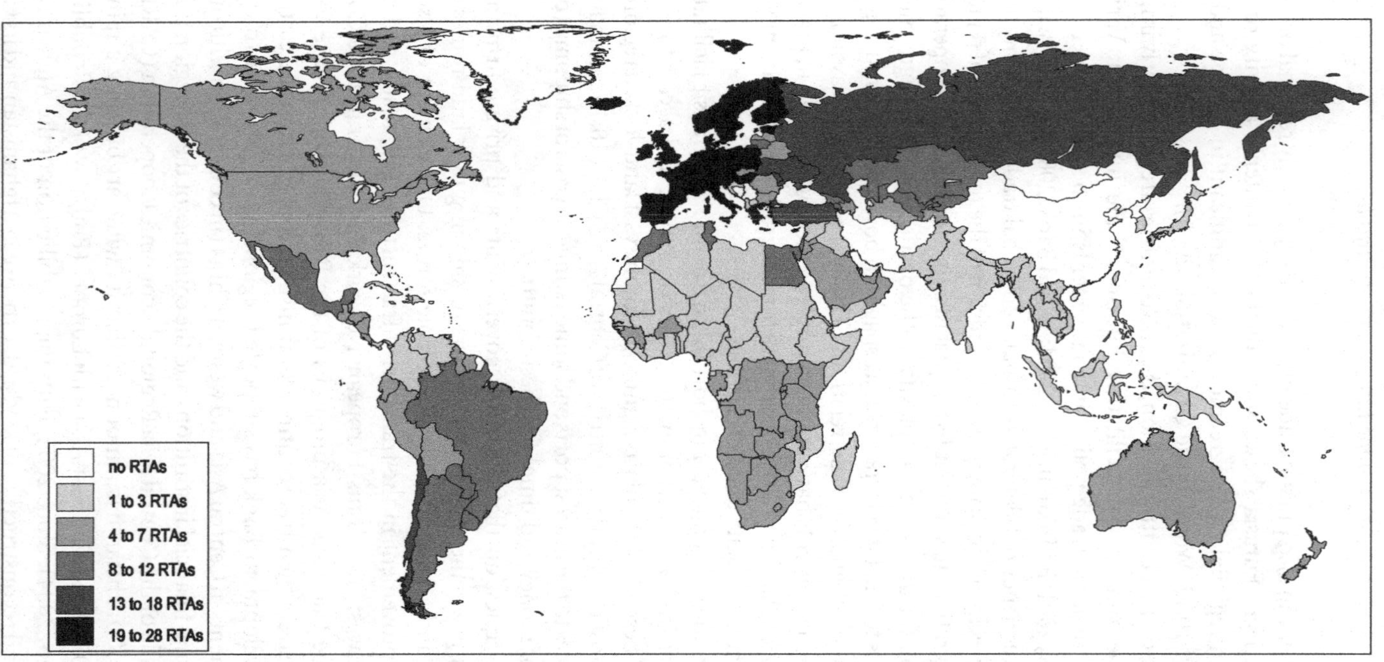

Chart 10.12. Regional trade agreements, globally, 2005. *Source*: WTO.

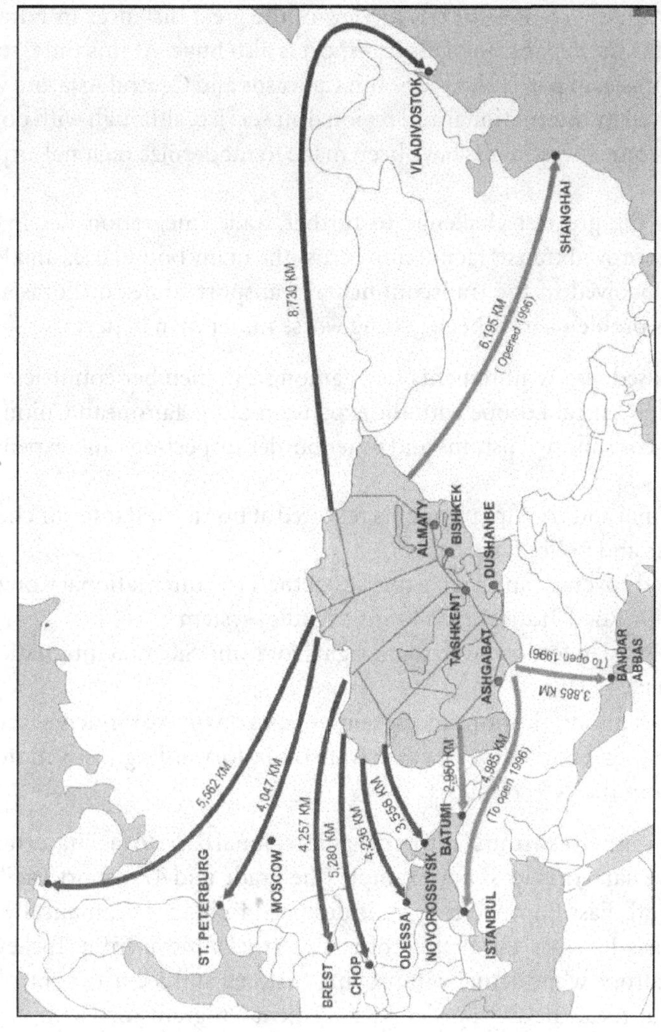

Chart 10.13. Transit links of Central Asian republics with world markets. *Source:* UNESCAP, 2003.

in Northeast Asia (NIRA, 2003). In view of the great distances in Eurasia, the scope for the expansion of air transport is also huge. At this time, some parts of Eurasia, in particular the South Caucasus and Central Asia, are very poorly served by international and regional air service, although with donor assistance some investments have been made to modernize regional airport facilities.

Perhaps the greatest challenge to further trade integration lies in the need for improved transit facilitation across the many boundaries and long distances involved in the transcontinental transport routes of Eurasia. In some ways problems have been getting worse rather than better:

- increased visa requirements (e.g., among CIS member countries, but also in Central Europe with the expansion of the European Union)[12]
- time-consuming customs and other border inspections and expensive fees
- informal and corrupt payments required at border and interior checkpoints and police barricades[13]
- limited coverage and high expenses of the TIR (International Convention for Road Transport in Transit Traffic) system
- high Russian fees for over-flight rights for trans-Siberian international flights[14]
- lack of communication among border posts on transcontinental routes
- lack of, or poorly developed, private trade-forwarding institutions in many of the CIS countries.

Various initiatives are under way on a subregional basis to facilitate transit in key Eurasian corridors. For example, the Trade and Transport Facilitation in South East Europe Program is designed to reduce dramatically the time it takes to cross the many borders as trucks move from Turkey to Western Europe while actually improving customs and security controls.[15] For Central Asia, the EU Border Management Program for Central Asia

[12] The EU required its new member countries, among them Poland and Hungary, to tighten visa and other entry requirements for border transit with their eastern neighbors (Oxford Analytica, 2005).

[13] This can cost around $1,500 per truck for crossing one country alone (Kazakhstan) (EBRD, 2003). When moving a generic consignment from Northern Europe to Tbilisi, Georgia, the Georgian leg of the journey accounts for almost half of the total transportation costs. It is estimated that 90 percent of the costs incurred in Georgia accrue to border guards, road police, and other such agencies (World Bank, 2003).

[14] According to a report in the *Financial Times* (March 15, 2005), European carriers paid Aeroflot, the Russian state airline, 250 million euros in 2003 for the rights to fly over Siberia.

[15] This program is financed by the World Bank. See http://www.ttfse.org.

is designed to help improve border management.[16] But much needs to be done to improve transit conditions so as to facilitate an expanded flow of trade throughout the Eurasian region.

In sum, there is already significant intra-regional trade across the Eurasian super-continent, but further trade expansion is possible and likely, especially if it is supported by improved trade policy (especially WTO access by the larger CIS countries), improved transport infrastructure, and enhanced trade facilitation. More work is needed to assess the probable investment requirements and the key priorities and sequencing of measures, and to estimate the possible gains from improved integration. In addition, improved cooperation among governments in the Eurasia region and key subregions will be essential to make sure major remaining obstacles to trade integration are removed or at least mitigated.[17]

Trade in Illicit Drugs

One more flow of trade is of special significance for the Eurasian region: the trade in illicit drugs.[18] Eurasia has an overwhelming share of the world's intravenous drug users, accounting for some 75 percent of the total. Its drug problem is principally opiates and their production. Over 60 percent of the world's illicit drug use involving opiates takes place in Eurasia, and well over 90 percent of the world's opiate production occurs in three countries of Eurasia – Afghanistan, Laos, and Myanmar (formerly Burma). Afghanistan alone produces an estimated three-quarters of the world's opium.

The principal flows of drugs in Eurasia are shown schematically in Chart 10.14. Exact quantification is difficult, but it is clear the illicit drug trade moves huge quantities of opiates across Eurasia. Although production of opium in the "Golden Triangle" of Southeast Asia appears to have declined somewhat in recent years, by all accounts, production in Afghanistan in 2003 and 2004 has reached near record levels (Newberg, 2005). The potential value of global opium production was estimated by the United Nations

[16] This program is financed by the European Union and implemented by UNDP. See www.eu-bomca.org/en.

[17] Various studies are currently under way that will help to address some of these issues. For example, the World Bank is carrying out a major study on integration of the Europe and Central Asia Region. UNDP and ADB are collaborating on a study of regional integration and cooperation in Central Asia that aims to estimate the benefits to Central Asian countries from transport and trade facilitation. While extremely useful pieces of the puzzle, even these studies remain partial in their coverage of the Eurasian integration process.

[18] Unless otherwise noted, the information and data provided in this section are drawn from the United Nations Office on Drugs and Crime (UNODC, 2004).

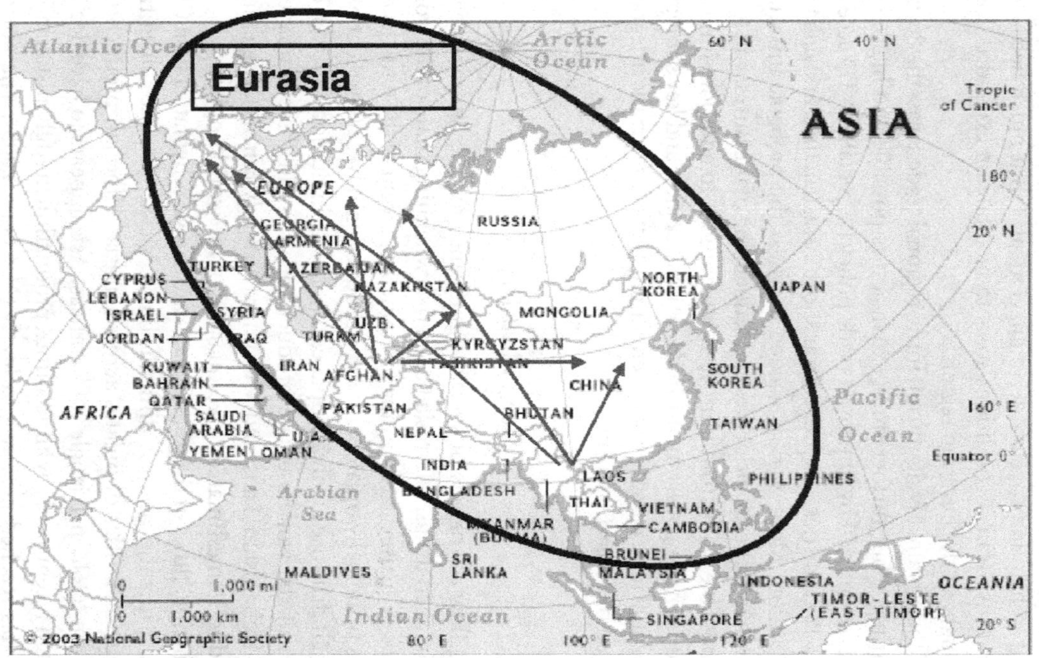

Chart 10.14. Drug flows in Central Asia. Reprinted with the permission of the National Geographic Society.

Office on Drugs and Crime at about $1.2 billion in 2003. In recent years, opiate use appears to have stabilized and may even be declining in Western Europe, but it has been increasing rapidly in Russia, which, according to U.N. estimates, is now the largest heroin market in Europe. In Asia, too, a stabilizing trend in drug use can be discerned, with the exception of China, where drug use appears to have increased at least through 2003. During that year the estimated number of drug users in China was in excess of one million, representing a fifteen-fold increase since 1990. An increasing share of the drug trafficking from Afghanistan appears to run through Central Asia. According to one estimate, there has been a thirty-fold increase in heroin seizures in Central Asia since 1993 (Osmonaliev, 2005).

Many efforts have been made to control the production, use, and trafficking of drugs in Eurasia, but they have had little impact on the flow of illicit drugs across the super-continent (Cornell, 2005; Swanstrom, 2005). Like elsewhere in the world, as long as high demand for illicit drugs continues to persist in Western Europe, Russia, and increasingly in China, it will be impossible to reduce production significantly in places such as Afghanistan and to reduce trafficking through Central Asia. Unfortunately, this trafficking in drugs has a very corrosive impact on the transit countries, as the illegal flow of drugs undermines already weak governments, fosters corruption and crime, and also leads to increased drug use and drug-related diseases, especially HIV/AIDS, locally. A concerted approach to the region-wide drug problem for the Eurasian super-continent therefore is a priority. But as long as the principal hubs of drug consumption do not control the demand for drugs, measures to limit production and transcontinental trafficking will have no real effect.

Investment and Capital Flows

Cross-border investment and capital flows, particularly foreign direct investment (FDI), have also become a force for integration in Eurasia. Until about two decades ago, there was almost no FDI or other capital flows to speak of in the region, except in Western Europe, Japan, and Southeast Asia. China and India had yet to start the process of liberalizing their economies, and the former Soviet Union, with its command economy and isolationist economic policies, was still intact. The opening of China and the fall of the Soviet Union, and the resulting reorientation of political alignments and trading patterns in Eurasia, have been accompanied by a surge in FDI outside the traditional areas. While Europe is still the largest recipient and source of FDI, investment growth is fastest east of Europe.

FDI and capital flows contribute to integration via two channels. First is the obvious channel: capital flows from one country to another create direct economic ties. Second, by promoting growth and technology diffusion, capital flows increase trade and economic cooperation, further enhancing integration. But there are also significant down-side risks from financial and capital market linkages:

- The potential contagion effect of one country's financial crisis on neighboring countries is perhaps the most clear. This became painfully obvious in 1997–1998, when the financial crisis that started in East and Southeast Asia had world-wide repercussions and affected Eurasia. For example, in the wake of the Korean financial crises, the withdrawal of Korean investors from the Russian government bond market contributed to the timing of the Russian financial crisis in 1998. The Russian crisis, in turn, affected Russia's neighbors through reduced trade and investments.
- Another down side of capital mobility is capital flight. For example, some $20 billion a year left Russia during the 1990s. Much of it probably found its first "resting place" in Western Europe (especially Cyprus and Switzerland).
- Finally, there is the monetary dimension of international financial linkages: Asian central banks have held large international foreign reserves, mostly in U.S. dollars. However, with the introduction of the euro and the depreciation of the dollar in recent years, there has been speculation that Asian central banks may wish to diversify their reserves by increasing their euro holdings relative to the dollar. The difficulties that the EU encountered in mid-2005 in ratifying its new constitution may have weakened such tendencies for the immediate future.

In the rest of this section we focus mostly on foreign direct investment as an important source of economic linkage and integration. Unfortunately, the data on FDI are weak, especially since they do not readily permit an assessment of regional and subregional FDI numbers and trends disaggregated by destination and source. Nonetheless, we have taken a first stab at the available numbers to see whether the stylized FDI flows shown in Chart 10.15 are broadly accurate.

Eurasia as a whole is a net foreign direct investor, albeit only slightly so. It is the repository of over 60 percent of the world's FDI stock (Chart 10.16). Within Eurasia, Europe is both the biggest investor and recipient of investment. Europe, China, and East and Southeast Asia together

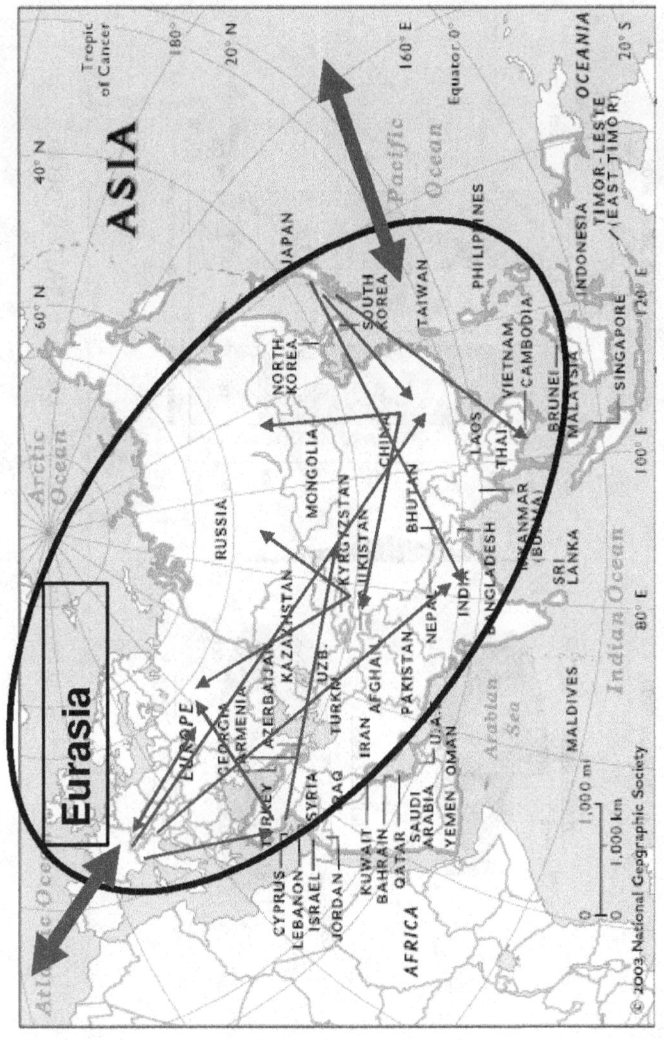

Chart 10.15. Eurasian capital flows. Reprinted with the permission of the National Geographic Society.

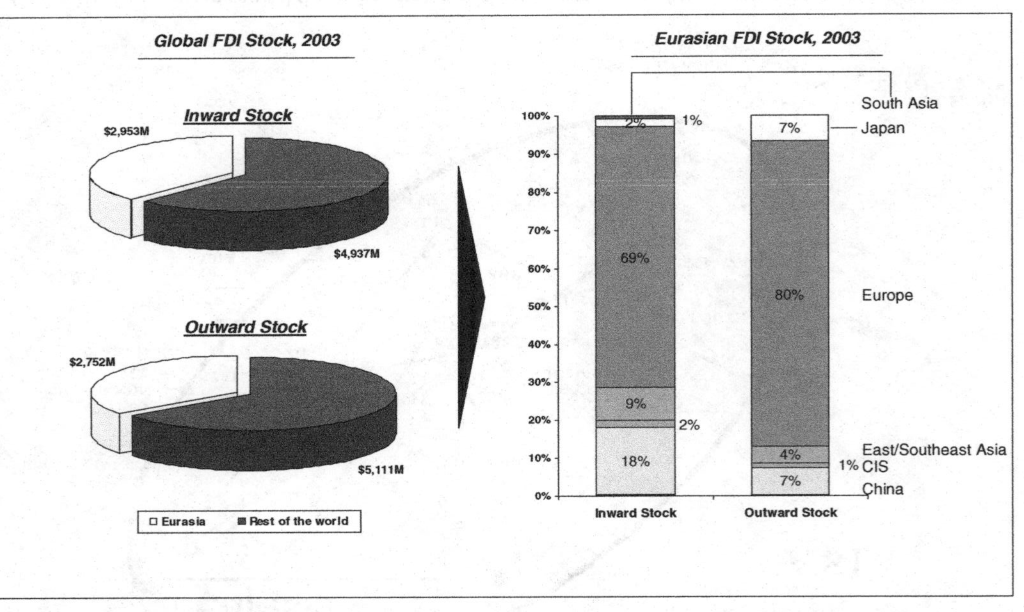

Chart 10.16. Global and Eurasian FDI stocks in 2003. *Sources*: UNCTAD, OECD.

account for almost the entire stock of FDI. Investment volumes in the CIS, Asia Minor, and South Asia are negligible by comparison, but these three regions also saw the greatest FDI growth from 1995 to 2003. For example, while FDI growth in Europe has averaged around 15 percent annually (for both inward and outward investments from 1995 to 2003), annual inward and outward FDI growth has been 31 percent and 43 percent, respectively, for the CIS. For South Asia, FDI growth rates have been 17 percent and 30 percent (Chart 10.17). In part this reflects growth from a low base.

We can derive a number of broad conclusions regarding the composition and direction of FDI trends for Eurasia. Traditionally, FDI that flows from the EU and Japan to the rest of Eurasia has been the most significant, albeit relatively small compared with the two-way flow of FDI to and from the rest of the world (especially the United States). Nonetheless, some new trends point to increased regional integration and diversification of capital flows within Eurasia. First, over the last twenty years there has been a rapid increase of European investment in China, and since 1998 there has been increased direct investment from Europe to Russia. Second, recently significant investment flows have also emerged from Russia to Central and Western Europe and to the rest of the CIS.[19] Third, there has been increased FDI from Turkey in the CIS, especially in Russia and Central Asia. And finally, China and India have started investing in the CIS, especially in the energy sector, as part of their strategy to increase their access to the Russian oil.[20]

This increased FDI engagement across borders in Eurasia is to be welcomed for a number of reasons. First, all available evidence, including research in the region itself, confirms that FDI on balance helps to improve productivity and growth. For example, Carstensen and Toubal (2004) have used panel data to examine the welfare effects of FDI in Central and Eastern

[19] Crane et al. (2005) has looked at Russian investments in the CIS and found that Russian firms are indeed increasingly investing in neighboring CIS countries. Russia has a considerable share of FDI inflows in Belarus, Moldova, Armenia, and Ukraine. Russian firms seem to be more adept than investors from Western industrialized countries in dealing with the poor business climate that widely prevails in the CIS countries. Crane also concludes that with the exception of the energy sector, the Russian government has not been directly involved in guiding foreign investments.

[20] Some observers are talking about the revival of the idea of a "Strategic Triangle" (attributed originally to former Russian Prime Minister Primakov) among China, India, and Russia in the political, energy, and commercial fields (Bajpaee, 2005; see also Blank, 2005; Cohen 2005; and Mitra, 2005, for growing energy investment links among Russia, China, and India).

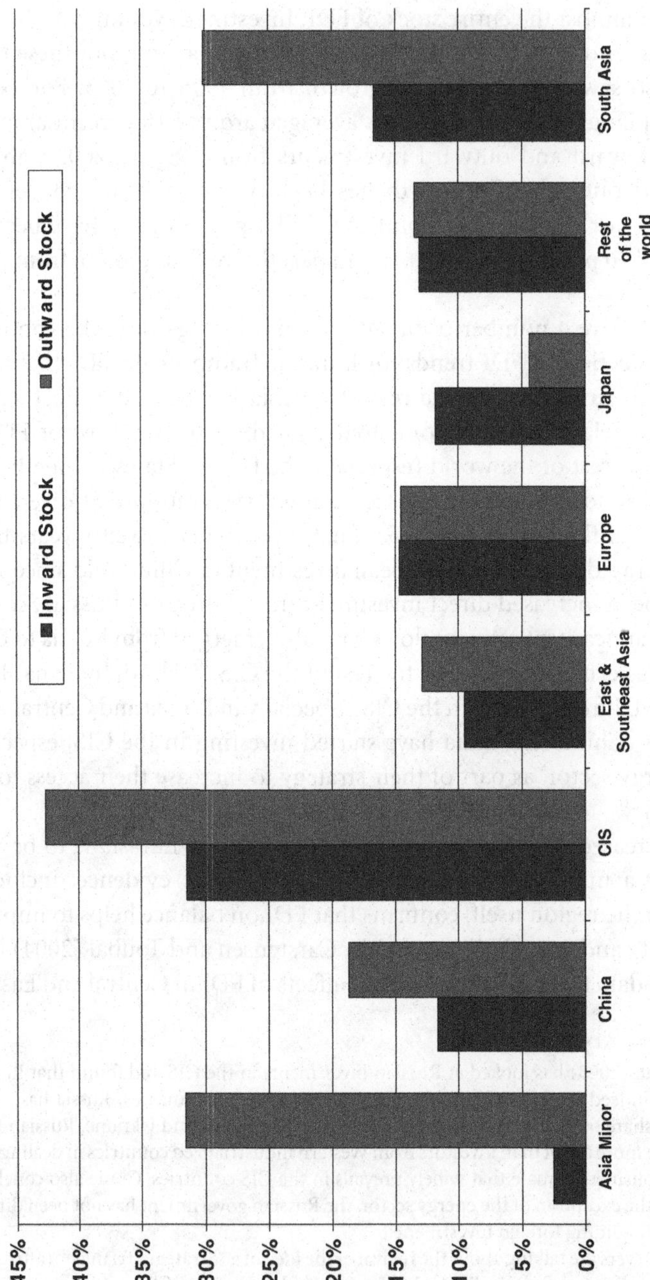

Chart 10.17. Growth of the FDI stock by region, 1995–2003. *Sources:* UNCTAD, OECD.

Europe, and find the link between FDI and growth to be statistically significant. And Campos and Kinoshita (2002) examined the impact of FDI on GDP growth based on panel data on twenty-five countries in East and Central Europe and the former Soviet Union between 1990 and 1998. They found that FDI has a positive and statistically significant causal impact on GDP growth. These findings imply that FDI – via the channel of higher economic growth and the resulting growth in trade – has the externality of encouraging further integration, not only between the two countries involved in a particular investment transaction but region-wide.

Of course, a major prerequisite for higher FDI in the lagging subregions (CIS, Indian subcontinent, Asia Minor) is a supportive local business and investment climate. Much remains to be done in this regard not only at the national level, but also at the provincial and municipal level; research on FDI has shown the importance of local business conditions.[21]

In conclusion, the recent growth of cross-border investments in Eurasia as part of the growing economic integration of the super-continent is welcome. Judging from the experience of economic integration in the EU, as well as between the United States and Europe and between the United States and East Asia, in the longer term it is the integration of firms through investments across borders that brings the greatest boost to trade and growth, as well as the strongest guarantee of stable long-term political relations.[22]

Migration

Population movements have been another important integrating factor in Eurasian and world history.[23] Historically, large Eurasian migrations, mostly from east to west, took place in prehistoric and ancient times. Then came significant voluntary and forced migration of Russians in Tsarist Russia (in the opposite direction), and subsequently the mostly forced movement of large

[21] See EBRD (2003) for the transition economies. For Vietnam, Meyer and Nguyen (2005) analyze the importance of local institutions and policies – including local education rates, industrial real estate availability, and passenger transport volumes – in attracting foreign direct investors. They find that such subnational institutional factors have a significant impact on FDI entry location and mode. Elsewhere in China, case studies have pointed out the importance of an active city government in reaching out to and attracting foreign investors (Wang and Meng 2004).

[22] For a discussion of the role of economic links as glue for stable long-term transatlantic relations, see Linn (2004).

[23] Much of the information summarized in this section is gleaned from Hill (2004c) and (Hill and Gaddy 2003). A major study on migration in Europe and Central Asia is under preparation at the World Bank and, once completed, should throw considerably more light on the issues tentatively explored in this section.

numbers of people in the Soviet Union.[24] More recently, Europe experienced large refugee flows as a result of wars during the twentieth century, and substantial migration post–World War II in response to economic opportunities. However, these migration flows within Eurasia do not compare in relative size or significance with the centuries-long history of transatlantic migration from Europe to the United States.[25] As with trade and capital flows, the Iron and Bamboo Curtains – and, in particular, restrictive immigration policies in Europe – acted as effective barriers to large movements of people on a transcontinental scale.

After the demise of the Soviet Union, there were initially some sizable movements of people, mostly of Russian origin, from the new CIS republics back to Russia. Hill and Gaddy (2003) cite estimates of around 3 million people. And in countries with war and civil disturbances, refugees and internally displaced people have often relocated within their own countries (Azerbaijan, Georgia, and Tajikistan). Since the early transition years, however, most of the migration movements have been for economic reasons. They fall into several streams, as shown schematically in Chart 10.18:[26]

- migration within the recently enlarged European Union and its immediate neighbors (especially Turkey, Southeast Europe, Ukraine, and Moldova)
- migration from South Asia to Western Europe, often in stages, via the CIS; in frequent cases, such migrants stay considerable periods in transit or settle along the way in the CIS countries, due to difficulties entering Central and Western Europe
- migration from Central Asia to Russia (and increasingly within Central Asia to Kazakhstan)
- migration within Russia from the cold northern and northeastern regions to central and south-central Russia
- migration within China and from China to far eastern Russia

Unfortunately, comprehensive and accurate data on Eurasian migration flows are scant. It is hoped that ongoing research will help to fill some of the gaps. From the information available (OECD, 2002; United Nations,

[24] Some non-Russians from the West, such as German settlers, were invited to various parts of Tsarist Russia and then further resettled, mostly in Central Asia, under Stalin (Janssen, 1997). There was also settlement of significant numbers of non-Russian settlers from the East, especially Koreans in Central Asia (Diener, 2004).

[25] There were also significant transpacific migration flows from Asia to the United States (Min, 2002).

[26] There are, of course, other migration flows not shown in Chart 10.18, particularly from Africa to Western Europe.

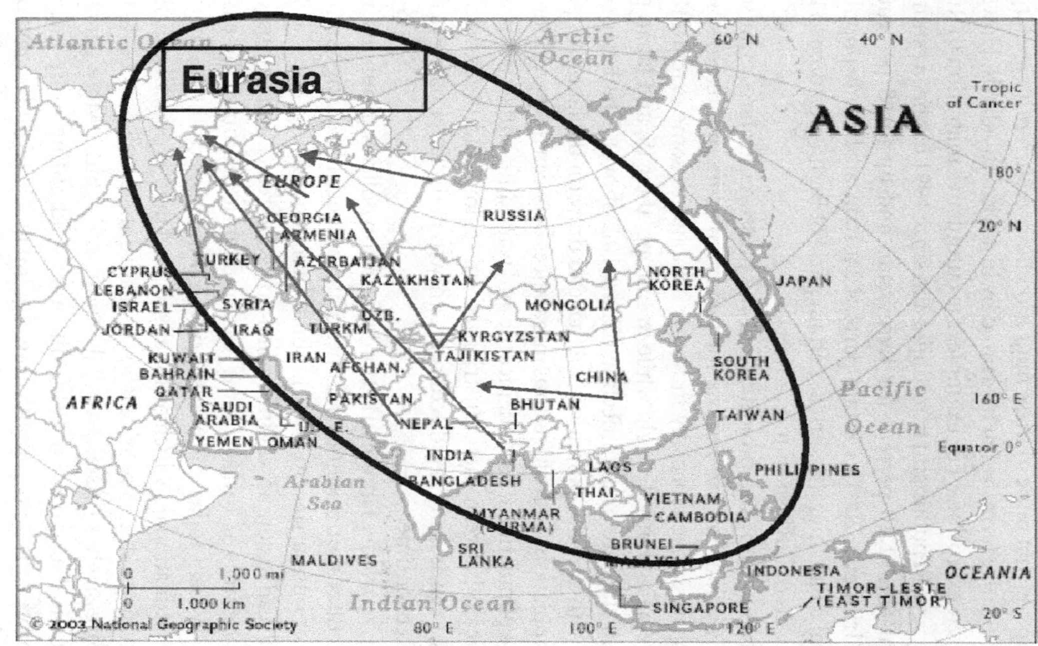

Chart 10.18. Migration flows in Eurasia. Reprinted with the permission of the National Geographic Society.

2002), it appears that none of these migration flows is currently very large in absolute or relative terms when measured by historical standards. However, there are a few exceptions. For example, the cumulative migration to Russia from the Kyrgyz Republic and from Tajikistan since 1991 has been estimated to represent almost 10 percent for Kyrgyzstan and up to 18 percent for Tajikistan (Irinnews, 2004). Certain parts of Moscow are heavily populated with Central Asian migrants, just as certain parts of Berlin are home to large concentrations of Turkish immigrants.

Looking ahead, one can project increasing pressures for larger transcontinental migration flows in Eurasia for two main economic reasons. First, population pressures, especially in South Asia and to some extent in East Asia, will remain relatively high, while in Europe, the CIS, and Japan populations will stagnate or even decline (Chart 10.2 above). The latter set of countries, with aging populations, will have to draw on the labor supply of younger populations to avoid serious imbalances between their working-age and old-age populations. Second, income and wage differentials will remain very significant between the industrialized subregions and the developing subregions, even as more rapid economic growth in the latter narrows these differentials over time.

However, restrictive labor market and migration policies, grounded in the economic, cultural, and political realities of the potential receiving countries, will act as serious barriers to labor mobility across borders in Eurasia. This, in turn, will lead to countervailing capital flows and relocation of jobs to the cheaper labor areas of Eurasia. Some fears and tensions around these issues are already evident today. Even in the new EU member countries there are fears that multinationals, which originally located their production facilities in Central Europe due to relative labor cost advantage, will now move their plants progressively to Asia, especially India and China. More generally, the tensions in Europe around this dilemma – admitting more migrants or losing more jobs – are a political reality today. They will become more pronounced as the distances across the Eurasian super-continent effectively become shorter and shorter.

Communication and Knowledge Sharing

One of the key factors in shrinking distances has been the development of modern communication and information technology. The most important element has been the development of the Internet. Eurasia is no exception in this regard. Chart 10.19 shows the degree of Internet penetration and growth in access for different subregions in Eurasia. Not surprisingly,

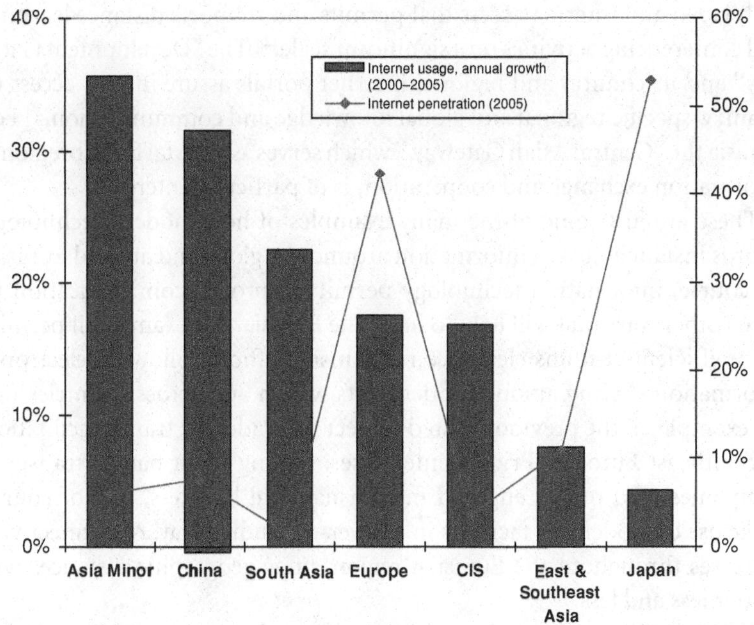

Chart 10.19. Eurasian Internet growth and penetration, 2000–2005. *Source*: Internet World Stats (http://www.internetworldstats.com).

Europe and Japan have the highest penetration rates, but the highest growth rates are in the other subregions, albeit from relatively low levels. Continued rapid growth in connectivity can be expected, as there have been significant improvements in the super-continent's coverage by communications satellites.

Special programs have been put in place to support connectivity, particularly in poorly served subregions, and institutions and programs have developed to provide access to world-wide knowledge, communication, and learning. For example, the "Virtual Silk Highway Project," organized with the support of the NATO Science Division and other donors, provides Internet access to the South Caucasus and Central Asian CIS countries.[27] By making available satellite access and providing support for the development of country-based networks of Internet providers, the project will increase information access in these land-locked countries. The World Bank–sponsored Global Development Learning Network has established learning centers in most of the countries of the Eurasia Region (and in the rest of the world),

[27] See http://www.silkproject.org.

with video and Internet access that permits and supports distance learning and conferencing activities on a significant scale.[28] The "Development Gateway" and its country and regional Internet portals assure instant access to country-specific regional and global knowledge and communication.[29] For Eurasia the "Central Asian Gateway," which serves as a portal for subregional information exchange and cooperation, is of particular interest.[30]

These are just some of the many examples of how modern technology affords instant access to information around the globe and around Eurasia. Of course, information technology permits improved communication in many other ways that will help to integrate Eurasia. For example, it permits more efficient customs clearance for transit traffic by allowing electronic information sharing among border posts within and across countries (as, for example, in the previously cited project for trade and transit facilitation in Southeast Europe). Private enterprises, among them banks, transport companies, and others engaged in transnational business, will of course make use of modern IT facilities in an ever-expanding way. As connectivity increases throughout the Eurasian region, huge geographic distances will matter less and less.

The Institutional Infrastructure, Politics of Regional Cooperation, and the Future of Regional Integration in Eurasia

In the preceding sections we have documented intensifying trends toward integration of economic activity and communication across Eurasia. Despite these trends, there is currently no overarching institutional framework for regional cooperation, nor should we expect one soon. However, overlapping initiatives for subregional cooperation and integration are expanding throughout the region. These are both a result of the increased economic integration and a factor driving closer integration.

The following are some prominent examples of regional cooperative institutions, none of which encompasses all Eurasia.

- ASEM (the Asia-Europe Meeting) is the largest group, with thirty-nine members, encompassing the (now-enlarged) EU, all Association of Southeast Asian Nations (ASEAN) countries, and China, Japan, and South Korea. The CIS and South Asia are not members.

[28] See http://www.gdln.org/index.html.
[29] See http://home.developmentgateway.org.
[30] See http://www.cagateway.org.

- The European Union (EU), with twenty-five members, is the most integrated subregional grouping, and with its planned further accessions in Southeast Europe will further increase its reach. The EU's "Neighborhood Policy" extends to six CIS countries as well as a number of North African and Middle Eastern countries.
- The CIS is a loose assemblage of thirteen republics of the former Soviet Union.
- Various smaller subregional groupings involve members of the CIS and some of their Eurasian neighbors; most notable are the Shanghai Cooperation Organization (SCO) with China, Russia, and four Central Asian members (Turkmenistan is not a member); the Central Asia Cooperation Organization (CACO), with the same membership as the SCO minus China; and the Economic Cooperation Organization, which includes the five Central Asian countries plus Afghanistan, Azerbaijan, Iran, Pakistan, and Turkey.
- Various East and Southeast Asian groupings, especially ASEAN and South Asian Association for Regional Cooperation (SAARC).
- In addition, there are a number of regional groupings supported by or involving multilateral institutions, such as the U.N. regional economic commissions for Europe (ECE) and Asia (ESCAP), the European Bank for Reconstruction and Development (EBRD), and the Asian Development Bank (ADB). They, as well as the World Bank, have in recent years become increasingly active in supporting subregional cooperation and integration initiatives. The Greater Mekong Subregion and the Central Asia Regional Economic Cooperation (CAREC) initiatives are prime examples of subregional cooperation efforts supported by multilateral institutions. Indeed, most aid donors active in the developing countries of Eurasia have now designed subregional approaches and strategies in key subregions (especially in Central Asia).

Many of these subregional institutional frameworks are not focused on the operational problems of supporting, funding and implementing specific programs designed to support integration or address key issues of Eurasia-wide concern (such as integration of the transport, transit, and energy infrastructure and regulatory frameworks). However, these interlocking forums do provide for regular contact and exchange at heads-of-state and ministerial levels. This helps to build trust, smoothes key bilateral relations, and over the long term probably supports selected initiatives that help with subregional and even Eurasia-wide integration.

This political and policy dialogue at the highest governmental level is important because it may help to answer a key question about the future. Will the increased interdependency and the unquestionable gains from economic integration, as well as a shared need for economic stability and prosperity, drive increased political cooperation and peaceful coexistence in the region? Or will long-standing political tensions and new competition for scarce resources, especially energy, create regional instability and serious barriers to the quick economic integration of Eurasia?

There are many potential sources of conflict within the region. In East Asia there are the tensions around North Korea, the competition between China and Japan, and the simmering tension between China and Taiwan. In South Asia, there is the long-standing conflict between India and Pakistan. Add to this the unstable situation in Afghanistan, the persistent tensions over Iran, and the deep-seated, violent conflicts of the rest of the Middle East, which can spill over into the Eurasian political scene. In the CIS there is the potential for conflicts in the South Caucasus and new unrest in Central Asia, and the latent competition between China and Russia. Even in Europe, there are difficulties with further EU enlargement, especially around Turkey's accession, and problems with the EU's strict control over its borders. All these possible sources of conflict might destabilize important parts of Eurasia with spill-over effects for the rest of the region and even globally.

Fortunately, there have been increased efforts within Eurasia to address many of these issues. The EU has become more actively engaged in its dialogue with key regional players (China, Russia, and Iran) and in the context of key subregional initiatives (ASEM, EU Neighborhood, the TACIS Central Asia regional strategy, etc.). Both China and Russia have shown increased interest in engaging Central Asia. India and Pakistan not only show signs of wanting to settle their long-standing Kashmir conflict, but also are increasingly looking to cooperate over access to the energy sources of Iran, Central Asia, and Russia. ASEAN and China in November 2004 agreed to closer cooperation in moving toward the creation of a free trade zone.[31] These tendencies toward peaceful cooperation bode well for a stable long-term future and continued economic integration.

Conclusions and Policy Implications

While the evidence on Eurasian economic integration remains partial and fragmentary, we conclude that the last twenty years have seen ever closer and

[31] As reported in *China Daily*, November 30, 2004. See http://www.chinadaily.com.cn/english/doc/2004–11/30/content_395778.htm.

more complex economic links throughout this enormous region. No doubt these trans-Eurasian links are not yet nearly as tight as they are across the Atlantic or the Pacific. But the trends are unmistakable. For better – or in some cases for worse – economic integration in Eurasia will continue at a fast pace, potentially catching up in terms of intensity with the economic integration that characterized development of transatlantic, transpacific, and trans-American economic relations. While competition for energy resources and political tensions may complicate and in some areas slow down this process, we are hopeful that Eurasia will find peaceful and cooperative solutions. The example of economic integration and political cooperation across the Atlantic and the Pacific over the last fifty years – despite the backdrop of past violent conflicts and competition tensions – offers hope for a similar outcome in Eurasia.

What are the policies that can help to bring about this favorable scenario?

- Major investments in transcontinental and subregional infrastructure are required to support increased regional trade and communication.
- These investments need to be accompanied by improvements in, and harmonization of, the policy and regulatory regimes for transit of goods, services, and people. Also important are "behind-the-border" reforms, especially improvements in the investment climate, more effective public administration, and reduced corruption.
- Early universal membership in the WTO is preferable to reinforcing the "spaghetti bowl" of (sub)regional trade agreements.
- Major investments in energy production and transport are needed, but should be matched by cross-border agreements on regulation and measures to improve energy efficiency so as to reduce pressures on energy prices and on the environment. Also, region-wide agreements are necessary to address competing claims for access to regional energy resources by key players (EU, China, India, Japan, United States).
- There is a need for a serious review of current illicit drug control policies region-wide, with a view toward combatting or at least better managing the use, production, and trafficking of illicit drugs.
- A better understanding of the role of migration is needed to support the long-term development of the various subregions, those with demographic deficits as well as those with population surpluses.
- Private and public knowledge networks, business, and civil society groups should increasingly take a transcontinental view of Eurasia,

rather than clinging to purely country or subregional perspectives. Of course, this should not be to the exclusion of linking with global and transoceanic networks.

The key actors in bringing about these policy actions are the governments of the largest countries in Eurasia. For the immediate future, it is likely that the EU will have to play a lead role in opening up a Eurasia-wide perspective of cooperation and integration. However, for the longer term, there is no question that China, the EU, India, and Russia will be the key players. They will have to pay particular attention to ensure that the fragile border regions of the South Caucasus and Central Asia become stable and prosperous parts of an integrated Eurasia. They must also ensure that the shared problems of an unstable Middle East and a poor and fractious Africa receive the world community's attention.

If the key players in Eurasia take on constructive roles in shaping a transcontinental integrated economy, then the United States can and should restrict itself to a relatively minor, supportive role. Should intra-Eurasian political frictions prevail, then a more active role by the United States might help to settle such conflicts in a minimally disruptive manner.

More generally, in light of the inevitable growth of China and India as strong economic and political players, and in light of the emergence of a new super-continental economic bloc in Eurasia, it would be desirable to develop global economic and political steering mechanisms that help to bind all major players together. One way to achieve this is to expand the membership of the Group of 8 (G8) summit mechanism, for example, by elevating the current ministerial-level G20 to a summit-level mechanism.[32]

Finally, key multilateral institutions, such as the U.N. agencies, the World Bank, and the regional development banks, will have to play an active role in aiding the regional integration of Eurasia, both at the subregional and at the overarching regional level. This will require cooperation among these agencies. But it will also require a clearer vision and action to cut across the internal bureaucratic boundaries of regional and subregional organizational units. There are encouraging signs that this is beginning to happen, but more concerted and effective steps are needed.

[32] The G20 consists of the major industrial and emerging market economies. It currently brings together ministers of finance and central bank governors, but there are proposals to elevate the G20 into a summit-level forum (Bradford and Linn, 2004).

References

Aitken, Brian J., and Ann E. Harrison. 1999. "Do Domestic Firms Benefit from Direct Foreign Investment? Evidence from Venezuela." *American Economic Review* 89, no. 3: 605–618.

Akiner, Shirin. 2001. "Regional Cooperation in Central Asia." In Patrick Hardouin, Reiner Weichhardt, and Peter Sutcliffe, eds., *Economic Developments and Reforms in Cooperation Partner Countries: The Interrelationship between Regional Economic Cooperation, Security and Stability*. NATO Colloquium, Romania.

Babetskii, Ian, Oxana Babetskaia-Kukharchuk, and Martin Raiser. 2004. "How Deep Is Your Trade? Transition and International Integration in Eastern Europe and the Former Soviet Union." EBRD Working Paper 83.

Bajpaee, Chietigj. 2005. "Setting the Stage for a New Cold War: China's Quest for Energy Security." *Power and Interest News Report*. Http://pinr.com/report.php?ac = view_report&report_id = 272&language_id = 1.

Blank, Stephen. 2005. "India's Energy Offensive in Central Asia." *Analyst*, Central Asia-Caucasus Institute, Johns Hopkins University. Http://www.cacianalyst.org/view_article.php?articleid = 3117.

Bradford, Colin I. Jr., and Johannes F. Linn. 2004. "Global Economic Governance at a Crossroads: Replacing the G-7 with the G-20." Policy Brief 131, Washington, D.C.: The Brookings Institution.

British Petroleum. 2004. *BP Statistical Review of World Energy 2004*. London: Beacon Press.

Campos, Nauro F., and Yuko Kinoshita. 2002. "Foreign Direct Investment as Technology Transferred: Some Panel Evidence from the Transition Economies." *The Manchester School* 70, no. 3: 398–419.

Carstensen, Kai, and Farid Toubal. 2004. "Foreign Direct Investment in Central and Eastern European Countries: A Dynamic Panel Analysis." *Journal of Comparative Economics* 32, no. 1: 3–22.

Chow, Edward C. 2004. "Russian Pipelines: Back to the Future?" *Georgetown Journal of International Affairs* 5, no. 1: 27–33.

Cohen, Ariel. 2005. "Russian Oil After YUKOS: Implications for the United States." Executive Memorandum 961. Washington, D.C.: The Heritage Foundation.

Cornell, Svante E. 2005. "Stemming the Contagion: Regional Efforts to Curb Afghan Heroin's Impact." *Georgetown Journal of International Affairs* 6, no. 1: 23–31.

Crane, Keith, D. J. Peterson, and Olga Oliker. 2005. "Russian Investment in the Commonwealth of Independent States." *Eurasian Geography and Economics* 46, no. 6: 405–444.

Diener, Alexander C. 2004. *Homeland Conceptions and Ethnic Integration Among Kazakhstan's Germans and Koreans*. Mellen Studies in Geography 13. Lewiston, N.Y.: Mellen Press.

Embassy of the Republic of Kazakhstan to the USA and Canada. 2004. *Kazakhstan News Bulletin* no. 1: 58.

Energy Information Administration. 2004a. *Azerbaijan Country Analysis Brief.* November.

Energy Information Administration. 2004b. *Caspian Sea Region Country Analysis Brief.* December.

Energy Information Administration. 2004c. *China Country Analysis Brief.* July.

Energy Information Administration. 2004d. *Kazakhstan Country Analysis Brief.* November.

Energy Information Administration. 2005. *Major Russian Oil and Natural Gas Pipeline Projects.* January.

European Bank for Reconstruction and Development (EBRD). 2003. *Transition Report 2003.* London: EBRD.

European Commission. 2004. "Helping to Tackle Non-Tariff Trade Barriers in South East Europe." Report to the Stability Pact Working Group on Trade. September.

Freinkman, Lev, Evgeny Polyakov, and Carolina Revenco. 2004. *Trade Performance and Regional Integration of the CIS Countries.* Washington, D.C.: The World Bank.

Hare, Paul, Alan Bevan, Jon Stern, and Saul Estrin. 2000. "Supply Responses in the Economies of the Former Soviet Union." Discussion Paper 2000/09. Department of Economics, Heriot-Watt University. Edinburgh: Centre for Economic Reform and Transformation.

Hill, Fiona. 2004a. "Energy Empire: Oil, Gas and Russia's Revival." Foreign Policy Centre, September.

Hill, Fiona. 2004b. "Pipelines in the Caspian: Catalyst or Cure-all?" *Georgetown Journal of International Affairs* 5, no. 1: 17–25.

Hill, Fiona. 2004c. "Eurasia on the Move: The Regional Implications of Mass Labor Migration from Central Asia to Russia." Presentation at the Kennan Institute, September 27. Http://www.brookings.edu/views/op-ed/hillf/20040927.pdf.

Hill, Fiona, and Clifford Gaddy. 2003. *The Siberian Curse: How Communist Planners Left Russia Out in the Cold.* Washington, D.C.: The Brookings Institution Press.

Hopkirk, Peter. 1980. *Foreign Devils on the Silk Road: The Search for the Lost Cities and Treasures of Chinese Central Asia.* London: Murray.

Hu, Albert G. Z., and Gary H. Jefferson. 2002. "FDI Impact and Spillover: Evidence from China's Electronic and Textile Industries." *The World Economy* 25, no. 8: 1063–1076.

Irinnews. 2004. "Central Asia: Special Report on Labor Migrants in Russia." Http://www.irinnews.org/S_report.asp?ReportID = 40107&SelectRegion = Central_Asia.

Janssen, Susanne. 1997. *Deutsche in Russland und Russlanddeutsche in den USA (1871–1928): Die politische, sozio-ökonomische und kulturelle Adaption einer ethnischen Gruppe im Kontext zweier Staaten* (Germans in Russia and Russian Germans in the United States (1871–1928): Political, Socio-economic and Cultural Adaptation of an Ethnic Group in the Context of Two States). Münster: Freie Universität Berlin, LIT Verlag.

Kelly, John. 2005. *The Great Mortality: An Intimate History of the Black Death, the Most Devastating Plague of All Time.* New York: HarperCollins.

Linn, Johannes F. 2004. "Economic (Dis)Integration Matters: The Soviet Collapse Revisited." Prepared for a conference on "Transition in the CIS: Achievements and Challenges," Moscow, September.

Linn, Johannes F., and Arthur Conan Doyle. 2004. "Europe and America: The Economic Ties that Bind." *Current History* 103, no. 676: 370–375.

Meyer, Klaus E., and Hung Vo Nguyen. 2005. "Foreign Investment Strategies and Sub-national Institutions in Emerging Markets: Evidence from Vietnam." *Journal of Management Studies* 42, no. 1: 63–93.

Min, Pyong Gap. 2002. *Mass Migration to the United States: Classical and Contemporary Periods*. Walnut Creek, Calif.: AltaMira Press.

Mitra, Pramit. 2005. "Indian Diplomacy Energized by Search for Oil." *YaleGlobal*, March 14. Http://yaleglobal.yale.edu/display.article?id = 5419.

Muzafarov, Damir R. 2001. "Problems of Economic Integration in Central Asia." In Patrick Hardouin, Reiner Weichhardt, and Peter Sutcliffe, eds., *Economic Developments and Reforms in Cooperation Partner Countries: The Interrelationship Between Regional Economic Cooperation, Security and Stability*. NATO Colloquium, Romania.

NEA Transport Research and Training. 2002. "Trade and Transport Facilitation Audit – Turkmenistan." Report for the World Bank, Washington, D.C.

Newberg, Paula R. 2005. "A Drug-Free Afghanistan Not So Easy." *Yale Global Online*. Http://yaleglobal.yale.edu/display.article?id = 5385.

NIRA (National Institute for Research Advancement). 2003. *Grand Design for Stability and Prosperity in Northeast Asia*. KRI International Corporation, Tokyo.

Organization for Economic Cooperation and Development (OECD). 2002. "Trends in International Migration." www.oecd.org/dataoecd.

Osmonaliev, Kairat. 2005. "Developing Counter Narcotics Policy in Central Asia: Legal and Political Dimensions." Central Asia-Caucasus Institute Silk Road Studies Program, SAIS, Washington, D.C.

Oxford Analytica. 2005. *Eastern Europe and European Union: Border Barriers*.

Rose, Andrew, Ben Lockwood, and Danny Quah. 2000. "One Money, One Market? The Effect of Common Currencies on International Trade." *Economic Policy* 15, no. 30: 7–45.

Schnitzer, Monika. 2002. "Debt vs. Foreign Direct Investment: The Impact of Sovereign Risk on the Structure of International Capital Flows." *Economica* 69, no. 273: 41–67.

Siddiqi, Toufiq A. 2004. "India and Pakistan: Pipe Dream or Pipeline of Peace?" *Georgetown Journal of International Affairs* 5, no. 1: 35–42.

Swanstrom, Niklas. 2005. "Multilateralism and Narcotics Control in Central Asia." *CEF Quarterly*, Winter.

Thomson, Peter. 2005. "The Outlook for Energy Trade between the CIS Countries and 'Western' Europe." Presentation at the Third International Congress on Restructuring the Energy Sector in Transition Countries held in Leipzig, Germany, March 8, 2005. Http://siteresources.worldbank.org/INTECAREGTOPENERGY/Resources/chapter6.pdf.

UNESCAP. 2003. *Transit Transport Issues in Landlocked and Transit Developing Countries*. Landlocked Developing Countries Series 1. New York: United Nations.

United Nations. 2002. *International Migration 2002*. UN Population Division.

United Nations Office on Drugs and Crime (UNODC). 2004. *World Drug Report 2004*. Vienna.

Wang, M. Y., and X. C. Meng. 2004. "Global-Local Initiatives in FDI: The Experience of Shenzhen, China." *Asia Pacific Viewpoint* 45, no. 2: 181–196.

Weatherford, John. 2004. *Genghis Khan and the Making of the Modern World*. New York: Three River Press.

Wilson, Dominic, and Roopa Purushothaman. 2003. "Dreaming with the BRICs: The Path to 2050." Goldman Sachs Global Economic Paper 99. New York: Goldman Sachs.

World Bank. 2003. *Georgia, an Integrated Trade Development Strategy*. Report 27264-GE. Washington, D.C.: The World Bank.

World Bank. 2004a. *Regional Electricity Export Potential Study*. Washington, D.C.: The World Bank.

World Bank. 2004b. *The Republic of Moldova: Trade Diagnostic Study*. Report 30998-MD. Washington, D.C.: The World Bank.

World Bank. 2004c. *Ukraine Trade Policy Study*. Report 29684. Washington, D.C.: The World Bank.

World Bank. 2005. *Global Economic Prospects 2005: Trade, Regionalism, and Development*. Washington, D.C.: The World Bank.

World Trade Organization. 2000. *Mapping of Regional Trade Agreements*. Committee on Regional Trade Agreements WT/REG/W/4.

Index